GREAT DESERT EXPLORERS

GREAT DESERT EXPLORERS

ANDREW GOUDIE
UNIVERSITY OF OXFORD

Royal Geographical Society
with IBG

Advancing geography
and geographical learning

SILPHIUM
PRESS

Produced by Silphium Press, an imprint of
The Society for Libyan Studies
c/o The British Academy
10–11 Carlton House Terrace
London SW1Y 5AH

www.societyforlibyanstudies.org

ISBN: 978-1-900971-45-4

Cover and interior design by Chris Bell, cbdesign
Edited by JMS Books LLP
Printed and bound in India by Imprint Press

CONTENTS

LIST OF FIGURES

127. Frémont's view of Pyramid Lake (RGS: From Frémont, J.C. 1845. *Report of the Exploring Expedition to the Rocky Mountains in the Year 1842, and to California in the year 1843–'44.* Washington, D.C.: Senate of the United States).

128. Death Valley. Below: As it is today (author's image). Right: As depicted by Manley.

129. The Major's bust at his memorial on the south rim of the Grand Canyon (author's image).

130. The Heart of Lodore, Green River: Frederick S. Dellenbaugh seated on the bank, 1871. Taken on John Wesley Powell's second expedition down the Colorado River, 1871–72 (RGS).

131. Powell's little boats in big rapids (RGS: Powell, J.W. 1961. *The Exploration of the Colorado River and its Canyons*, 250. New York, NY: Dover Publications).

132. Powell dangling from trousers (RGS: Powell, J.W. 1961. *The Exploration of the Colorado River and its Canyons*, 169. New York, NY: Dover Publications).

133. Point Sublime, Grand Canyon, from Clarence Dutton (this panoramic image of Point Sublime by William Henry Holmes was one of several included in Clarence E. Dutton's 1882 publication *Tertiary History of the Grand Canon District*).

134. Explorers' routes in the Sahara and West Africa (Map drawn by Sebastian Ballard).

135. Hugh Clapperton (RGS).

136. Sketch of Lake Chad. (RGS: Denham, D. 1828. *Narrative of travels and discoveries in northern and central Africa in the years 1822, 1823 and 1824.* 3rd Edition. London: John Murray).

137. Major Gordon Laing. Engraving by S. Freeman (RGS).

138. René Caillié (RGS: Caillié, R. 1830. Travels through Central Africa to Timbuctoo, volume 1, frontispiece).

139. Caillié meditating on the Koran and taking notes (RGS: Caillié, R. 1830. *Travels through Central Africa to Timbuctoo*, volume 2, 73).

140. Timbuktu as portrayed by Caillié (RGS: Caillié, R. 1830. *Travels through Central Africa to Timbuctoo*, volume 2, 75).

141. An oasis in the far south of Morocco (author's image).

142. Heinrich Barth (RGS).

143. Barth's caravan entering Timbuktoo. (Engraving by Eberhard Emminger (1808–85). From Denham, D. 1828. *Narrative of Travels and Discoveries in Northern and Central Africa in the Years 1822, 1823 and 1824.* 3rd Edition. London: John Murray).

144. Henri Duveyrier (RGS: Duveyrier, H. 1864. *Les Toureg du nord*, frontispiece).

145. The Citroens (RGS: Haardt and Audouin-Dubreuil. 1924. *Across the Sahara by motor car: from Touggourt to Timbuctoo.* London: T. Fisher Unwin).

146. The route of the first crossing of the Sahara by motor car. (Map drawn by Sebastian Ballard).

147. The routes of Monod in the Sahara (Map drawn by Sebastian Ballard).

PREFACE

THERE ARE MANY BOOKS on exploration but remarkably few on desert exploration. Moreover, some of the great desert explorers are now very little remembered or appreciated in comparison, say, with those who ventured to the poles, climbed Everest, or sought the source of the Nile. Yet, crossing unknown deserts is no less challenging. In this volume I present short biographies of around 60 of the most interesting, intrepid and important explorers of the world's greatest deserts. I could have included many more, but I have tried to treat a range of different deserts and to include a range of nationalities. I have also concentrated on explorers from the last three centuries, which means that I have, for example, not featured one of the greatest of all desert explorers, the Berber Abu 'Abdallah ibn Battúta, who travelled huge distances in the fourteenth century in Asia and Africa. Nor have I included either Qiu Chuji, who at the behest of Genghiz Khan travelled from China into Central Asia in the thirteenth century, or Felix Fabri who traversed the deserts of the Levant in the 1480s, or the members of the Spanish Coronado expedition who discovered the Grand Canyon in 1540, or Bento de Góis, the Portuguese Jesuit who travelled from India to China at the start of the seventeenth century. I have however tried to include some of the more neglected figures. Some explorers have been excluded, often with regret, either because they are already so well known, or because they tended to follow in the footsteps of others, or because they were essentially travellers or writers rather than explorers, their prime aim not being to expand our knowledge of desert landscapes and desert people. My subjects are treated in order, firstly by the desert they are most closely associated with, and secondly by their date of birth. I have also provided a very brief introduction to each desert region. I have included many original quotations as so many of my subjects have written with greater facility and panache than I am able to achieve.

I reserve special thanks for the excellent work undertaken on this volume by Victoria Leitch, the expert drawing of the maps by Sebastian Ballard, and the assistance of Alasdair Macleod and the Royal Geographical Society with the provision of images.

Andrew Goudie
May 2016

THE EXPLORERS

ARABIA, THE MIDDLE EAST AND IRAN

J.L. Burckhardt (Swiss), 1784–1817. Burckhardt discovered Petra and Abu Simbel, and visited Mecca.

F.R. Chesney (British), 1789–1872. The great explorer of the Euphrates, Chesney used paddle steamers to seek an alternative route to India.

G.F. Sadlier (also **Sadleir**) (British), 1789–1859. A professional soldier who made the first recorded crossing of Arabia from east to west by a European.

J.R. Wellsted (British), 1805–1842. Wellsted surveyed the Red Sea coastline and the interior of Oman.

R.F. Burton (British), 1821–1890. Sir Richard Burton made a pilgrimage to Medina and Mecca.

W.G. Palgrave (British), 1826–1888. Traveller and diplomat, Palgrave was the first European to cross Arabia from north-west to south-east and managed to penetrate Riyadh.

A. Blunt (British), 1837–1917. The 15th Baroness Wentworth explored the Middle East in the company of her husband and was the first European woman to cross the Nafud Desert.

W.S. Blunt (British), 1840–1922. Part of the husband and wife team, who were horse breeders and travellers in Mesopotamia and Arabia.

C.M. Doughty (British), 1843–1926. Perhaps the most important British explorer in Arabia, Doughty made observations of great anthropological and archaeological value.

G.N. Curzon (British), 1859–1925. As part of the Great Game, Lord Curzon travelled the length of Persia seeking political intelligence.

P.M. Sykes (British), 1867–1945. A soldier, diplomat and author, Sir Percy Sykes travelled widely in southern and eastern Persia but also in Kashgar.

G.M.L. Bell (British), 1868–1926. An explorer, archaeologist, kingmaker and spy.

G.E. Leachman (British), 1880–1920. A military intelligence officer, Leachman roamed widely over Iraq and Arabia.

W.H.I. Shakespear (British), 1878–1915. A British soldier engaged in military intelligence in Arabia.

H. St J.B. Philby (British), 1885–1960. Philby converted to Islam and lived in Arabia. He was the second European to cross the Rub' al Khali or Empty Quarter.

B.S. Thomas (British), 1892–1950. A British administrator who was the first European to cross the Rub' al Khali.

W.P. Thesiger (British), 1910–2003. A perennial nomad, photographer, traveller and writer, Sir Wilfred Thesiger built on the achievements of Philby and Thomas in the Empty Quarter.

SOUTH AMERICA

W. Bollaert (British), 1807–1876. A chemist, with an interest in the great nitrate deposits of the Atacama, Bollaert is thought to have been the first European to cross that driest of world deserts.

AUSTRALIA

C. Sturt (British), 1795–1869. Sturt opened up much of Central Australia and discovered many of its greatest rivers and creeks.

P.E. Warburton (British), 1813–1889. He made a crossing of the Great Sandy Desert from Alice Springs to the Indian Ocean in Western Australia.

E.J. Eyre (British), 1815–1901. Eyre discovered Lake Torrens and crossed from South to Western Australia.

J.M. Stuart (British), 1815–1866. He led the first successful traverse of the Australian mainland from south to north and back, undertaking six major expeditions in all.

R.O'H. Burke (Irish), 1821–1861. A policeman in Victoria, Burke made a pioneering and fatal expedition with Wills across Australia from Melbourne towards the Gulf of Carpentaria.

W.J. Wills (British), 1834–1861. Wills, a surveyor, made a pioneering and fatal expedition with Burke across Australia from Melbourne towards the Gulf of Carpentaria.

J. Forrest (Australian), 1847–1918. A native-born explorer of Western Australia.

CHINA AND CENTRAL ASIA

N.M. Prezahlsky (Russian), 1839–1888. A hunter and explorer who visited Lop Nor and many other parts of Central Asia.

M.A. Stein (Hungarian), 1862–1943. Archaeologist and explorer, Sir Aurel Stein mounted various expeditions to East Turkestan and along the Silk Route.

F.E. Younghusband (British), 1863–1942. Soldier, mystic and explorer, Sir Francis Younghusband crossed the Gobi Desert and then the Himalayas via Kashgar and the Muztagh Pass to Kashmir.

S.A. Hedin (Swedish), 1865–1952. During four expeditions to Central Asia, Hedin found the sources of some of the great rivers of Asia, visited Lop Nor and the Tarim Basin, discovered ancient cities and made important collections.

E. Huntington (American), 1876–1947. Huntington sought evidence for climate change in Central Asia and developed his ideas of environmental determinism.

E. and F. French (British). Sisters Evangeline (1869–1960) and Francesca (1873–1960) were missionaries who travelled in the Gobi Desert with Mildred Cable.

M. Cable (British), 1878–1952. Member of the China Inland Mission, Mildred Cable took the gospel across the Gobi Desert with Evangeline and Francesca French.

R.C. Andrews (American), 1884–1960. Led a series of major expeditions across Mongolia and the Gobi Desert in which he made dramatic discoveries of dinosaur fossils.

ETHIOPIA AND ERITREA

W. Munzinger (Swiss), 1832–1875. A pioneer explorer of Abyssinia, Egypt and Sudan, who traversed the Afar region.

L.M. Nesbitt (British), 1891–1935. A mining engineer, Nesbitt traversed the great Danakil Depression, which he described as 'The Hell-Hole of Creation'.

INDIA AND PAKISTAN

J. Tod (British), 1782–1835. A soldier and political officer, Tod was posted to the Rajput states and became the expert on the 'Annals and Antiquities of Rajasthan'.

A. Burnes (British), 1805–1841. Soldier Sir Alexander Burnes travelled up the Indus, crossed from India to Bukhara, and made journeys to Kabul, where he perished.

LIBYA AND EGYPT

W.G. Browne (British), 1768–1813. Browne traversed large parts of North Africa.

F.K. Hornemann (German), 1772–c.1801. A pioneer explorer of the Libyan Desert and Sahara, from east to west.

W.J. Bankes (British), 1786–1855. Bankes made pioneering journeys up the Nile from Cairo to Wadi Halfa in search of antiquities.

F.G. Rohlfs (German), 1831–1896. Among his many travels in North Africa, Rohlfs was the first European to cross the Great Sand Sea on the borders of Libya and Egypt and to enter the secret oasis of Kufra.

G. Nachtigal (German), 1834–1885. Nachtigal crossed the Sahara and Sudan, visiting regions previously unknown to Europeans, and made important ethnographic observations and contributions to tropical medicine.

J. Ball (British), 1872–1941. Surveyor and geologist, Dr Ball pioneered the use of the Model T Ford in numerous excursions in the Libyan Desert, where he produced maps of previously unmapped territory.

A.E.P.B. Weigall (British), 1880–1934. Chief Inspector of Antiquities for Upper Egypt, Weigall undertook major archaeological field trips which took him through the little-known Eastern Desert of Egypt from the Nile to the Red Sea.

A. Hassanein (Egyptian), 1889–1946. Courtier, diplomat and politician Hassanein made a journey to the secret oasis of Kufra with Rosita Forbes, and then undertook a lengthy trip by camel to Uweinat.

C. Williams (New Zealander), 1876–1970. Pioneered the use of Model T Fords in the Light Car Patrols in the First World War.

L.E. Almásy (Austro-Hungarian), 1895–1951. Beginning his career as a test driver of cars, Almásy became a true explorer and pioneered new routes in pursuit of the lost oasis of Zerzura. He also discovered many major rock art sites.

R.A. Bagnold (British), 1896–1990. Bagnold was a professional soldier who used cars to explore the Western Desert and commanded the Long Range Desert Group.

SOUTHERN AFRICA

F.M.J. Welwitsch (Austrian), 1806–1872. One of the greatest of the naturalist explorers, Welwitsch travelled the Namib Desert in Angola and discovered that extraordinary plant species, *Welwitschia*.

F. Galton (British), 1822–1911. Biostatistician, geneticist and eugenist, Sir Francis Galton led an expedition from the coast of the Namib Desert to the interior.

W.L. Hunt (American), 1838–1929. Also known as The Great Farini, hunt was a showman who walked through the Kalahari.

B.E.H. Clifford (New Zealander), 1890–1969. A colonial governor, Sir Bede Clifford became the first white man to cross the Kalahari Desert using motor transport.

NORTH AMERICA

J.S. Smith (American), 1799–1831. A hunter, trapper and fur trader, Smith was the first European American to travel from the Great Salt Lake to the Colorado River and the Mojave.

J.C. Frémont (American), 1813–1890. Frémont crossed Nevada, Oregon and the Great Basin to California, combining adventure, science and the gaining of practical information for emigrants.

W.L. Manly (American), 1820–1903. Manly discovered Death Valley and explored the Mojave Desert.

J.W. Powell (American), 1834–1902. The great explorer and geologist of the Grand Canyon and the Colorado Plateau.

NORTH AFRICA

B.H. Clapperton (British), 1788–1827. Clapperton crossed the Sahara and discovered Lake Chad with Walter Oudney and Dixon Denham.

A.G. Laing (British), 1794–1826. Laing sought the Niger River and travelled from Libya across the Sahara to Timbuktu.

R.A. Caillié (French), 1799–1838. Travelled across the Sahara, from the Niger via Timbuktu to Fez in Morocco.

H. Barth (German), 1821–1865. Barthe was a notable explorer of the Sahara and the Lake Chad region.

H. Duveyrier (French), 1840–1892. While still a teenager, Duvreyier made a visit to the Sahara, and on that and subsequent journeys he became an expert on the Tuareg in Libya and neighbouring areas.

G.M. Haardt (French), 1884–1932. Engineer and First World War veteran, Haardt crossed the Sahara with Audouin-Dubreuil by motor transport.

L. Audouin-Dubreuil (French), 1887–1960. A veteran of the First World War and pioneer of Saharan motoring using Citroen vehicles with Georges-Marie Haardt.

T.A. Monod (French), 1902–2000. A polymath explorer of the Sahara over seven decades.

INTRODUCTION

MOTIVES

MANY DIFFERENT MOTIVES have enticed people to deserts. For some, like Moses, Elijah, David, St John the Baptist, Jesus, the monks of Santa Katarina in Sinai, or missionaries like Charles de Foucauld, the motive has been spiritual and religious. For others, often of rather different persuasion – engineers, surveyors, railway route planners, locust control officers, arms pedlars and oil men – the motives have been material and financial. Some go for academic reasons – botanists, geologists, geomorphologists, ethnographers, and archaeologists. For men like Wilfred Thesiger and T.E. Lawrence, the attraction has, in part, been to find and live with that sometimes elusive 'noble Arab'. Certainly Lawrence preferred Arab company to 'the feral smell of English soldiers: that hot pissy aura of thronged men in woollen clothes'. Some go to deserts to seek out the remains of ancient civilizations, places like Petra – that 'long-lost rose-red city half as old as time'. Some, like David Roberts and Thomas Baines, went to paint. A few go for pure adventure, namely to attempt some spectacular first crossing of a sand sea by spitting camel or a Model T Ford. For others, however, it is the stark clarity and beauty of desert landscapes that is so mesmerizing. Still others have gone chasing myths, as was the case with the search for the mythical oasis of Zerzura in the Libyan Desert. Yet another category consists of spies seeking intelligence in contested areas like Central Asia. This volume includes examples of all these types.

The means of travel used by the desert explorers were varied, and again I have tried to include a range.

Some of the great desert explorers have been women. In some cases they travelled with their husbands (such as Mabel Bent and Anne Blunt) or their brothers (for example, Ella Sykes). Their contributions were, however, not merely as passive partners. Others travelled intrepidly and independently (such as Freya Stark, Isabelle Eberhardt, Gertrude Bell, Mildred Cable and Eva and Francesca French, Rosita Forbes and Alexandrine Tinné). It is intriguing that so many of them operated in Islamic lands.

Although some great desert explorers lived to a considerable age (notably Ardito Desio to 104, Freya Stark to 100, Rupert Harding-Newman to 99, Théodore Monod to 98, Ralph Bagnold to 94, Claud Williams to 94, Wilfrid Thesiger to 93 and William Leonard Hunt to 91), a substantial number died tragically young, either because they suffered from disease, or because they were murdered. Desert exploration could be a terminal occupation.

Explorer	Cause of death	Age
Andersson, Charles	Stomach and other disorders	40
Barth, Heinrich	Stomach disorder	44
Bent, Theodore	Malaria	45
Browne, William	Murdered	45
Burckhardt, Johann	Dysentery	32
Burke, Robert	Starvation	40
Burnes, Alexander	Murdered	36
Caillié, René	Consumption and fever	38
Clapperton, Hugh	Fever and dysentery	39
Davidson, John	Murdered	38
Douls, Camille	Murdered by Tuareg	35
Eberhardt, Isabelle	Killed in flash flood in Algeria	27
Flatters, Paul	Beheaded by Tuareg	48
Forsskål, Peter	Malaria	31
Garcés, Francisco	Killed in Yuma uprising	43
Gibson, Alfred	Disappeared	*c*.24
Giulietti, G.M.	Killed by Afar tribesmen	34
Hornemann, Friedrich	Not known	28
Laing, Alexander Gordon	Decapitation or strangling	32
Leachman, Gerard	Shot during revolt	40
Leichardt, Ludwig	Not known	*c*.34

Explorer	Cause of death	Age
Munzinger, Werner	Murdered	43
Overweg, Adolf	Malaria	29
Richardson, James	Malaria	42
Ritchie, Joseph	Fever	*c.*30
Shakespear, William	Decapitated	37
Smith, Jedediah	Murdered	32
Stroyan, Willie	Murdered by Somalis	30
Stuart, John	Stroke	50
Tinné, Alexandrine	Murdered by Tuareg	33
Vogel, Eduard	Beaten to death	26
Von Bary, Erwin	Not known	31
Wellsted, James	Fever, attempted suicide, madness	37
Wills, William	Starvation	27

Consider the fate of the Danish expedition to Arabia, which set sail in January 1761. In May 1763 the expedition's argumentative philologist, von Haven, died in Yemen, and shortly afterwards so did its gifted young naturalist Peter Forsskål, a pupil of Linnaeus. From Mocha the expedition continued to Bombay (Mumbai), but its artist and engraver, Georg Baurenfeind, together with Lars Berggren, a soldier, died en route and its medical officer, Christian Kramer, soon after disembarkation. This meant that Carsten Niebuhr, whose constitution was remarkable, was the only surviving member of a team of six.

> 'The wind blows from the east nine months in the year ... driving the sand in clouds before it...'

It is therefore not perhaps suprising that some writers have found deserts deeply unattractive. as this extract from Mary Somerville's *Physical Geography* (1858 edition, p. 92) plainly shows with respect to the Sahara:

This desert is alternately scorched by heat and pinched by cold. The wind blows from the east nine months in the year; and at the equinoxes it rushes in a hurricane, driving the sand in clouds before it, producing the darkness of night at midday, and overwhelming caravans of men and animals in common destruction.

The French geographer, Elisée Reclus (*The Earth*, 1871, p. 94–5) gave a sense of even deeper despair:

> Even the flea itself will not venture into these dreadful regions. The intense radiation of the enormous white or red surface of the desert dazzles the eyes; in this blinding light every object appears to be clothed with a sombre and preternatural tint. Occasionally, the traveller, when sitting upon his camel, is seized with the *râgle*, a kind of brain-fever, which causes him to see the most fantastical objects in his delirious dreams. Even those who retain the entire possession of their faculties and clearness of their vision, are beset by distant mirages. … When the wind blows hard, the traveller's body is beaten by grains of sand, which penetrate even through his clothes and prick like needles.

THE NATURE OF DESERTS

Deserts receive only meagre amounts of rain. Whereas even the driest parts of Britain have around 500 mm of rainfall per year, there are many desert weather stations that normally record less than one-tenth of that figure. Extremely low levels of precipitation are a particular feature of some coastal deserts, but in Egypt there are also stations where the mean annual precipitation only amounts to 0.5 mm. Years may go by in such areas of extreme aridity when no rain falls at all. On the other hand, from time to time deserts may be subjected to short spells of intense rainfall that may generate flash floods, which can be dangerous for unwary travellers. Indeed, maximum falls in 24 hours may approach or exceed the long-term annual precipitation values. In July 1981, Bassi in the Thar Desert of India received 560 mm in 24 hours, 93 per cent of its mean annual rainfall. In the Atacama Desert, storms in the summer of 2001 produced over 400 mm of rainfall in areas where the mean annual rainfall was around 150 mm. In April 2006, the desert town on Luderitz in southern Namibia received 102 mm, about six times its average annual rainfall. In June 2007, Cyclone Gonu struck eastern Oman, and dumped up to 610 mm in one storm in an area where the mean annual rainfall is around 70 mm.

Deserts have a wide range of temperature conditions. Interior deserts can be subjected to extremes of temperature, both seasonally and diurnally, that are not equalled in any other climatic region, while coastal deserts tend to have relatively low seasonal and diurnal ranges. In the case of coastal deserts, the climate is modified and moderated by the presence of cold currents and upwelling. Temperature ranges over the year are low – Callao, in the Peruvian desert, has an annual range of only 5°C. Daily ranges in such stations are also low, often around 11°C, and only about half what one would expect in the Sahara. The annual temperature values are also generally moderate (around 19°C in the Atacama, and 17°C in the Namib).

By contrast, great extremes of temperature occur in interior deserts, with maximum shade temperatures exceeding 50°C. Satellite-borne sensors now enable us to have a global picture of maximum land surface temperatures and areas such as western North America, the Sahara, Egypt, India, the Middle East, the Gobi and much of Australia, regularly exceed 60°C. Tracts of the Iranian deserts regularly exceed 70°C in the summer months. Air temperatures in excess of 37°C may occur for many days on end in the summer, but because of the clear skies there may be a marked reduction of temperature at night, and daily ranges of 17–22°C are normal. In the winter months, in high-altitude interior deserts, frost can occur frequently.

Extremely arid areas cover about 4 per cent of Earth's land surface, arid about 15 per cent and semi-arid about 14.6 per cent. Combined, these amount to almost exactly one third of the total land surface area of the planet. The deserts occur in five great provinces separated by either oceans or equatorial forests. The largest of these by far includes the Sahara and a series of other deserts extending eastwards through Egypt and Arabia to central Asia and China. The southern African province consists of the coastal Namib and the interior Karoo and Kalahari. The South American dry zone is confined to two strips – the Atacama along the west coast and the cooler Patagonian Desert along the south east coast. The North American desert province occupies much of Mexico and the south-western United States, including the Mojave and Sonoran deserts. The fifth and final province is in Australia.

Because deserts are so dry and vegetation cover so limited, there is little to protect the desert surface against the action of wind. Where there are high winds, with plenty of abrasive sand operating on susceptible surfaces, wind erosion may be important. Indeed, the examination of air photographs and satellite imagery has revealed that extensive areas of bedrock in many deserts have huge bowed, or arcuate, grooves with relative relief of more than 100 m; these run for tens of kilometres and are aligned with the prevailing winds. Such areas of grooved ground are called *yardangs* and were first described by Swedish geographer Sven Hedin when he encountered them in Central Asia. Many desert depressions also appear to have an aeolian origin: streamlined in shape, occuring in lines, with dunes on their lee sides resulting from the deposition of sands excavated by winds from the hollows. That wind action is a significant factor in creating desert landscapes is perhaps best indicated by the occurrence of *dust storms* produced by the deflation of fine materials (especially silt) from unvegetated desert surfaces. Dust storms (Figure 1), which have local names such as *khamsin, haboob* or *simoon,* may be of sufficient intensity to reduce visibility to below 1,000 m on 20–30 days in the year, and are large enough (up to 2,500 km long) to be seen on satellite imagery. Many explorers' accounts give graphic descriptions of the nature of such storms and the hardships they posed. Examples included Johann Burckhardt in Sudan, William Bollaert in the Atacama, Francis Younghusband in Turkmenistan, and René Caillié, Dixon Denham and Hugh Clapperton in the Sahara.

Figure 1. *A sand and dust storm at Jazirat al Hamra, United Arab Emirates (author's image).*

Although the romantic view of deserts envisages landscapes dominated by ever-changing sand dunes, with oases, camels and men in flowing robes, only about one-third to one-quarter of the world's deserts are covered by aeolian sand, so its role in deserts should not be exaggerated. Indeed, in the American deserts, sand dunes occupy less than 1 per cent of the surface area. Nonetheless, great *ergs*, or seas of sand, are found nowhere else on earth, and they form some of the most beautiful, repetitive and regular landforms that our planet (and, indeed, Mars) has to offer (Figure 2). Particularly large ergs occur in Arabia and the Sahara. The explorer who was perhaps most struck by the characteristics of these dunes was the great Ralph Bagnold.

Desert stream channels or valleys are called wadis (or, in North Africa, *oueds*) (Figure 3), and while they are normally dry they can be subjected to large flows of water and sediment, as was dramatically described in the Sahara by Henri Duveyrier and by Johann Burckhardt in Arabia. Isabelle Eberhardt was killed in a flash flood in Algeria. Such flows, as one might expect from the character of desert rainfall, are sporadic in time and space. In the Sahara there is an average of one flood a year in the semi-arid parts, but in the more arid core some of the wadis may go ten years without carrying water.

Figure 2. (right) *Crescentic barchan dunes in the Kharga depression, Libyan Desert (author's image).*

Figure 3. (opposite) *A typical desert wadi in the Hajar Mountains, United Arab Emirates (author's image).*

CHAPTER 1
ARABIA, THE MIDDLE EAST AND IRAN

Figure 4. (opposite) *Arabia (map drawn by Sebastian Ballard).*

ARABIA, as Jack Philby remarked in *A Pilgrim in Arabia*, 1946 (p. 7), is situated at the very crossroads of human destiny. It is also an area that has 'mothered the three great religions of the One God and nursed them until they could go forth to conquer the world'.

The Middle East is also an area of remarkable landscape diversity. It possesses old shields of great antiquity and relative stability, large rift structures, the lowest point on Earth's surface, outpourings of recent volcanic lavas, high mountains and escarpments, magnificent folded rocks, large domes of salt, the world's largest coastal marshes, called *sabkhas*, salty lakes and seas, huge alluvial fans and enormous sand seas.

Much of this diversity and distinctiveness can be attributed to the interaction of a number of plates, for the tectonic setting of this area is one both of complexity and great activity. The Middle East is on, or close to, a group of plate boundaries: in the south-west, the African plate, and to the east, the Arabian plate. The two are moving apart along the Red Sea and the Gulf of Aden. The Arabian plate is pushing northwards, colliding with the Turkish and Eurasian plates, and producing crustal deformation in the shape of multiple ripples of synclines and anticlines in the Zagros Mountains of Iran and elsewhere. The Red Sea, the Gulf of Suez, the Gulf of Aqaba, and the Afar Depression form one of the most remarkable groupings of tectonic phenomena on Earth and give a valuable insight into the process by which the breakup of continental crust can lead to the generation of new ocean crust material. Indeed, most of the most spectacular relief in the Middle East and north-eastern Africa is related to the tectonic movements resulting from the opening of the Red Sea.

Climate also contributes to the diversity of the Middle East. The southern part is directly influenced by the great Asian monsoon and may, therefore, receive summer rain and winds from the south and south-west. By contrast, the northern part comes under the influence of winter cyclones, which track from the west and bring winter precipitation. The north of the region tends to have greater annual precipitation totals, as do some of the higher mountain ranges in the south, such as those of Yemen and Oman. There is, however, a great tract of country in eastern Iran, southern Jordan, Syria, Iraq and the Arabian Peninsula, where precipitation totals are less than 100 mm per year. Extensive portions of Arabia have rainfall that is less than a third of that figure.

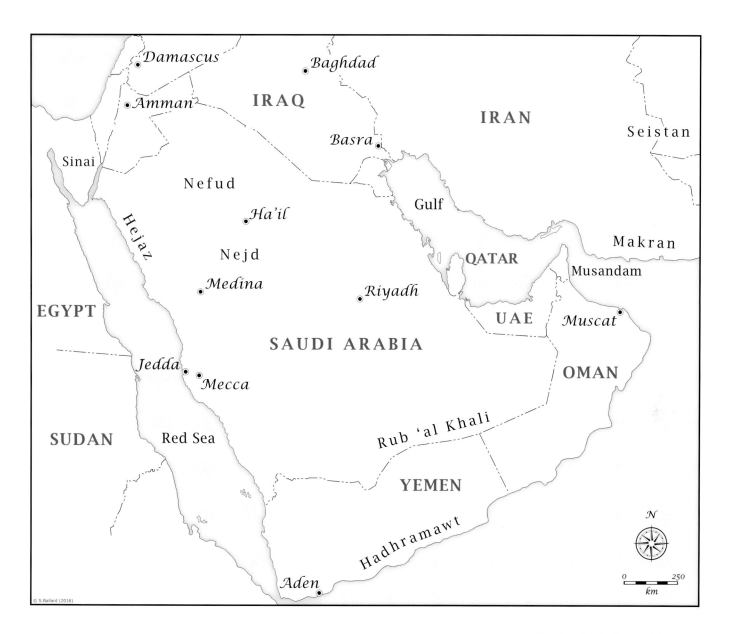

The Arabian Peninsula (Figure 4) is essentially a great tilted block, which is highest in the west and slopes gradually eastward. This pattern is broken only in the southeast by the Oman highlands. The peninsula can be divided into the following landform regions: (1) the western and southern highlands; (2) the Nejd; (3) the sand areas (Great Nafud, Dahana and Rub' al Khali); (4) the Syrian Desert; (5) the Persian (Arabian) Gulf lowlands; and (6) Oman.

The western and southern highlands rise in elevation from 460 m to 3,700 m in Yemen. The northern segment, from the Gulf of Aqaba to south of Mecca, is known as the Hejaz. It has a general elevation of 600–900 m, with some mountains attaining 1,850–2,700 m. Many ephemeral streams rise in these highlands and flow onto the narrow coastal plain, called the Tihama. Southward, the highlands continue into Asir, but at a considerably higher elevation. The mountains of Yemen in the south-western corner of Arabia are the highest of the peninsula. Eastward, through the Hadhramawt (Hadramut), the rugged highlands gradually decline to 600 m in Dhofar. The Nejd tableland lies to the east of the western highlands and is bordered on its north, east and south by sand seas: the Great Nafud in the north and the Rub' al Khali in the south.

Arabia's sand seas are enormous and stretch almost down the whole latitudinal extent of the peninsula from Kuwait to Oman. They account for nearly a third of its land area, covering not far short of 800,000 km². The Rub' al Khali itself, with an area of between 500,000 km² and 600,000 km², is often called the Empty Quarter. It is the biggest active sand sea in the world and is approximately the size of France. Some if its linear ridges can be up to 300 km long. It was almost unknown to outsiders until Bertram Thomas, Jack Philby and Wilfred Thesiger crossed it by camel in the middle of the twentieth century.

North of the Great Nafud is the Syrian Desert, which stretches into Iraq, Jordan and Syria. The most dissected part is the divide area between the Persian Gulf (also known as the Arabian Gulf) and the Euphrates drainage basin.

The Persian Gulf lowlands extend from the head of the Gulf to the fjord-like coast of the Musandam Peninsula of Oman. Largely a low plains area (less than 180 m in elevation), the relief is broken in a few places by elevated ridges or escarpments. The immediate coast is fringed with coral reefs, bars, and marshes and lagoons (sabkhas).

Oman has a series of rugged mountain ranges parallel to the coast. The Jebal al Akhdar, visited in the 1830s by James Wellsted, attains a height of over 3,000 m.

The Arabian deserts had all the usual problems of heat and water shortage, but for Europeans and Christians there was also the problem of having to cope with Islam in general and with Wahhabism in particular. The latter is a religious movement or branch of Sunni Islam, variously described as 'orthodox', 'ultraconservative', 'austere', 'fundamentalist' or 'puritanical'. Initially, it was a revivalist movement instigated by an eighteenth century theologian, Muhammad ibn Abd al-Wahhab from Nejd. The movement gained unchallenged precedence in most of the Arabian Peninsula through an alliance between Muhammad ibn Abd al-Wahhab and the House of Muhammad ibn Saud.

Much of the nineteenth and early twentieth century exploration of the area was undertaken by the British, and the names of notable, though sometimes forgotten explorers include George Sadlier (Sadleir), Richard Burton, Charles Doughty, James Wellsted, Gifford Palgrave, Jack Philby, Bertram Thomas, Gerard Leachman, William Shakespear, Wilfrid Scawen Blunt and his wife Anne, Theodore Bent and his wife Mabel, Gertrude Bell, Freya Stark, Major A.L. Holt, Gerald de Gaury (a great photographer), Percy Cox and Wilfred Thesiger. However, various Europeans were also active, including German Carsten Niebuhr in the service of Denmark, Baron Nolde of Austria, Swiss explorer Johann Burckhardt, Georg August Wallin, from Finland, Joseph Halévy, an Ottoman Jew, and Alois Musil, a Czech.

Across the Gulf lies Iran. This, too, is a country of great deserts, with the huge Dasht-e-Kavir (the Great Salt Desert) in the interior, the Lut Desert, with its dramatic yardangs, in the south, the edge of the Seistan Basin in the east (extending into Afghanistan and Pakistan), the rugged Makran Coast, and the anticlines and synclines of the Zagros Mountains in the west. This was territory, which, inter alia, attracted two great figures of the British Empire, George Curzon and Percy Sykes. Other great explorers of the desert borders of Persia and Afghanistan included Captain Charles Christie and Lieutenant (later, Sir) Henry Pottinger (in 1810), Captain Metcalfe MacGregor and Captain R.B. Lockwood (in 1875), the surveyors of the Indo-Afghan Boundary Commission, such as G.P. Tate (in the 1880s and 1890s), and the dashing Harry de Windt (in 1890). They all deserve to be better known.

JOHANN LUDWIG BURCKHARDT

I**N HIS TRAGICALLY SHORT LIFE,** Johann Burckhardt (Figure 5) was the first European to visit two of the world's greatest historical sites: Abu Simbel in Nubia, southern Egypt, and Petra in Jordan. He also made a celebrated pilgrimage to Mecca. Burckhardt was born in Lausanne, Switzerland, in 1784, and educated in Germany, where, at the University of Göttingen, he was taught by the great naturalist and anthropologist Professor J.H. Blumenbach. However, desirous of being an explorer he moved to England in 1806, with an introduction from Blumenbach to Sir Joseph Banks, the influential naturalist and explorer. Banks was the leader of The Association for Promoting the Discovery of the Interior Parts of Africa (commonly known as the African Association), which was founded in London in 1788. It was a club dedicated to the exploration of West Africa, with the mission of discovering the origin and course of the Niger River and the location of Timbuktu. With Banks's support Burckhardt persuaded this august and aristocratic body to back a mission he wanted to make and when they did so he prepared himself by studying languages – including Arabic – surgery and science, first in England – including Cambridge – and then in Syria. He also learnt to behave like a Muslim, wore Arabic dress, and prepared himself by taking long walks in hot weather and consuming only modest amounts of food. Burckhardt called himself Shaikh Ibrahim ibn Abdullah.

In June 1812, disguised as a Syrian, he crossed Palestine to the south of the Dead Sea and entered the Nabatean city of Petra through the narrow chasm for which it is so famous (*Travels in Syria and the Holy Land*, 1822, pp. 422–4):

I perceived a chasm about fifteen or twenty feet in breadth, through which the rivulet flows westwards in winter; in summer its waters are lost in the sand and gravel before they reach

Figure 5. (opposite) *Portrait of Johann Burckhardt (RGS).*

the opening, which is called El Syk (Arabic). The precipices on either side of the torrent are about eighty-feet in height; in many places the opening between them at top is less than at bottom, and the sky is not visible from below. … After proceeding for twenty-five minutes between the rocks, we came to a place where the passage opens, and where the bed of another stream coming from the south joins the Syk. On the side of the perpendicular rock, directly opposite to the issue of the main valley, an excavated mausoleum came in view, the situation and beauty of which are calculated to make an extraordinary impression upon the traveller, after having traversed for nearly half an hour such a gloomy and almost subterraneous passage as I have described. It is one of the most elegant remains of antiquity existing in Syria; its state of preservation resembles that of a building recently finished, and on a closer examination I found it to be a work of immense labour.

Later, in 1812, Burckhardt set course for Suez and Cairo (Figure 6). He hoped to join a caravan to Fezzan, a region in present-day Libya, whence he hoped to explore the sources of the Niger. This ultimate aim he never achieved. Dressed in the commonest of garments, as an Arab peasant or small trader, with a blue cotton blouse covering a coarse shirt, loose white trousers, a calico turban, and slippers, he travelled down the Nile Valley en route to Old Dongola and came across the great temples of Rameses II at Abu Simbel (Ebsambal) (*Travels in Nubia*, 1819):

Having, as I supposed, seen all the antiquities of Ebsambal, I was about to ascend the sandy side of the mountain by the same way I had descended; when having luckily turned more to the southward, I fell in with what is yet visible of

SKEIKH IBRAHIM (J. L. BURCKHARDT.)
In his Arab Bernous.
Sketched at Cairo in Feb.ʸ 1817. by H. Salt Esq.

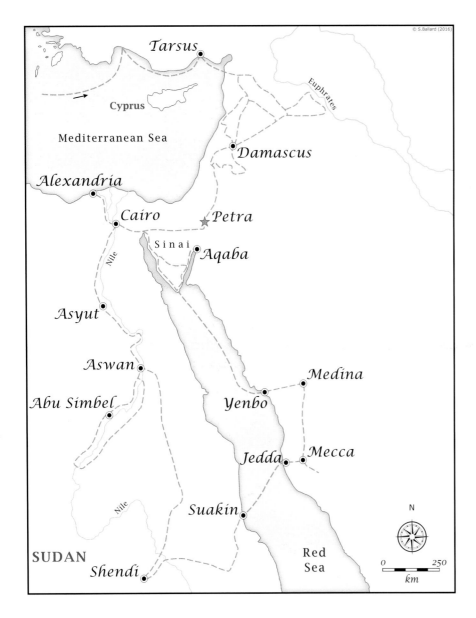

four immense colossal statues cut out of the rock, at a distance of about two hundred yards from the temple; they stand in a deep recess, excavated in the mountain; but it is greatly to be regretted, that they are now almost entirely buried beneath the sands, which are blown down here in torrents. The entire head, and part of the breast and arms of one of the statues are yet above the surface; of the one next to it scarcely any part is visible, the head being broken off, and the body covered with sand to above the shoulders; of the other two, the bonnets only appear.

Their discovery drew many later travellers to the area, including William Bankes and Amelia Edwards. In 1814 Burckhardt travelled across the Nubian Desert to Suakin, a Sudanese port on the Red Sea. There he experienced a *semoum* (simoon or dust storm):

I have repeatedly been exposed to the hot wind, in the Syrian and Arabian deserts, in Upper Egypt and Nubia. The hottest and most violent I ever experienced was at Suakin, yet even there I felt no particular inconvenience from it, although exposed to all its fury in the open plain. For my own part I am perfectly convinced that all the stories which travellers or the inhabitants of the towns of Egypt and Syria relate of the Semoum of the desert, are greatly exaggerated, and I never could hear of a single well authenticated instance of its having proved mortal either to man or beast. I never observed that the Semoum blows close to the ground, as commonly supposed, but always observed the whole atmosphere appear as if in a state of combustion; the dust and sand are carried high into the air, which assumes a reddish, or blueish, or yellowish tint, according to the nature and colour of the ground, from which the dust arises. The yellow however always, more or less, predominates. The most disagreeable effect of the Semoum on man is, that it stops perspiration, dries up the palate, and produces great restlessness. I never saw any person lie down flat upon his face to escape its pernicious blast, as Bruce describes himself to have done in crossing this desert; but during the whirlwinds the Arabs often hide their faces with their cloaks, and kneel down near their camels to prevent the sand or dust from hurting their eyes. Camels are always much distressed, not by the heat but by the dust blowing into their large, prominent, eyes.

'Camels are always much distressed, not by the heat but by the dust blowing into their large, prominent, eyes.'

From Suakin he sailed across to Jeddah, and made his way to Mecca. He stayed two months and suffered from a severe bout of fever before returning to Cairo. He gave very full descriptions of Jeddah, Mecca, Medina and other parts of the Hejaz. On route to Mecca he experienced a flash flood (*Travels in Arabia*, 1829, pp. 166–8):

On the road from Shedad, which lies along the lower plains, between sharp mountains, we were surprised by a most violent shower of rain and hail, which obliged us to halt. In a very short time the water poured down in torrents from the mountains; and when the hail ceased, after about an hour, we found that the rain, which still continued, had covered the Wady Noman with a sheet of water three feet deep, while streams of nearly five feet in breadth crossed the road with an impetuosity which rendered it impossible for us to pass them. In this situation we could neither advance nor retreat, knowing that similar currents would have been formed in our rear; we therefore took post on the side of the mountain, where we were sure of not being washed away, and where we could wait in security till the subsiding of the storm. The mountains, however, soon presented on their sides innumerable cascades, and the inundation became general; while the rain, accompanied with thunder and lightning, continued with undiminished violence.

Figure 6. (opposite)
Burckhardt's journeys from 1809–1817 (map drawn by Sebastian Ballard).

Burckhardt described the people and drew attention to their tattoos (p. 183):

'All the male natives of Mekka and Djidda are tattooed with a particular mark, which is performed by their parents when they are forty days of age.'

All the male natives of Mekka and Djidda are tattooed with a particular mark, which is performed by their parents when they are forty days of age. It consists of three long cuts down both cheeks; and two on the right temple, the scars of which, sometimes three or four lines in breadth, remain through life. It is called Meshále. The Bedouins do not follow this practice; but the Mekkawys pride themselves in the distinction, which precludes the other inhabitants of the Hedjaz from claiming, in foreign countries, the honour of being born in the holy cities. This tattooing is sometimes, though very seldom, applied to female children.

In fact, a subsequent study by Sinclair (Tattooing–Oriental and Gypsy, 1908) showed that the tattooing of men and women was extraordinarily widespread, not least among the Bedouin in the Middle East, with the procedure very often being undertaken by gypsies.

Burckhardt also found that the inhabitants of the Holy City and its environs had certain vices:

They outwardly appear more religious than their southern neighbours. They are much more rigid in the observance of their sacred rites, and public decorum is much more observed at Medina than at Mekka: the morals, however, of the inhabitants appear to be much upon the same level with those of the Mekkans; all means are adopted to cheat the hadjys. The vices which disgrace the Mekkans are also prevalent here; and their religious austerity has not been able to exclude the use of intoxicating liquors. These are prepared by the negroes, as well as date-wine, which is made by pouring water over dates, and leaving it to ferment. On the whole, I believe the Medinans to be as worthless as the Mekkans, and greater hypocrites. They, however, wish to approach nearer to the northern Turkish character; and, for that reason, abandon the few good qualities for which the Mekkans may be commended.

He was also interested in the eunuchs of Medina:

The black eunuchs, unlike those of Europe, become emaciated; their features are extremely coarse, nothing but the bones being distinguishable; their hands are those of a skeleton, and their whole appearance is extremely disgusting. By the help of thick clothing they hide their leanness; but their bony features are so prominent, that they can be distinguished at first sight. Their voice, however, undergoes little, if any change, and is far from being reduced to that fine feminine tone so much admired in the Italian Singers.

In 1816 he explored Sinai, partly to avoid an outbreak of the plague in Cairo and partly because he wanted to visit Mount Sinai and Akaba. Burckhardt visited such places as Wadi Feiran, Sharm el Sheik and the monastery at Santa Katharina (Figure 7) (*Travels in Syria and the Holy Land*, 1822, pp. 490–1):

> We alighted under a window, by which the priests communicate with the Arabs below. The letter of recommendation which I had with me was drawn up by a cord, and when the prior had read it, a stick tied across a rope was let down, upon which I placed myself, and was hoisted up. Like all travellers I received a cordial reception and was shewn into the same neatly furnished room in which all preceding Europeans had taken up their abode.

He described the interior (pp. 541–2):

Figure 7. *Santa Katharina Monastery, Sinai (author's image).*

> The convent contains eight or ten small court-yards, some of which are neatly laid out in beds of flowers and vegetables; a few date-trees and cypresses also grow there, and great numbers of vines. The distribution of the interior is very irregular, and could not be otherwise, considering the slope upon which the building stands; but the whole is very clean and neat. There are a great number of small rooms, in the lower and upper stories, most of which are at present unoccupied. The principal building in the interior is the great church, which, as well as the convent, was built by the Emperor Justinian, but it has subsequently

undergone frequent repairs. An abundance of silver lamps, paintings, and portraits of saints adorn the walls round the altar; among the latter is a saint Christopher, with a dog's head. The floor of the church is finely paved with slabs of marble.

He also climbed up Mount Moses, also known as Mount Sinai. However, back in Cairo in 1817 Burckhardt contracted dysentery having eaten contaminated fish, and died at the age of 32. His funeral was Muslim and was conducted with all proper regard to his rank as haji, scholar and sheikh. His influence lived on, for among those he inspired was German explorer and geographer Gerhard Rohlfs. Burckhardt's diaries were published in three volumes by John Murray for the African Association, and are remarkable not only as a record of his travels but also of the countryside and peoples that he encountered.

BIBLIOGRAPHIC REFERENCES AND FURTHER READING

Burckhardt, J.L. 1819. *Travels in Nubia.* London: John Murray.

Burckhardt, J.L. 1822. *Travels in Syria and the Holy Land.* London: John Murray.

Burckhardt, J.L. 1829. *Travels in Arabia.* London: John Murray.

Christie, T.L. 1967. Shaikh Burckhardt: explorer. *Saudi Aramco World*, 18 (5), 15–17.

Freeth, Z. and Winstone, V. 1978. *Explorers of Arabia.* London: Allen and Unwin.

Hogarth, D.G. 1905. *The Penetration of Arabia. A Record of the Development of Western Knowledge Concerning the Arabian peninsula.* London: Alston Books.

Kiernan, R.H. 1937. *The Unveiling of Arabia.* London: Harrap.

Sabini, J. 1981. *Armies in the Sand. The Struggle for Mecca and Medina.* London: Thames and Hudson.

Sim, K. 1981. *Jean Louis Burckhardt. A Biography.* London: Quartet Books.

Sinclair, A.T. 1908. Tattooing—Oriental and Gypsy. *American Anthropologist*, 10(3), 361–386.

FRANCIS RAWDON CHESNEY

FRANCIS CHESNEY was born in Ulster in 1789. He was an officer in the Royal Artillery and was wiry, tough, brave, confident, determined, devout and devoted to duty. He was also irritable, obstinate, dogmatic, argumentative, loquacious and bad tempered. Perhaps most remarkably of all, he was no more than 1.55 m (5 feet 1 inch) tall (Figure 8).

His interest in exploration began in 1829 when he was sent to Constantinople (now Istanbul) with some rockets for the Turkish sultan. The British Ambassador in Constantinople, Sir Robert Gordon, was concerned about the growing French influence at the Court of Mohammed Ali Pasha, of Egypt. Thus he invited Chesney to travel to Egypt and Syria, to report on the situation there and particularly to assess whether it might be possible to improve communications between Britain and India, either via the Red Sea or overland from a port on the Mediterranean across the Syrian Desert to the Persian Gulf. As a consequence, in 1830, already over 40 years old, Chesney reconnoitred the southern part of the Sinai Peninsula and went up the Nile to Wadi Halfa. Later in the year he proceeded to Syria, crossing the desert via Palmyra to Anah on the Euphrates. There he constructed a raft mounted on inflated sheepskins and went down the river as far as Hit. Having transferred to a faster local boat he proceeded to the Shatt al-Arab at Basra and then

Figure 8. *Francis Chesney (RGS: Chesney and O'Donnell, 1885).*

on to Bushire. He then decided to explore Persia and Anatolia and eventually reached London in the autumn of 1832. He had become convinced that the security of the British Empire depended on the exploitation of the Euphrates route to India, using river steamers. This became his main preoccupation until his death 40 years later in 1872.

King William IV, the first patron of the newly established Royal Geographical Society (RGS), was an enthusiastic supporter of Chesney's dream and in 1834 Parliament voted to allocate money so that Chesney could carry out the project. Two paddle steamers were laid down at the Laird shipyard in Birkenhead, vessels that could be dismantled and transported in portable sections overland. The personnel for the expedition were selected, and comprised 50 officers and men, including sappers, artillerymen, mechanics and experts on steam boilers. In February 1835, this large expedition sailed from the Mersey to the Bay of Antioch. The plan was to sail as far as possible up the Orontes River and then to carry the dismantled ships overland to the Euphrates. Unfortunately, the Orontes proved not to be navigable because of its strong currents and shallow rapids, so everything had to be transported laboriously over a distance of 225 km of hills and desert. This was an almost incredible exercise, for one of the steamers was 31.4 m long, and the other 21.3 m long. To move the heavy iron plates, the large boilers, the paddle wheels, the masts and many other supplies was a herculean ordeal. They had to create their own road through the steep foothills that barred their way to the Syrian plains. The portage took them nearly a year, instead of the estimated one month, and cost the lives of eight men. A particularly difficult stretch was 'The Hill of Difficulty' (*Narrative of the Euphrates Expedition*, 1868, p. 194):

'...we soon found that the sharp angles and abruptness of the descent made this all but impracticable...'

We had four artillery wagons, twenty-seven waggons and sledges … and numerous 'arabas' or carts of the country, with which to transport the steamers' boilers – the heaviest of which weighed seven tons – and all our ponderous materials. … A zigzag path having been made, we confidently expected that, with 40 pairs of oxen and 100 men to each sledge, the boilers might reach the crest of the ridge one at a time, the whole of our available strength of animals and men being applied to each separately. But we soon found that the sharp angles and abruptness of the descent made this all but impracticable: with less enterprise and perseverance on the part of the officers and men it must have been quite so. They were, however, fertile in expedients. Anchors were fixed firmly in the ground a little distance in advance, towards which the boiler was drawn by pulleys and drag-ropes inch by inch; at certain places jack-screws were used to raise the sledge; and by these process, tedious though they were, the summit was attained step by step.

By April 1836, the two vessels – the *Euphrates* and the *Tigris* – had been reassembled at Birecik on the Turkish frontier and the expedition set off downstream. On 21 May it suffered a dreadful calamity. A violent windstorm, accompanied by dense clouds of sand, dust and rain, overwhelmed the *Tigris*, and 22 lives were lost. Miraculously Chesney himself survived, and was found in a field. Undeterred and undaunted, he carried on downriver in the *Euphrates* and eventually reached Basra in the middle of June (Figure 9). He had proved that the Euphrates was navigable from a point about 190 km from the Mediterranean to the Gulf. After crossing to

Figure 9. *The Steamers* Euphrates *and* Tigris *passing Thapsacus (RGS: Chesney, 1868).*

Bushire for repairs, he decided to try and navigate the Euphrates upstream, but his progress was blocked by the Lamlum marshes and by the breakdown of one of the engines. In retrospect it seems odd that Chesney should have selected to start the expedition going down the river rather than up. The obvious way to have tested whether the Euphrates was navigable was to take the vessels by sea to Basra rather than hauling them across hills and deserts. It was little use to know whether the ships could pass downstream if they could not go up. In 1838 the RGS awarded Chesney its Founder's Medal, but others criticised him on grounds of the cost of the expedition, the loss of the *Tigris*, and the extensive casualty list. He received scant recognition or reward from the British Government.

The use of steamers in Mesopotamia continued, however, after Chesney's return home. H. Blosse Lynch of the Indian Navy (Chesney's second in command) used the *Euphrates* to explore the Tigris from its source in Armenia to Baghdad. A company was set up in Baghdad to promote commercial navigation, so that by 1840, four steamers were regularly sailing between Basra and Baghdad. In 1856 Chesney returned to Constantinople, and again in 1862, to try and press for the construction of a railway from the Mediterranean, across the desert to the Euphrates and then down to the Gulf. He was not successful.

BIBLIOGRAPHIC REFERENCES AND FURTHER READING

Brinton, J. 1969. Wreck on the Tigris. *Saudi Aramco World*, 20, 24–29.

Chesney, F.R. 1868. *Narrative of the Euphrates Expedition*. London: Longmans Green.

Guest, J.S. 1992. *The Euphrates Expedition*. London: Kegan Paul.

Jones, D.D. and Grissom, J.W. 1949. Francis Rawdon Chesney: a reappraisal of his work on the Euphrates route. *Historian*, 11, 185–203.

Lane-Poole, S. 2004. Chesney, Francis Rawdon (1789–1872). *Oxford Dictionary of National Biography online*.

Marshall-Cornwall, J. 1965. Three soldier-geographers. *Geographical Journal*, 131, 357–365.

Rawlinson, H.C. 1871/2. Address to the Royal Geographical Society. *Proceedings of the Royal Geographical Society of London*, 16, 291–377.

GEORGE FORSTER SADLIER

GEORGE FORSTER SADLIER (sometimes, and probably correctly, spelt Sadleir), was born in Cork, Ireland, in 1789, and became the first European to cross Arabia from east to west. He became a soldier at the age of 16 and joined the 47th Regiment of Foot, in which he was to serve abroad continuously for over 22 years, some of it in India, and some of it in Persia.

In 1818, the pasha of Egypt's second son, Ibrahim, in an effort to suppress the Wahhabis in Arabia, overran their eastern stronghold and capital, Dar'iya. Sadlier was chosen by Lord Hastings, governor general and commander in chief in India, to convey to Ibrahim an address of congratulations and a sword of honour. The British wanted to ingratiate themselves with the victor, to encourage the complete reduction of Wahhabi power, and to seek Ibrahim's assistance in dealing with the pirates who infested the ports along the southern shores of the Arabian Gulf, such as Ras al-Khaimah. The expedition was in a sense futile, because the Egyptians, including Ibrahim, wanted nothing more than to leave the Nejd and to return in triumph with their spoils of war to Egypt. Nonetheless, Sadlier dutifully set off from Bombay in April 1819, and reached Muscat in Oman in May of that year (Figure 10). He then crossed to the Persian side of the Gulf and landed at Bushire before crossing back to Qatif. He left Qatif on 28 June and began his pioneering journey of over a thousand miles and 84 days duration to Yanbu on the Red Sea. Eventually, near Medina, he managed to meet up with the elusive Ibrahim and presented him with his sword and address of congratulations. The Egyptian no longer had an interest in the Nejd, had no interest in the Persian Gulf pirates and was extremely non-committal, so that Sadlier learnt little of Egyptian intentions.

In spite of knowing very little Arabic, the heat and lack of water, illness, incompetent guides and exasperating delays, he had fulfilled his orders. Dutifully, this reluctant, conscientious,

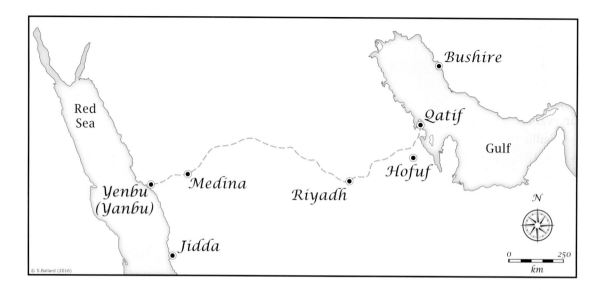

Figure 10. *Sadlier's route from the Persian Gulf to the Red Sea (map drawn by Sebastian Ballard).*

stiff-necked explorer, who wore his braided, high-collared uniform throughout the heat of an Arabian summer, had kept his diary (Sadler, 1866) with scrupulous care, noting the names of villages and tribes, and the physical features of the country. As David Hogarth was to write in 1905: 'If the Englishman saw with somewhat unsympathetic eyes, he saw what was; and, as it was, he recorded it. Other Europeans, more scientific and observant, were to come after him to Nejd, but none on whose report we may surely rely.'

While most early travellers in Arabia tended to like the people and the landscape of Arabia, Sadlier liked neither. To him, as to many British soldiers, the indigenous people were unimportant and distasteful. In his diary entry for 6 July 1819 (Sadlier 1866), he wrote of the Bedouin:

The procrastination, duplicity, falsity, deception, and fraudulence of the Bedouin cannot be described by one to an European in language which would present to his mind the real character of these hordes of robbers. To attempt to argue with them on the principles of justice, right, or equity is ridiculous; and to attempt to insist in their adhering to promises or agreements is equally fruitless, unless you possess the means of enforcing compliance.

He was also appalled by the Turks and their 'numerous and depraved soldiery' who forced Arab women into common prostitution. He also disliked his final stop, the port of Yanbu, which he described as miserable, tottering, having impure air caused by dunghills, burying grounds and receptacles for dead horses and camels, and well water which emitted as abominable a smell as the bilge water of a ship. As for Ibrahim Pasha, whom he sought, he was another ghastly foreigner with 'an avaricious disposition, and an insatiable desire to shed human blood'.

Sadlier sailed from Jeddah in a British warship, the *Prince of Wales*, and reached Bombay on 8 May, 1820. Although he had failed in is intended mission, Sadlier had become the first European ever to cross the whole Arabian Peninsula. After completing his army service, he returned to Cork, became sheriff, married for the first time at the age of 60, and migrated to New Zealand, where he died in December 1859.

BIBLIOGRAPHIC REFERENCES AND FURTHER READING

Edwards, F.M. 1957. George Forster Sadleir. *Journal of the Royal Central Asian Society*, 44, 38–49.

Hogarth, D.G. 1905. *The Penetration of Arabia. A Record of the Development of Western Knowledge Concerning the Arabian Peninsula.* London: Alston Books.

Kiernan, R.H. 1937. *The Unveiling of Arabia.* London: Harrap.

Sabini, J. 1981. *Armies in the Sand. The Struggle for Mecca and Medina.* London: Thames and Hudson.

Sadlier, G.F. 1866. *Diary of a Journey Across Arabia from El Khatif in the Persian Gulf to Yambo in the Red Sea, during the Year 1819.* Bombay: Education Society Press.

JAMES RAYMOND WELLSTED

J AMES WELLSTED, born in 1805, was a British naval officer who surveyed the coastlines of the Red Sea and the interior of Oman. He is now largely forgotten, but his two-volume work *Travels in Arabia* (1838) is an immense store of detailed information on areas that Europeans had scarcely visited before. Between 1830 and 1833, he sailed in the *Palinurus*, a brig of the East India Company, which made a detailed survey of the Gulf of Aqaba and the northern part of the Red Sea. Between 1833 and 1834 the same vessel was used to survey the southern coast of Arabia and the island of Socotra. In 1835, with Lieutenant F. Whitelock (whose assistance he perhaps underplayed), also of the Indian Navy, he obtained permission to travel to Muscat in Oman, and ventured into the interior (Figure 11).

On this journey, Wellsted (*Travels in Arabia*, 1838, Volume 1, pp. 6–7) was impressed by the imam of Muscat:

He possesses a tall and commanding figure; a mild, yet striking countenance; and an address and manner courtly, affable, and dignified. In his personal habits, the Imam has preserved the simplicity of his Bedowin origin; he is frugal almost to abstemiousness; he never wears jewels; his dress, excepting in the fineness of the materials, is not superior to that of the principal inhabitants; and he is attended, on all occasions, without pomp or ostentation. It is noticed by the Arabs, as an instance of the warmth of his affections, that he daily visits his mother, who is still alive, and pays, in all matters, implicit obedience to her wishes. In his intercourse with Europeans, he has ever displayed the warmest attention and kindness.

Equally, he was impressed by Muscat itself (p. 12):

The town of Maskat is situated at the extremity of a small cove in the gorges of an extensive pass, which widens from this point as it advances into the interior. On either side, the cove hills, to the height of from three to five hundred feet, rise almost perpendicularly from the sea, and appear lined with forts, which, considering they belong to the vicinity of an Arab town, are in a tolerable state of repair. … To persons arriving from seaward, Maskat with its fort and contiguous hills, have an extraordinary and romantic appearance.

Inland from Sur, Wellsted received hospitality from the local women (p. 47):

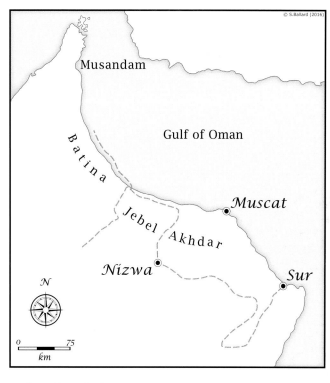

Figure 11. *Wellsted's routes (Map drawn by Sebastian Ballard).*

I had scarcely seated myself on a skin, spread on the ground in one of these dwellings, when some young and very pretty females entered, bringing with them a huge bowl of milk. Out of compliment to them I took a long draught; but no, this was insufficient. Was it bad?—try again, and again! In vain I extolled it to the skies; I was not permitted to desist until I had swelled almost to suffocation, and sworn by the beard of the Prophet that I could and would take no more. They were then delighted, and we became such excellent friends that, with the assistance of a few presents and some fair speeches, we parted with expressions of mutual regret.

He also seemed to gain great exhilaration both from the Bedouin and the desert landscape (p. 72):

The air was cold and pure, the sun just sufficiently high to render its warmth agreeable, while the wild appearance and movements of my Bedowin friends gave an exhilarating novelty to my sensations: even the very solitude of the scene rendered it the more pleasing. While sweeping across these solitary and boundless wastes, although destitute of trees, mountains, and water, or any of the features common to softer regions, there is something in their severely simple features, their nakedness and immensity, which reminds me of the trackless ocean, and impresses the soul with a feeling of sublimity. The aspect of my companion is in perfect keeping with the peculiar attributes of his native land. His sinewy form, and clean and compact limbs, are revealed by the scantiness of his garments: his dark and ruddy countenance is lighted up by the kindling of his resolute eye: his demeanour is honest and frank, and his whole appearance breathes a manly contempt of hardships.

Among his interesting observations on the economy of the country are his remarks about the *falaj* irrigation systems, in which water is transported by underground tunnels from the mountains to the oases of the plains (pp. 92–3):

> The greater part of the face of the country being destitute of running streams on the surface, the Arabs have sought in elevated places for springs or fountains beneath it; by what mode they discover these I know not; but it seems confined to a peculiar class of men who go about the country for the purpose; but I saw several which had been sunk to the depth of forty feet. A channel from this fountain-head is then, with a very slight descent, bored in the direction in which it is to be conveyed, leaving apertures at regular distances, to afford light and air to those who are occasionally sent to keep it clean. In this manner water is frequently conducted from a distance of six or eight miles, and an unlimited supply is thus obtained. These channels are usually about four feet broad, and two feet deep, and contain a clear rapid stream. Few of the large towns or oases but had four or five of these rivulets or feleji running into them. The isolated spots to which water is thus conveyed possess a soil so fertile, that nearly every grain, fruit, or vegetable, common to India, Arabia, or Persia, is produced almost spontaneously.

'The air was cold and pure, the sun just sufficiently high to render its warmth agreeable...'

He visited the Jebel Akhdar, which he thought misnamed (pp. 138–9):

> The Jebel Akhdar occupy from east to west, which is their greatest length, a distance of thirty miles. At right angles to this they are intersected by narrow deep valleys, along which, during the rainy season, on either side, the torrents descend, and lose themselves, either in the sandy soil which crosses the plains, or pour their waters into the ocean. The maximum

breadth of the chain is fourteen miles, and the northern and southern declivities are very rapid. Taken generally, it will be seen by my narrative of our route, that the range by no means deserves the appellation it has received, "Green," for a great proportion of its surface is bare limestone rock, which presents in some places naked tabular masses, and in others, the shallow, earthy deposit lodged in the hollows is as poor as the worst part of the plains; but the valleys with several hollows are extensively cultivated, and supply such an abundance of fruit, &c., that many writers have considered them as common to the whole range, and hence is derived its present appellation.

In the mountains he encountered the Beni Riyam people and noted the effects of alcohol (p. 144):

In their persons, although more athletic and robust than their neighbours of the plains, they have not the usual healthy and hardy look of mountaineers, but, on the contrary, their faces are wrinkled and haggard, and appear as if suffering from premature decay. I have little doubt but this is owing to an immoderate use of wine, which they distil from their grapes in large quantities, and partake of openly and freely at their several meals. They defend the practice by asserting that the cold renders it necessary.

'... the shallow, earthy deposit lodged in the hollows is as poor as the worst part of the plains; but the valleys with several hollows are extensively cultivated, and supply such an abundance of fruit, &c...'

Like some other Arabian explorers, Wellsted found a medical kit was advantageous, though his dispensing of opium may raise an eyebrow (p. 155):

During my progress in this country, with a view to initiate myself into their manners and domestic life, I mixed much with the Bedowins, frequently living and sleeping in their huts and tents. On all occasions I was received with kindness, and often with a degree of hospitality above, rather than below, the means of those who were called upon to exercise it. The medical character which I assumed proved then of much service to me. … My practice proved very extensive, and, if not travelling, the early part of the day was thus occupied. I always carried with me a large quantity of pills made of ambergris mixed with opium, and found, on

> 'I always carried with me a large quantity of pills made of ambergris mixed with opium...'

account of the stimulating property which the former is supposed to possess, that I could not, to an Arab, make a more acceptable present.

Although Wellsted's travels in Oman are his finest achievement, he also described in great detail the coastlines of Arabia and even ventured to Berbera in Somalia, and along the coast of Yemen. As with the people of Oman, he was generous about the Somalis (*Travels in Arabia*, Volume 2, p. 431):

They are a fine race, easily recognised from all other classes by their martial bearing and appearance, for in general they are remarkably tall, a short person being rarely seen. Their limbs are clean and well made, their nose slightly aquiline; but otherwise their features are very regular, and expressive of that boldness and freedom which really belongs to the Sumali character. Their skins are dark and glossy, and they have a custom of changing the colour of their hair from its natural blackness to an auburn tinge, by allowing it to remain for some hours plastered with chinam. To what absurdities does not the caprice of fashion lead mankind!

In 1837 in Muscat, suffering from severe fever, Wellsted shot himself in the mouth with a double-barrelled gun, but survived, though horribly injured. In bad health, physically and mentally, he retired to England, and died in London in 1842, aged only 37. His achievements were recognised in his lifetime; he was, for example, elected a fellow of the Royal Society in 1837. He wrote beautifully and is notable for the enthusiasm he displayed both for the landscapes he travelled through and the people that inhabited them.

BIBLIOGRAPHIC REFERENCES AND FURTHER READING

Al-Hajri, H.S. 2003. *Oman through British Eyes: British Travel Writing on Oman from 1800 to 1970* (Doctoral dissertation, University of Warwick).

Hamilton, A. 2010. *An Arabian Utopia: the Western Discovery of Oman.* Oxford: Oxford University Press and Arcadian Library.

Hogarth, D.G. 1905. *The Penetration of Arabia. A Record of the Development of Western Knowledge Concerning the Arabian peninsula.* London: Alston Books.

Kiernan, R.H. 1937. *The Unveiling of Arabia.* London: Harrap.

Laughton, J.K. 2004. Wellsted, James Raymond (1805–1842). *Oxford Dictionary of National Biography online.*

Ward, P. 1987. *Travels in Oman.* Cambridge: Oleander Press.

Wellsted, R. 1836. Observations on the coast of Arabia between Ras Mohammed and Jiddah. *Journal of the Royal Geographical Society,* 6, 51–96.

Wellsted, J.R. 1838. *Travels in Arabia.* 2 volumes. London: John Murray.

SIR RICHARD FRANCIS BURTON

SIR RICHARD BURTON (1821–1890) (Figure 12), a gifted linguist, anthropologist, soldier and sexologist, was one of the greatest explorers of the Victorian age. Best known for his explorations in the Great Lakes area of eastern Africa and his endeavours with Speke to find the source of the Nile, he was also a noted traveller in Arabia.

Born in Hertfordshire to an Irish father and an English mother, he became accustomed to a vagabond life as a boy, was partial to duelling and swordsmanship, and 'rode, smoked, gambled and experimented with all the available forms of profligacy' (*The Wilder Shores of Love*, Lesley Blanch, 1954, p. 21). He was sent to Trinity College, Oxford, and read Arabic. However, he loathed the college, his fellow students and the city, and was eventually expelled (sent down). He is said to have shown his resentment by departing the college by driving his horse and carriage through the college flowerbeds. It was determined that he should join the Indian Army, and he sailed for Bombay as an ensign in June 1842. In India he learnt many languages and became exposed to the life of the local people and picturesque landscapes. He experimented with cannabis and opium, and acted as a secret agent in Sind, in present-day Pakistan, where he mixed with the tribes, often disguised as a Pathan or Persian. One of the secret tasks with which he was entrusted by Sir Charles Napier, the conqueror of Sind, was to report on various sexual practices, including pederasty, and in due course this became the subject of a paper he wrote on the distribution of this 'Persian' vice across the 'Sotadic Belt' of the Old World. This phase in his life is beautifully evoked by Christopher Ondaatje (*Sindh Revisted*, 1996).

Tiring of army life, Burton, known to his fellow officers as 'Ruffian Dick' or the 'White Nigger', decided he wished to visit Arabia, and in particular to visit the holy cities of Medina and Mecca. With the support of the Royal Geographical Society, where Sir Roderick Murchison

Figure 12. (opposite) *Richard Burton (RGS: Sir Richard Francis Burton from the portrait by Lord Leighton in the National Portrait Gallery).*

was an ally, and of the East India Company, he was given leave to fulfil this ambition.

In a decree of AD 629 Mohammed had ruled the holy cities to be out of bounds to all infidels, and any non-believer found there could be executed. The journey was, therefore, fraught with danger. His aim was to be the first unconverted Englishman to go there. As Burton recognised, some Europeans, such as Burckhardt, had been there before him, as had some announced Islamic converts. Burton also wished to establish himself as an authority on Arabia and to remove what he called 'that opprobrium to modern adventure, the huge white blot which in our maps still notes the Eastern and Central regions of Arabia'.

In preparation, Burton honed his language skills, had himself circumcised in the Islamic rather than the Jewish manner, grew a beard, shaved his head, and darkened his skin with walnut juice. He portrayed himself as an Afghan doctor and assumed the role of a dervish, recognised by Islamic culture as a role for the socially and psychologically marginal. In July 1853, he made his way from Egypt, across the Red Sea to the Arabian port of Yanbu, which he found as 'in no wise remarkable', and to be inhabited by races who were 'bigoted and quarrelsome'. From there he proceeded to Medina

by donkey, a means of transport necessitated by having infected his foot by stepping on a sea urchin on the Red Sea coast. He spent a month in Medina, touring the shrines, most notably the Prophet's tomb and the Prophet's Mosque.

Burton was greatly struck by the date trees of Medina *Personal Narrative of a Pilgrimage to El-Medinah and Meccah* (1855–6):

> Their stately columnar stems, here, seems higher than in other lands, and their lower fronds are allowed to tremble in the breeze without mutilation. These enormous palms were loaded with ripening fruits; and the clusters, carefully tied up, must often have weighed upwards of eight pounds. They hung down between the lower branches by a bright yellow stem, as thick as a man's ankle.

He described the buildings and foods of the city, and discussed the costs of different types of slave:

> A little black boy, perfect in all his points, and tolerably intelligent, costs about a thousand piastres; girls are dearer, and eunuchs fetch double that sum. The older the children become, the more their value diminishes. … The Abyssinian, mostly Galla, girls, so much prized because their skins are always cool in the hottest weather, are here rare; they seldom sell for less than £20, and they often fetch £60.

At Medina he joined a seven thousand-strong 'Damascus caravan' of hajis (pilgrims) and they traversed the barren and desolate terrain to Mecca, using the Darb el Sharki. This inland road had never before been travelled by a European.

In Mecca he was able to visit the Grand Mosque, the Kaabah and the sacred Black Stone, and passed through all the rituals and ceremonials demanded of a pilgrim, before returning to Egypt via Jeddah. He noted than many Meccans have black concubines but that the consumption of alcohol, noted by Burckhardt, had ceased. He felt that the Meccans had some undesirable characteristics, including being covetous spendthrifts, excessively proud and coarse of language.

Burton's remarkable journey is written up in his *Personal Narrative of a Pilgrimage to Al-Madinah and Meccah*, first published in 1855, and which was described by R.H. Kiernan

(*The Unveiling of Arabia*, 1937, p. 164) as being 'marked out from all other works on Arabia by its graphic description, humour, grimness, insight into Arab and all Semitic thought, vast knowledge of Easter manners and habits, vigorous, trenchant style, and highly individualistic opinions'.

Burton was accompanied throughout his journey by someone he generally referred to as 'the boy Mohammed'. This youth, originally from Mecca, had met up with him in Cairo *Personal Narrative of a Pilgrimage to El-Medinah and Meccah* (1855–6):

> He is a beardless youth, of about eighteen, chocolate-brown, with high features and a bold profile. … His figure is short and broad, with a tendency to be obese, the result of a strong stomach and the power of sleeping at discretion. He can read a little, write his name, and is uncommonly clever at a bargain. Meccah had taught him to speak excellent Arabic … to be eloquent in abuse, and to be profound at Prayer and Pilgrimage.

Unlike some of the other British explorers, Burton was appreciative of the Bedouin (Badawi) of the Hejaz:

> The best character of the Badawi is a truly noble compound of determination, gentleness and generosity. Usually they are a mixture of worldly cunning and great simplicity, sensitive to touchiness, good-tempered souls, solemn and dignified withal, fond of a jest, yet of a grave turn of mind, easily managed by a laugh and a soft word, and placable after passion, though madly revengeful after injury.

'The best character of the Badawi is a truly noble compound of determination, gentleness and generosity.'

Later in life, after the near fatal debacle in Somalia (in which his young colleague Willie Stroyan was killed) and his African exploits in the source regions of the Nile, for which he received the RGS Founder's Medal in 1859, Burton had a career as a diplomat, serving in such diverse postings as Fernando Po, an island in Equatorial Guinea, Santos in Brazil, Damascus and Trieste. This great man, who was striking physically and overpowering intellectually, died in that last posting in 1890, but his remarkable stone tomb, in the form of an Arab tent, can be seen in the St Mary Magdalen Roman Catholic cemetery in Mortlake, West London.

BIBLIOGRAPHIC REFERENCES AND FURTHER READING

Blanch, L., 1954. *The Wilder Shores of Love*. New York: Carroll and Graf.

Brodie, F.M. 1967. *The Devil Drives*. London: Eyre & Spottiswoode.

Burton, R.F. 1854. Journey to Medina, with route from Yambu. *Journal of the Royal Geographical Society of London*, 24, 208–225.

Burton, R.F. 1874. *Personal Narrative of a Pilgrimage to Mecca and Medina*. B. Tauchnitz.

Ghose, I. 2006. Imperial Player: Richard Burton in Sindh. In T.Youngs (ed) *Travel Writing in the Nineteenth Century: Filling the Blank Spaces*, Chapter 5. London: Anthem.

Godsall, J.R. 1993. Fact and fiction in Richard Burton's *Personal Narrative of a Pilgrimage to El-Medinah and Meccah* (1855–6). *Journal of the Royal Asiatic Society (Third Series)*, 3, 331–351.

Kiernan, R.H. 1937. *The Unveiling of Arabia*. London: Harrap.

McLynn, F. 1990. *Burton: Snow upon the Desert*. London: John Murray.

Ondaatje, C. 1996. *Sindh Revisited. A Journey in the Footsteps of Captain Sir Richard Francis Burton*. London: Harper Collins.

WILLIAM GIFFORD PALGRAVE

GIFFORD PALGRAVE (Figure 13) was born in London in 1826. His father Sir Francis Palgrave, born Francis Ephraim Cohen, was a Jew who converted to the Church of England. Francis Palgrave set up the Public Record Office, while one of Gifford's uncles was the first director of Kew, Sir William Hooker. Giffy, as he was known to his family, had a glittering academic career at Charterhouse and Oxford, but this did not stop him from joining the army in India. It was in India that he became a Roman Catholic and then a Jesuit missionary, first in India and then in the Lebanon and Syria. Under the name of M. l'Abbé Michel Sohail, eventually, with Vatican permission and employed supported by Napoleon III, he became a French agent. The reason why he should want to forward the imperial ambitions of France is not clear.

In 1862 and 1863, disguised as a Syrian Christian physician, adopting the name Selim Abu Mahmoud al-'Eis, he set off in the stifling heat of mid-summer on a journey from north west to south east across Arabia (Figure 14), accompanied by a Syrian Jesuit teacher called Barakat. Like Charles Doughty, he felt that a medical disguise would help to allay 'native suspicion'. On the other hand, this meant he could take no scientific instruments, undertake sketching

Figure 13. *William Gifford Palgrave (RGS).*

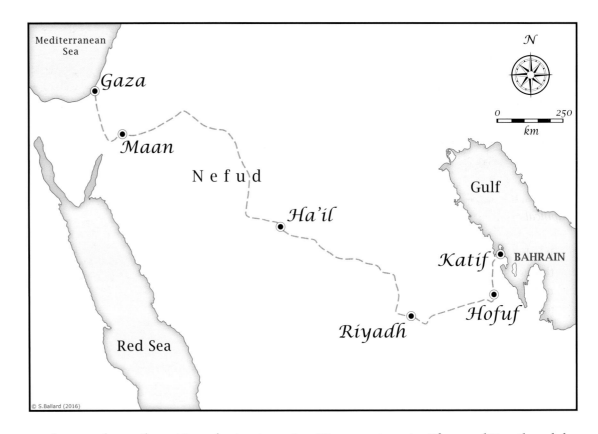

Figure 14. *Palgrave's routes 1862–1863 (Map drawn by Sebastian Ballard).*

or photography, or the writing of extensive notes. His was not a scientific expedition though he had some perceptive things to say about various natural phenomena, including dunes and water supplies. His destinations were Ha'il (the Rashids' capital) and Riyadh, a city that no European except Sadlier had ever penetrated and the heartland of Wahhabi Islam. The Wahhabis were a reformed, puritanical and fundamentalist sect who regarded even orthodox Sunnis as libertarians. They were xenophobic and their fanaticism and isolation in the heart of Arabia had bred a deep distrust of outsiders. Following the succumbing of Medina, Mecca, Lhasa, Bokhara and Timbuktu to the nineteenth-century explorers, Riyadh was at the time arguably the last of the great 'forbidden cities'.

Palgrave travelled through Gaza to to Ma'an, in southern Jordan. In Ha'il, he mixed easily with all levels of society and was able to write extensively about its character and its people. He spent seven weeks in Riyadh, but to avoid imminent death had to slip away in haste. He gives a full description of the city but disapproved of the oppressive control exercised by a kind of religious police whom he called 'zealators'. From there, he travelled through the Yamama and Hasa to Katif (Qatif), where he sighted the Persian Gulf eight months after his departure from Gaza. He visited Bahrain, Qatar, Bandar Abbas (in Persia), parts of the Trucial States (now the United Arab Emirates), including the village of Aboo-Debee (Abu Dhabi), and Oman.

Palgrave was also not especially fond of deserts and referred to their 'hopeless, irremediable sterility and desolation' (*The Journal of the Royal Geographical Society of London*, 1864, p. 113). He noted that water was a problem:

> It is, however, an unfortunate but a most characteristic feature of Arabia, that, through the whole of its vast extent, no single flowing river worthy of the name is to be found. I am aware that some compassionate geographers supply a few, bit I regret to say that they have been in this respect more liberal than Nature.

'It is, however, an unfortunate but a most characteristic feature of Arabia, that, through the whole of its vast extent, no single flowing river worthy of the name is to be found.'

He recognised that when rain fell, as it does, it was soon absorbed into the crevasses or the loose soil, charging subterranean groundwater reservoirs, which then emerged as springs, especially near the eastern coastline. Palgrave was also interested in the great sand deserts (p. 117), with 'their loose and deep sand, generally heaped up in enormous ridges or waves, whose invariable direction is from north to south'. He gave a good and largely correct description of the distribution of the sand seas in Arabia, but also described the problems of crossing them (p. 120):

> The prodigious depth of their sandy stratum, often not less than many hundred feet … renders water, of course, out of the question for the most part; and this, along with the extreme heat of such tracts, the want of pasture, the total absence of anything like shade or shelter, and the labour of wading now up, now down, through the mountain-waves of loose and scorching sand, render their passage no easy and even no very safe matter, especially in the hot summer months.

Most interestingly of all, he noted that many of the dunes occurred as 'gigantic and regular furrows', and tried to come up with an explanation (p. 120):

> The symmetrical undulations of the sand have found in their parallelism with the axis of the earth a tolerably plausible explanation, derived from the inequality of the rotator movement of the globe when communicated through the hard rocky base to the loose and sliding mass of sand above.

'Gaiety and fondness for social amusement, industry and commercial activity, are characteristic of the Omanite race...'

Palgrave was not one of those travellers who was besotted with the Bedouin. Indeed, in contrast to town Arabs, he found them to be treacherous, ignorant, coarse, immoral, aimless and degraded. He described them as 'wandering and brigandish herdsmen' (p. 115). By contrast he remarked that the inhabitants of the oasis of Kasim (p. 127) were a 'fine and tall race of men', whose 'braided locks falling on either side of a handsome and open countenance, give them a somewhat rakish appearance'. He was also impressed by the admirable and tasteful crafts practised in Hasa. His most favourable comments were, however, on Oman (p. 149–150):

> In no other part of Arabia did I meet with stronger marks of advanced and long-established civilization than in 'Oman. Large stone-built houses, three and even four stories high, with ample and variously carved vestibules, vaulted passages, painted walls, and copious furniture for every use; hospitality and courteous welcome, outdoing even that of Nejd; politeness in conversation, cleanliness and ornament in dress, and much else of the same nature. … Gaiety and fondness for social amusement, industry and commercial activity, are characteristic of the Omanite race: they are mild, good-humoured and cheerful. The women of this province are of remarkable and far-famed beauty.

In 1865 he published his lively two-volume work *Personal Narrative of a Year's Journey through Central and Eastern Arabia*. His account was the subject of some doubt, not least in London, and in the interests of a good story he may have been guilty of some embroidery. Indeed, Philby thought that Palgrave never reached Riyadh and suggested that the second half of his tale at least was a gigantic concoction.

After his great journey, Palgrave, described by Freeth and Winstone (*Explorers of Arabia*, Allen and Unwin, 1978, p. 152) as an 'Englishman of exceptional talent: an Arabic scholar, a man of cultivated and sensitive intelligence, a writer of splendidly evocative prose...', renounced both Roman Catholicism and his links with Napoleon III, and served in the British foreign service in a huge range of sometimes bizarre postings, including the West Indies, Trebizond, Manila, Bulgaria, Bangkok and Uruguay (where he died of bronchitis in 1888).

BIBLIOGRAPHIC REFERENCES AND FURTHER READING

Brent, P. 1978. *Far Arabia. Explorers of the Myth.* Newton Abbot: Readers Union.

Freeth, Z. and Winstone, V. 1978. *Explorers of Arabia.* London: Allen and Unwin.

Hogarth, D.G. 1905. *The Penetration of Arabia. A Record of the Development of Western Knowledge Concerning the Arabian Peninsula.* London: Alston Books.

Keay, J. 1982. *Eccentric Travellers.* London: John Murray.

Kiernan, R.H. 1937. *The Unveiling of Arabia.* London: Harrap.

Palgrave, W.G. 1864. Observations made in Central, Eastern, and Southern Arabia during a journey through that country in 1862 and 1863. *Journal of the Royal Geographical Society*, 34, 111–154.

Palgrave, W.G. 1865. *Personal Narrative of a Year's Journey through Central and Eastern Arabia (1862–63).* 2 volumes. London: Macmillan.

Thompson, J. 2004. Palgrave, William Gifford (1826–1888). *Oxford Dictionary of National Biography online.*

Tidrick, K. 1990. *Heart Beguiling Araby. The English Romance with Arabia.* London: I.B. Tauris.

ANNE AND WILFRID BLUNT

LADY ANNE BLUNT (Figure 15), the 15th Baroness Wentworth, and her philandering, hedonistic and adulterous husband, Wilfrid Scawen Blunt (Figure 16), were great breeders of Arab horses and notable explorers of the Middle East. Like the Bents in southern Arabia and the Bakers in East Africa, they were a formidable married team. Anne (1837–1917) was a granddaughter of Lord Byron and she married Wilfrid (1840–1922), a poet and diplomat, in 1869. The relationship was not entirely successful. Anne suffered numerous miscarriages and Wilfrid enjoyed many mistresses, often simultaneously. Peter Brent in *Far Arabia. Explorers of the Myth* (p. 147) says that his deepest and most powerful relationship was with 'Skittles' (Catherine Walters), 'one of the most famous of those *grandes horizontales* whose courtesan proficiency, displayed in Paris, laid low with passion and venereal disease so many of the kings, nobility and *nouveaux riches* of the late nineteenth century'. When he moved one of his mistresses, Dorothy Carleton, into their home in 1906, Anne decided it was time to separate from him.

It was Wilfrid's ill health that first brought the couple to the Levant in 1873 and initiated their interest in the Arabs. Wilfrid admired the simple religious faith of the Bedouin and the lack of bureaucracy in their society. Their fascination was further whetted by an expedition they carried out from Syria to the Euphrates in 1878 (*Bedouin Tribes of the Euphrates*, 1879, Harper & Brothers, NY, co-authors), on which they collected some Arab horses that they took back to Wilfrid's family estate at Crabbet Park in Sussex. *Bedouin Tribes of the Euphrates* is a pleasant enough volume but contains little very significant geographical information. It is, however, interesting on Arabian horses, the advantages that camels possess over horses and gives a clear picture of how Anne Blunt regarded the Bedouin. On the one hand she points to their tendency in middle age to lead a rather inactive life and to their love of money, but on the other she refers to the fact that they

Figure 15. (opposite) *Portrait of Lady Anne Blunt in Arab costume (RGS: Lady Anne Blunt. 1881).*

are essentially humane and never take life needlessly, are sober and honest, are devoted to their children, obey their laws, and are hospitable and egalitarian.

Later in the same year they set off again to Damascus with the intention of penetrating deep into Arabia. One notable feature of their journey was that they travelled without subterfuge, as Europeans openly exercising their curiosity. They carried compass and barometer and were free to take notes. They did, however, wear Arab clothes, not as a disguise but with the practical intention of not attracting too much attention. They were accompanied in their travel by Muhammad ibn Aruk, whom they had met on their Euphrates expedition, and who was desirous of finding a wife in the Nejd. They were motivated by no great geographical ambition but by an affection for the Bedouin and the desert. On their journey to the Nejd (*A Pilgrimage to Nejd, the Cradle of the Arab Race*, Lady Anne Blunt, 1881) (Figure 17), they covered some 640 km of stony desert between Damascus and Al-Jawf in northern Arabia and were ambushed in a *ghazu* (raid) by Bedouin, but they were eventually able to demonstrate their friendly intentions. They also suffered a sandstorm (Chapter 4 of Lady Blunt's book):

> Sandstorms are evidently common here, for the Tell Guteyfi, which is of black volcanic boulders like the Harra, is half smothered in sand. We saw it looming near us in the thick air, and soon after were almost hidden from each other in the increasing darkness. The sun shone feebly at intervals through the driving sand, but it was all we could do to keep the caravan together, and not lose sight of each other. At one moment we had all to stop and turn tail to the wind, covering our eyes and heads with our cloaks, waiting till the burst was over. Nothing could have faced it. Still we were far from having any idea of danger, for there really is none in these storms, and had plenty of time to notice how very picturesque the situation was, the camels driven along at speed, all huddled together for protection, with their long necks stretched out, and heads low, tags and ropes flying, and the men's cloaks streaming in the wind, all seen through the yellow haze of sand which made them look as though walking in the air. The beasts looked gigantic yet helpless, like antediluvian creatures overwhelmed in a flood.

Thereafter they crossed the Great Nafud, which they described as being the colour of rhubarb and magnesia, to Ha'il, where they called upon the emir, Muhammad ibn Rashid, who, although

'We saw it looming near us in the thick air, and soon after were almost hidden from each other in the increasing darkness.'

Figure 16. (opposite) *Wilfrid Scawen Blunt as he appeared in Vanity Fair January 31, 1885.*

notorious for his cruelty, treated them with kindness. The Blunts observed dunes with regularly spaced, crescentic hollows in the Great Nafud sandsea (Chapter 8):

> The most striking features of the Nefûd are the great horse-hoof hollows which are scattered all over it (Radi calls them *fulj*). These, though varying in size from an acre to a couple of hundred acres, are all precisely alike in shape and direction. They resemble very exactly the track of an unshod horse, that is to say, the toe is sharply cut and perpendicular, while the rim of the hoof tapers gradually to nothing at the heel, the frog even being roughly but fairly represented by broken ground in the centre, made up of converging water-courses. The diameter of some of these fuljes must be at least a quarter of a mile, and the depth of the deepest of them, which we measured to-day, proved to be 230 feet, bringing it down very nearly exactly to the level of the gravelly plain which we crossed yesterday, and which, there can be little doubt, is continued underneath the sand.

They were not sure of their origin, and debated whether the hollows were due to wind or water action. At Jubba (Jobba) the Blunts surmised correctly – as recent palaeoenvironmental studies have shown – that it had once been the site of a large lake (Chapter 9):

> JOBBA is one of the most curious places in the world, and to my mind one of the most beautiful. Its name Jobba, or rather Jubbeh, meaning a well, explains its position, for it lies in a hole or well in the Nefûd; not indeed in a fulj, for the basin of Jobba is on quite another scale, and has nothing in common with the horse-hoof depressions I have hitherto described. It is, all the same, extremely singular, and quite as difficult to account for geologically as the fuljes. It is a great bare space in the ocean of sand, from four hundred to five hundred feet below its average level, and about three miles wide; a hollow, in fact, not unlike that of Jôf, but with the Nefûd round it instead of sandstone cliffs. That it has once been a lake is pretty evident, for there are distinct water marks on the rocks which crop up out of its bed just above the town; and, strange to say, there is a tradition still extant of there having formerly been water there.

Figure 17. *The Blunts' route in Arabia, 1879 (Map drawn by Sebastian Ballard).*

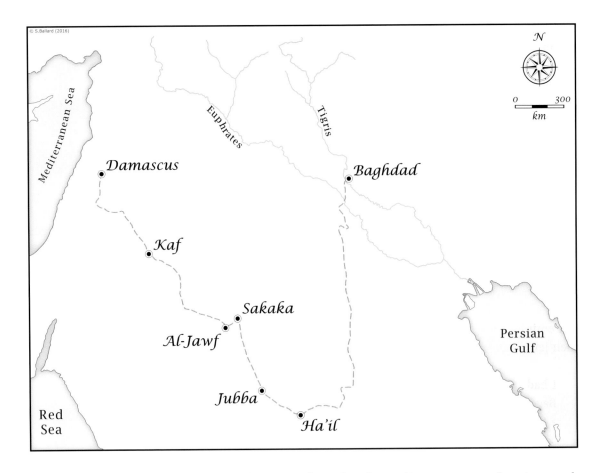

The Blunts, as had Georg August Wallin some three decades earlier, encountered various rock paintings scratched into the desert varnish that coated the local sandstone (*Proceedings of the Royal Geographical Society*, 1880, p. 86):

> The rocks of Aalem, like those of Jof, Jubbeh, and indeed all the outlying peaks north and east of Jebel Aja, are of sandstone, varying in colour from yellow to red and purple, but weathered black on the upper surface. On many of these I discovered letters, in the character which is,

I believe, now called Phoenician, together with the conventional drawings of camels, ibexes and goats usually found accompanying them. Some of these are sufficiently ancient to be now included in the black weathering of the rocks. Others appear more modern. I also found one inscription in old Arabic, but nothing that could suggest Classic or Christian times. The cross, which constantly occurs in Phoenician inscriptions, is evidently no more than a letter of the alphabet. Others in the same way resemble Greek.

Lady Blunt's description of the emir of Ha'il, Muhammad ibn Rashid, is brilliant (Chapter 10):

His countenance recalled to us the portraits of Richard the Third, lean, sallow cheeks, much sunken, thin lips, with an expression of pain, except when smiling, a thin black beard, well-defined, black knitted eyebrows – eyes deep-sunk and piercing, like the eyes of a hawk, but ever turning restlessly from one of our faces to the other, and then to those beside him. It was the very type of a conscience-stricken face, or one which fear an assassin. His hands, too, were long and caw-like, and never quiet for an instant.

The emir let Anne visit the harem, where she was able to meet the ladies. She was much struck by their jewellery (Chapter 10):

I had nearly forgotten to mention the nose-ring, here much larger than I have seen it at Bagdad and elsewhere, measuring an inch and a half to two inches across. It consists of a thin circle of gold, with a knot of gold and turquoises attached by a chain to the cap or lappet before described. It is worn in the left nostril, but taken out and left dangling while the wearer eats and drinks. A most inconvenient ornament, I thought and said, and when removed it leaves an unsightly hole, badly pierced, in the nostril, and more uncomfortable-looking than the holes in European ears. But fashion rules the ladies at Haïl as in other places, and my new acquaintances only laughed at such criticisms. They find these trinkets useful toys, and amuse themselves while talking by continually pulling them out and putting them in again. The larger size of ring seemed besides to be a mark of high position, so that the diameter of the circle might be considered the measure of the owner's rank, for the rings of all inferiors were kept within the inch.

From Ha'il the Blunts joined a huge caravan that was making for Persia, composed of as many as 4,000 camels, and headed for Baghdad, where for the first time in almost three months, they were able to sleep in a proper bed. The Blunts described the way in which Persians rode in the desert (Chapter 13):

> A Persian riding on a camel is the most ridiculous sight in the world. He insists on sitting astride, and seems absolutely unable to learn the ways and habits of the creature he rides; and he talks to it with his falsetto voice in a language no Arabian camel could possibly understand. The jokes cut on the Persians by the Arabs never cease from morning till night. The better class of pilgrims, and of course all the women except the very poor, travel in *mahmals* or litters—panniers, of which a camel carries two—covered over like a tradesman's van with blue or red canvas. One or two persons possess *tahtera-vans*, a more expensive kind of conveyance, which requires two mules or two camels, one before and one behind, to carry it. In either of these litters the traveller can squat or even lie down and sleep. The camels chosen for the mahmals are strong and even-paced; and some of these double panniers are fitted up with a certain care and elegance, and the luxuries of Persian rugs and hangings. A confidential driver leads the camel, and servants sometimes walk beside it. One of the pilgrims keeps a man to march in front with his narghi-leh, which he smokes through a very long tube sitting in the pannier above.

'A Persian riding on a camel is the most ridiculous sight in the world.'

Anne was the first European woman to penetrate the heart of the Arabian peninsula, to cross the Great Nafud Desert and to visit the town of Ha'il. In 1881 the Blunts bought the estate of Shaikh Obeyd in Egypt and until their separation divided their time between this home and Crabbet Park. Anne did much to save the Arab horse breed, was competent in Arabic and translated some of the finest pre-Islamic verse into English, was a decent watercolourist (taught by John Ruskin) and an accomplished violin player. She displayed bravery and perseverance, but was perhaps a little lacking in imagination. She seems not to have emulated her husband's nocturnal activities. David Hogarth, the doyen of historians of Arabian exploration, says that her narrative of the journey to the Nejd is notable for its sobriety and accuracy as well as for its observation and sympathy. Anne died of dysentery in Cairo in 1917, aged 80, and Wilfrid followed her shortly afterwards, dying in England, in 1922, aged 82.

Wilfrid was a complex individual. A conservative English aristocrat, he had been a fierce champion of the cause of the Arabs, the Egyptians, the Irish (for which he was imprisoned) and the Indians against British domination, but showed clear anti-semitic tendencies. He was for a while a fervent Catholic, but later in life considered converting to Islam. He is said to have ruled all those around him with the absolutism of a Turkish Sultan, and to have consumed hashish and morphine. With a body that his grandson regarded as beautiful as Byron's, he attracted beautiful women but also the admiration of intelligent men, such as T.E. Lawrence and George Curzon. He was the great uncle of Anthony Blunt, the Cambridge spy, one of whose co-traitors was Kim Philby, the son of another great Arabian explorer.

BIBLIOGRAPHIC REFERENCES AND FURTHER READING

Blunt, A. 1879. *Bedouin Tribes of the Euphrates*. London: John Murray.

Blunt, W.S. 1880. A visit to Jebel Shammar (Nejd). New routes through Northern and Central Arabia. *Proceedings of the Royal Geographical Society and Monthly Record of Geography*, 2, 81–102.

Blunt, A. 1881. *A Pilgrimage to Nejd, the Cradle of the Arab Race*. London: John Murray.

Brent, P. 1978. *Far Arabia. Explorers of the Myth*. Newton Abbot: Readers Union.

Freeth, Z. and Winstone, V. 1978. *Explorers of Arabia*. London: Allen and Unwin.

Kiernan, R.H. 1937. *The Unveiling of Arabia*. London: Harrap.

Hogarth, D.G. 1905. *The Penetration of Arabia. A Record of the Development of Western Knowledge Concerning the Arabian Peninsula*. London: Alston Books.

Longford, E. 2007. *A Pilgrimage of Passion: the Life of Wilfrid Scawen Blunt*. London: I.B. Tauris.

Tidrick, K. 1990. *Heart Beguiling Araby. The English Romance with Arabia*. London: I.B. Tauris.

Tuson, P. 2014. *Western Women Travelling East 1716–1916*. Oxford: The Arcadian Library in association with the Oxford University Press.

Winstone, H.V.F. 2003. *Lady Anne Blunt: A Biography*. Manchester: Barzan Publishing.

CHARLES MONTAGU DOUGHTY

CHARLES DOUGHTY (Figure 18), Arabian explorer, travel writer and poet, was born into a religious family, in Suffolk, England, in 1843. Originally it was intended that he would join the Royal Navy but he was rejected on the grounds of a slight speech impediment. A dedicated patriot, this disappointed him, but as a result he attended Cambridge University and became a geologist, writing papers on such topics as the flint implements of East Anglia and the glaciers of Norway. After graduation in 1865, Doughty started to study old English literature, in order to write an epic about early Britain as a patriotic substitute for his lost naval career. He also studied in some of the great European universities, including Louvain and Leiden, and undertook various travels in Europe and the Middle East, and studied Arabic in addition.

In 1875 Doughty went to Petra, where he learnt about the Nabatean inscriptions and rock-cut tombs at Medain Salih, a place that lay deep in the desert, not far from the pilgrim route

Figure 18. *Portrait of Charles M. Doughty (RGS: by John R. Freeman, c.1880–1926).*

Figure 19. *Doughty's route 1876–1878 (Map drawn by Sebastian Ballard).*

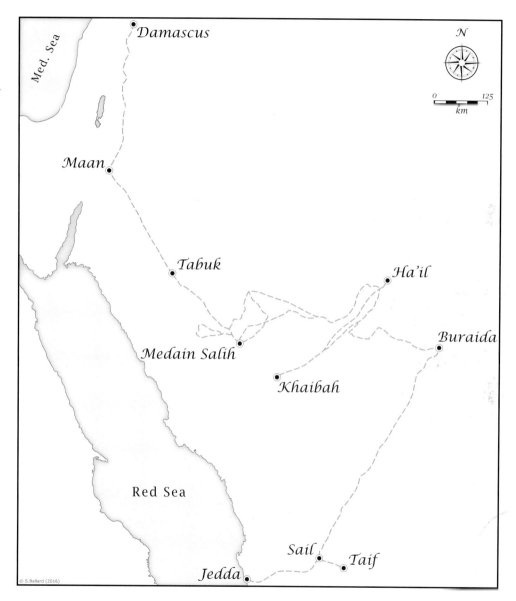

to Mecca and Medina. Deciding that he wanted to study these, in 1876 he set off from Damascus to enter Arabia. He was to wander there for almost two years and published the results in his monumental [two-volume] *Travels in Arabia Deserta*, Cambridge University Press, which appeared in 1888. The motives for this journey are not entirely clear but may have had something to do with his interests in geology and spirituality.

Tall, red headed and with a luxuriant beard, Doughty set off from Damascus (Figure 19) with a great pilgrim caravan of 6,000 haji and their accompanying 10,000 camels. He carried with him no letters of introduction and was short of money. Though dressed as a Syrian, and calling himself Khalil, he made no secret of being a Christian (a *Nasrâny*), and thus an infidel, and an Englishman. He also carried a medicine chest, reasoning that a doctor would always receive a warm welcome. He first travelled in a southerly direction to Ma'an, before reaching Medain Salih where, fulfilling his initial aim, he made copies of the inscriptions. However, he did not then go home. Instead he struck out eastwards into the high desert of the Nejd to live with the nomads. He visited Ha'il, which Palgrave had visited 14 years earlier, and the oasis of Khaybar, where he stayed for three and a half months. Eventually, weakened by bilharzia, he reached Taif, Jeddah and the Red Sea coast.

In spite of its somewhat archaic style, *Arabia Deserta* came to be widely admired and is regarded as a great example of fine travel writing. It also gives a very important account of Arabian society in the last quarter of the nineteenth century. Among the great admirers of *Arabia Deserta* was T.E. Lawrence, who, in an introduction to the 1921 edition, wrote:

The more you learn of Arabia, the more you find in *Arabia Deserta*. The more you travel there the greater your respect for the insight, judgment and artistry of the author. … It is the first and indispensable work on the Arabs of the desert. … There is no sentiment, nothing merely picturesque, that most common failing of oriental travel books. Doughty's completeness is devastating. There is nothing we would take away, little we could add. He took all Arabia for his province, and has left to his successors only the poor part of specialists.

Lawrence also admired Doughty himself for his effort and endurance, his wisdom and his patience. He also wrote about how Doughty interacted with the Arabs of the desert:

Doughty went among these people dispassionately, looked at their life, and wrote it down word for word. By being always Arab in manner and European in mind, he maintained a perfect judgment, while bearing towards them a full sympathy which persuaded them to show him their inmost ideas.

Doughty devoted his later life to family and poetry, received honorary degrees from both Oxford and Cambridge universities, and belatedly, in 1912, received the Founder's Medal from the RGS. He died aged 80, in Kent, in 1926. Throughout his life he was a great patriot and Christian, who despised the teachings and practice of Islam.

BIBLIOGRAPHIC REFERENCES AND FURTHER READING

Bevis, R. 1972. *Spiritual Geology: C.M. Doughty and the Land of the Arabs.* Victorian Studies, 163–181.

Brent, P. 1978. *Far Arabia. Explorers of the Myth.* Newton Abbot: Readers Union.

Canton, J. 2011. *From Cairo to Baghdad. British Travellers in Arabia.* London: I.B. Tauris.

Doughty, C.M. 1888. *Arabia Deserta.* Cambridge: Cambridge University Press.

Freeth, Z. and Winstone, V. 1978. *Explorers of Arabia.* London: Allen and Unwin.

Hogarth, D.G. 1905. *The Penetration of Arabia. A Record of the Development of Western Knowledge Concerning the Arabian Peninsula.* London: Alston Books.

Kiernan, R.H. 1937. *The Unveiling of Arabia.* London: Harrap.

Tabachnick, S.E. 2004. Doughty, Charles Montagu (1843–1926). *Oxford Dictionary of National Biography online.*

Tidrick, K. 1990. *Heart Beguiling Araby. The English Romance with Arabia.* London: I.B. Tauris.

GEORGE NATHANIEL CURZON

GEORGE NATHANIEL CURZON (1859–1925) (Figure 20), marquis of Kedleston, once described as a man 'with the complexion of a milkmaid, the stature of an Apollo and the activity of an Under-Secretary', was of very significant importance in the history of the British Empire. He was inter alia viceroy of India, foreign secretary, acting prime minister, a fellow of the Royal Society, chancellor of Oxford University, a sworn enemy of Field Marshal Kitchener, and an associate of Oscar Wilde, Wilfrid Blunt and Rudyard Kipling. Even as a young man he was fascinated by the Great Game during which Britain and Russia sized each other up on the borderlands of India. This was a prime motive for his explorations, though he also sought 'the beautiful and the romantic' and 'relics of a dead civilization, or a glorious but forgotten past'. He loved the way 'Majestic ruins that tell of a populous and mighty past rear their heads amid deserted wastes and vagabond tents'

Great man though he undoubtedly was, he has not always been accorded acclaim for his personal qualities, either by contemporaries or by historians. Sir Harold Nicolson wrote (*Curzon: the Last Phase*, 1934, Constable, p. 19) that Curzon possessed a 'highly developed competitive, or even combative instinct', and averred: 'Never did his enjoyment of foreign travel become so acute as when it enabled him to correct the imperfect information or the erroneous hypotheses of previous travellers.'

It is a paradox, however, that others regarded Curzon as a great friend and were in turn treated with civility. This is particularly true of Younghusband, the soldier, explorer and mystic, who (*Geographical Journal*, 1928, p. 498), reported that 'for explorers he had an admiration in which not the slightest taint of his superiority was to be traced'. Curzon was one of the few true friends that he possessed. They met in 1891 and their friendship persisted for 34 years.

Though superior, haughty, inelastic, critical and satirized for being a man who appeared to be used to processing with elephants, Curzon's merits should not be forgotten. Even Nicolson (*Foreign Affairs*, 1928) refers to 'his splendid activities of mind and soul', his 'prodigies of industry', and 'his genius for presentation'. David Hogarth (1926, *George Nathaniel Curzon, Marquis Curzon of Kedleston*, British Academy, p. 2) refers to his 'meticulously accurate recording'. These were essential qualities for a great explorer.

There were two notable elements to Curzon's contribution to desert exploration and survey: his own considerable feats; and his encouragement of others. Curzon himself had a great love of travel. He owed his initial enthusiasm to a master at Eton, Oscar Browning, 'who liked the company of lively-minded young men on his rambles round Europe'. Curzon accompanied him to the French Riviera and northern Italy. However, the most important part of his career in travel and exploration started in 1887–88 when he embarked on a world tour which took him from North America to the Far East and the Indian sub-continent, where he managed to reach Peshawar and the Khyber Pass. In 1888–89 he visited Russia and proceeded to Bokhara (known as a place where one could be 'done to death', like Charles Stoddart and Arthur Conolly in 1842, on charges of spying, Samarkand, Tashkent and the Caspian Sea. The sand desert beyond the ancient city of Merv had 'the appearance of a sea of troubled waves, billow succeeding billow in melancholy succession'. As a result of this substantial journey, Curzon produced a series of publications, including his encyclopedic *Russia in Central Asia in 1889 and the Anglo-Russian Question* (1889), Longmans, Green, and Co. He gave sage advice to those thinking of following in his footsteps (Curzon, *Russia in Central Asia in 1889 and the Anglo-Russian Question*, p. 56):

Figure 20. (opposite) *The Lord Curzon of Kedleston, President of the RGS 1911–13 (RGS: From the portrait by Sir John Sargent in the Royal Geographical Society's house).*

A frying pan, a kettle, a teapot must be carried and can be bought in any Persian bazaar. … Crosse and Blackwell's tinned soups are quite excellent. … Soup in tablets or powders are good in their way and economise space but require more trouble in cooking. Sardines, potted meats, chocolate or cocoa and good tea and coffee are useful adjuncts which should be procured in Europe. … A small medicine chest or case should be carried; and the maladies against which the stranger must chiefly provide are fever, diarrhea and dysentery. Chlorodyne and quinine form the nucleus of any such medical outfit.

In 1889–90 Curzon set off again (Figure 21), this time to Persia, which he regarded (prophetically) as being one of 'the pieces on a chessboard upon which is being played out a game for the dominion of the world' (Curzon, *Persia and the Persian Question*, 1892, Longmans, Green & Co., p. 3). On what was essentially a three-month-long journey to gain geopolitical intelligence, he rode some 1,400 km through the frontier province of Khorasan and thence to the Persian capital, Teheran. Then he rode another 1,290 km to Bushire on the south-west coast and remarked: 'The Union Jack fluttering from the summit of the Residency flag-staff is no vain symbol of British ascendency.' He particularly disliked the track from Shiraz to the coast, noting: 'It is a road that has been selected quite at haphazard, simply because somebody started it. … Very often it follows the steepest and least practicable of the various available lines … a monument to the apathy and resolution of the Persian character.' The main result of this three-month journey was the production of the monumental two-volume work, *Persia and the Persian Question* (1892), widely regarded as one of the most authoritative and thoroughly referenced books on the country. Curzon stated its aims simply (p. 5):

> 'I shall endeavour to do here for Persia what far abler writers have done for most other countries of equal importance…'

I shall endeavour to do here for Persia what far abler writers have done for most other countries of equal importance, but what for two hundred years no single English writer has essayed to do for Iran, viz. to present a full-length and life size portrait of that Kingdom.

Travelling by horse, accompanied by only a small retinue, cooking his own dinners and staying in primitive post-houses or *Chapah Khanehs*, he travelled through some of the most arid parts of Persia. He pronounced Persian wine as very nasty but found 'exquisite solace' from 'the perfumed inhalations' of a Persian water pipe. As a traveller, Curzon must have presented an unusual spectacle to the people through whose lands he passed, his travel kit for the higher and colder regions consisting of a Norfolk jacket, breeches, boots at least two sizes too large, an ingenious hat, a Cardigan waistcoat, blue spectacles, galoshes, a flask of spirits and a full-skirted frock coat.

It was wearing such garb that in 1894 he made his remarkable journey through the Pamirs and Afghanistan to the source of the Oxus River (Amu Darya). Over a period of six months he travelled just short of 2,900 km, either on horseback or on foot, much of it over ground of great difficulty. In May 1895 he was rewarded with the Patron's Medal from the RGS 'for his travels and researches in Persia, in French Indo-China, in the Hindu Kush and Pamirs, and his investigation of the sources of the Oxus'. By the age of 35, in spite of severe physical disabilities produced by curvature of the spine and the need to endure a steel brace, Curzon had produced a massive output of material on large parts of Asia, had acquired an unparalleled personal knowledge of the countries bordering British India and had performed feats of great personal courage.

After his appointment as viceroy of India in 1898, extensive exploration was no longer possible. However, it was at this time that he became important as a patron of exploration by others. Curzon sanctioned Aurel Stein's first journey in Central Asia and made preliminary arrangements for the second. He encouraged the Seistan Boundary Commission of MacMahon in 1905–6 and the travels of the Swedish explorer, Sven Hedin. Hedin's *Central Asia and Tibet* (1903) Hurst and Blackett, Ltd.[C6.3] is dedicated to Curzon. Ellsworth Huntington was another great geographer and traveller who acknowledged his debt to Lord Curzon in furthering travel to the drylands of Central Asia during the classic years of scientific exploration in that area. In March 1925 Curzon suffered a severe haemorrhage of the bladder. Surgery was unsuccessful and he died in London on 20 March 1925 at the age of 66.

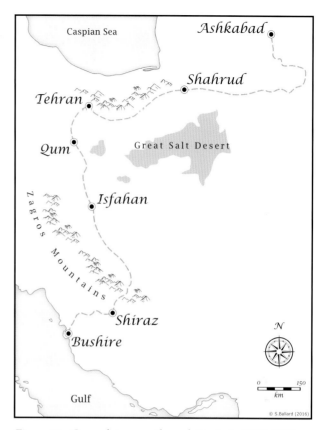

Figure 21. *Curzon's journey through Persia in 1889–1890 (Map drawn by Sebastian Ballard).*

BIBLIOGRAPHIC REFERENCES AND FURTHER READING

Curzon, G.N. 1889. *Russia in Central Asia in 1889 and the Anglo-Russian Question*. London: Longmans, Green and Co.

Curzon, G.N. 1892. *Persia and the Persian Question*. 2 vols. London: Longmans, Green and Co.

Curzon, G.N. 1896a. The Pamirs and the source of the Oxus. *Geographical Journal*, 8, 1: 15–54; 2: 97–119; 3: 239–64.

Curzon, G.N. 1896b. Makran. *Geographical Journal*, 7, 5: 557.

Gilmour, D. 1994. *Curzon*. London: John Murray.

Hedin, S. 1903. *Central Asia and Tibet*. London: Hurst and Blackett.

Hogarth, D.G. 1926. *George Nathaniel Curzon, Marquis Curzon of Kedleston, 1859–1925*. London: British Academy.

Huntington, E. 1907. *The Pulse of Asia*. Boston and New York: Houghton Mifflin Co.

King, P. (ed.). 1986. *Curzon's Persia*. London: Sidgwick and Jackson.

Nicolson, H. 1928. Curzon. *Foreign Affairs*, 7: 221–33.

Nicolson, H. 1934. *Curzon: the Last Phase 1919–1925*. London: Constable.

Rose, K. 1969. *Superior Person, A Portrait of Curzon and His Circle in Late Victorian England*. London: Weidenfeld and Nicolson.

Wright, D. 1987. Curzon and Persia. *Geographical Journal*, 153, 343–350.

Younghusband, F. 1928. in *Geographical Journal*, 71, 5: 4

SIR PERCY MOLESWORTH SYKES

SIR PERCY SYKES (1867–1945) was a diplomat, soldier, explorer and author (Figure 22). He was born in Canterbury and educated at Rugby and the Royal Military College, Sandhurst. He became interested in Persia, a sphere of influence of both Britain and Russia, and started to participate in the Great Game when, in 1892, he was sent in disguise on an intelligence gathering trip to Samarkand in Russian Turkestan. In the following year he went to Persia itself, and became consul for Kerman and Persian Baluchistan. Percy also served with Colonel Thomas Holdich on the Perso-Baluch (Baluchistan) Boundary Commission. In 1898 he founded the British consulate of Seistan and Kain in the far east of the country and surveyed a large part of that little-known area. After service in the Boer War he returned to Persia, to consular posts in Kerman and Mashad. Sykes went to France early in the First World War and in 1915 was sent to Kashgar in Central Asia to enable Sir George Macartney, who had been there as consul general, almost without a break for 24 years, to take some leave. The following year he was sent once again to Persia, with the rank of brigadier general, and led a large force – most of it raised locally, the South Persia Rifles – to deal with the German infiltration of southern Persia. When the war ended Sykes left Persia, and retired from the army in 1920, aged 52. In all he had spent 26 years in Persia.

Figure 22. *Percy Sykes disguised as a Russian in Baku, 1892 (from Antony Wynn. 2003.* Persia in the Great Game, *plate 6. London: John Murray).*

Percy travelled extensively, often in the company of his intrepid sister, Ella (Figure 23). She had, like Gertrude Bell, been educated at Lady Margaret Hall, Oxford University, and was herself a gifted writer on Persia and one of the first European women to travel widely in that country. Her book *Through Persia on a Side-Saddle*, which appeared in 1898, was much admired.

Sykes was clear about the importance of his work in Persia (in the preface to his book *Ten Thousand Miles in Persia; or, Eight Years in Iran*, John Murray, 1902:

> I can claim, without fear of contradiction, that in the present generation no Englishman, and indeed no European, has travelled more extensively in Eastern and Southern Persia than myself, while my official position has given me exceptional opportunities, such as are rarely if ever enjoyed by unofficial travellers, of meeting the better classes of natives, and thereby of obtaining accurate information.

He was not enamoured with the Baluchi inhabitants of eastern Persia, describing them (p. 307 as a 'feckless, lazy and almost hopelessly backward race'. On the other hand, he admired the Persians for (p. 457) he had 'almost everywhere been the recipient of ungrudging hospitality and courteous consideration'. He concluded:

> Although by no means blind to the defects of a nation which was great and ruled the world when we were but savages, yet, sitting at home surrounded by trophies, the result of many an exciting stalk, with the walls covered with the exquisite old tiles and products of the loom which no European manufacture can rival, I feel that I can lay down my pen with all good wishes to my many Persian friends, and with a hearty and sincere FLOREAT PERSIS.

In Seistan (Sistan), Sykes noted the power of the 'wind of 120 days', which though unpleasant, kept the ever-present malaria at bay whilst it blew. He also noted (p. 381) that its shallow lakes were subject to flooding and described the villages:

> All the villages in Sistan are built on dung-hills … the reason being, that when the country is inundated, the villages form islands. Imagine a collection of squalid, dome-shaped mud huts, with a manure heap and a donkey in front, and the type of Sistan village is grasped.

To the south-east of Seistan, Sykes also described a huge dry lake, the Gaud-i-Zirra. (p. 365), 160 km in length and 48 km in width.

Percy and his sister seem to have enjoyed their sojourn in Kashgar, though in the spring months the violent dust and sandstorms were troublesome. He recognised that they were the cause of the extensive deposits of fertile loess (windblown silt), which occurred in the area. He was struck by the beauty of local inhabitants:

'... and as he smiled and salaamed to us I thought he looked like a fairy prince.'

Many of the young Kashgari women were most attractive in appearance, and some of the little girls quite lovely, their plaits of long hair falling from under a jaunty little embroidered cap, their big dark eyes, flashing teeth and piquant olive faces reminding me of Italian or Spanish children. One most beautiful boy stands out in my memory. He was clad in a new shirt and trousers of flowered pink, his crimson velvet cap embroidered with gold, and as he smiled and salaamed to us I thought he looked like a fairy prince.

Sykes was, on the one hand, a good horseman and polo player, an excellent and almost obsessive shot, and a hardy, out-of-doors man. On the other hand, he was erudite, extremely well read, and conversant in both Persian and Arabic. In addition to writing a major book on the history of Persia, he also wrote a major review of the history of world exploration. He received the RGS Patron's Medal in 1902.

Fit and active to the end, he collapsed on a hot summer day in 1945, while carrying his suitcase between Waterloo Station and his London club, the Athenaeum, and died in Charing Cross Hospital.

BIBLIOGRAPHIC REFERENCES AND FURTHER READING

Sykes, E.C. 1898. *Through Persia on a Side-Saddle*. London: A.D. Innes & Co.

Sykes, P.M. 1902. *Ten Thousand Miles in Persia; or Eight Years in Iran*. London: John Murray.

Sykes, E.C. and Sykes, P.M. 1920. *Through Deserts and Oases of Central Asia*. London: Macmillan.

Tuson, P. 2014. *Western Women Travelling East 1716–1916*. Oxford: The Arcadian Library in association with the Oxford University Press.

Wynn, A. 2003. *Persia in the Great Game*. London: John Murray.

GERTRUDE MARGARET LOWTHIAN BELL

GERTRUDE BELL (Figure 24) was a traveller, campaigner against female suffrage, archaeologist, diplomat and spy. She was born in County Durham, England, in 1868, and had access to considerable private means through her family's ownership of steel, aluminium, chemical and coal enterprises. She had a remarkable career at Lady Margaret Hall, Oxford University, where, in spite of her prowess in a whole range of sports, she obtained a first class degree in modern history, the first woman to achieve that particular distinction at Oxford. Bell was slender, with piercing green eyes, a long pointed nose, a ramrod posture and a mass of auburn hair, and was a lifelong smoker of cigarettes. She travelled extensively in Persia and the Alps, and was an intrepid mountaineer. However, with the dawn of the new century, she began a sequence of travels and archaeological research in Arabia and the Middle East, including a crossing of the Syrian Desert, which led to the publication of her classic book published 1907, *The Desert and the Sown*. It garnered great acclaim, detailing as it did the journey of a lone Englishwoman, who was an accomplished scholar, linguist and writer. She expressed the feelings that created her enthusiasm for desert travel (p. 1):

To those bred under an elaborate social order few such moments of exhilaration can come as that which stands at the threshold of wild travel. The

Figure 24. *Gertrude Bell (RGS).*

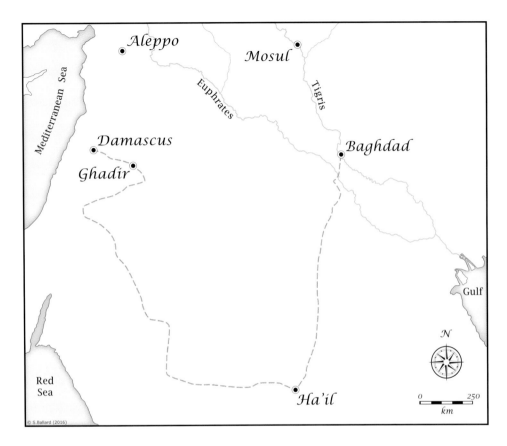

gates of the enclosed garden are thrown open, the chain at the entrance of the sanctuary is lowered, with a wary glance to right and left you step forth, and behold! the immeasurable world. The world of adventure and of enterprise, dark with hurrying storms, glittering in raw sunlight, and unanswered question and an unanswerable doubt hidden in the fold of every hill. Into it you must go alone, separated from the troops of friends that walk the rose alleys, stripped of the purple and fine linen that impede the fighting arm, roofless, defenceless, without possessions.

In 1909 Bell surveyed the Roman and Byzantine fortresses on the banks of the Euphrates in Mesopotamia. From Aleppo, Syria, she travelled via the Hittite capital at Carchemish on the west bank of the Euphrates to Mesopotamia and Baghdad, before going upstream to Mosul and then crossing to Konya in Turkey. This was her most important journey of exploration, described in *Amurath to Amurath* (1911). Dur-

Figure 25. Gertrude Bell's journey to Hail 1914 (Map drawn by Sebastian Ballard).

ing 1911 she made a further expedition to Mesopotamia, while in 1913–1914 she travelled by camel to Ha'il, an oasis in the heart of central Arabia (Figure 25). She used scientific instruments throughout her journey, making observations of latitude, temperature and pressure, and took excellent photographs on her very expensive cameras, including panoramas of many archaeological sites, some of which have now been eroded or pilfered. Indeed to Bell, scientific endeavour was more important than mere adventure. She was never able to write a full account of her journey to Ha'il, and the task was left to David Hogarth, who put together – from diaries, letters and recollections of conversations – a narrative of the journey after her death (*The Geographical Journal*, 70, 1927).

Howell, in his 2006 book *Daughter of the Desert* (p. 117) has summarised the magnitude of Bell's 1911 and 1913 expeditions:

> Taken together, her journeys encompassed most of Syria, Turkey and Mesopotamia. ... She covered more than ten thousand miles on the map, but she went over hills and mountains, searched for fords, took detours to ancient sites and to make contact with sheiks. Over six hundred days she must have journeyed at least 20,000 miles in the saddle.

She was awarded the RGS Founder's Medal in 1918, an honour only twice previously conferred on a woman.

Bell's mode of travel in the desert was relatively lavish, as described by Howell (2006, p. 131):

> She packed couture evening dresses, lawn blouses and linen riding skirts, cotton shirts and fur coats, sweaters and scarves, canvas and leather boots. Beneath layers of lacy petticoats she hid guns, cameras and film, and wrapped up many pairs of binoculars and pistols as gifts for the more important sheikhs. She carried hats, veils, parasols, lavender soap, Egyptian cigarettes in a silver case, insect powder, maps, books, a Wedgwood dinner service, silver candlesticks and hairbrushes, crystal glasses, linen and blankets, folding tables and a comfortable chair – as well as her travelling canvas bed and bath.

In 1915, after the outbreak of the First World War and at the instigation of David Hogarth, Gertrude joined the military intelligence department in Cairo, the aim of which was to hasten the departure of the Turks from Arabia and to develop links with the Arabs that would strengthen British influence once the First World War was over. Among those with whom she worked was T.E. Lawrence (Figure 26). In 1916 she went to Basra, on the staff of Sir Percy Cox and became a high-ranking colonial admin-istrator. She played a crucial part in the establishment of the modern state of Iraq (as well as the setting up of its national museum in Baghdad), and in the assumption of the Iraqi throne by King Faisal. She was often called 'the uncrowned queen of Iraq'. However, in 1926, unlucky in love (and not for the first time), she died in the Iraqi capital, after suffering from depression and having taken an overdose of sleeping tablets. Some ascribed her death to natural causes, and

'Beneath layers of lacy petticoats she hid guns, cameras and film, and wrapped up many pairs of binoculars and pistols as gifts for the more important sheikhs.'

her obituary in the *Times* (13 July 1926) suggested that it was due to overwork and 'an unflinching sense of duty which, except for two very short holidays at home, kept her for nearly ten years almost continuously at Baghdad, even during the torrid heat of the Mesopotamian summers, when the thermometer stands for weeks together about and above 120 deg. in the shade'. She had lived life to the full in a man's world.

Some people disliked Gertrude. Sir Mark Sykes stated that she was a 'silly chattering windbag of conceited, gushing, flat-chested, man-woman, globe-trotting, rump-wagging, blethering *ass*!' (quoted by Wallach in *Desert Queen*, 1996, p.73). However, her friend David Hogarth penned a fulsome obituary of her in *The Geographical Journal* (1926, p. 363), remarking:

No other woman of recent time has combined her qualities – her taste for arduous and dangerous adventure with her scientific interest and knowledge, her competence in archaeology and art, her distinguished literary gift, her sympathy for all sorts and conditions of men, her political insight and appreciation of human values, her masculine vigour, hard common sense and practical efficiency – all tempered by feminine charm and a most romantic spirit.

Figure 26. *Gertrude Bell with T.E. Lawrence in Cairo, 1921 (courtesy of the Gertrude Bell Archives, Newcastle University).*

BIBLIOGRAPHIC REFERENCES AND FURTHER READING

Bell, G. 1907. *The Desert and the Sown*. New York: E.P. Dutton.
Bell, G. 1911. *Amurath to Amurath*. London: William Heinemann.
Hogarth, D.G. 1926. Obituary. Gertrude Lowthian Bell. *Geographical Journal*, 68, 363–368.
Hogarth, D.G. 1927. Gertrude Bell's Journey to Hayil. *Geographical Journal*, 70.
Howell, G. 2006. *Daughter of the Desert*. London: Macmillan.
Lukitz, L., Bell, Gertrude Margaret Lowthian (1868–1926). *Oxford Dictionary of National Biography*, Oxford University Press, 2004, article 30686.
Tuson, P. 2014. *Western Women Travelling East 1716–1916*. Oxford: The Arcadian Library in association with the Oxford University Press.
Wallach, J. 1996. *Desert Queen*. London: Weidenfeld and Nicholson.

GERARD LEACHMAN
AND WILLIAM SHAKESPEAR

GERARD EVELYN LEACHMAN, known to his friends as Gerald, was born in Hampshire in 1880. He was one of a group of British soldiers, who, as tough intelligence officers, scouted around Arabia. Educated at Charterhouse, he went to Sandhurst, and then saw service in the Boer War. He was subsequently posted to India and in 1907 was assigned to military intelligence in Simla. There he learnt Arabic and German and studied intelligence reports from Arabia. He arrived in southern Iraq in 1909 to begin his career in the field. In early 1910 Leachman travelled on horseback 2,100 km through Persia, Turkish Kurdistan, Armenia and Syria. Later in the same year, wearing Arab dress, he undertook a journey into the desert south of Baghdad, for which the Royal Geographic Society awarded him its Gill Medal, in 1911 (Figure 27).

In 1912 the RGS funded a modest expedition to central Arabia. Leachman travelled from Damascus to Qasim (Figure 28), Riyadh, Hasa and Bahrain, a journey of nearly 2,250 km. He brought back the first photographs of the Saudi royal family and developed personal links with Ibn Saud himself. During the Great War he was posted to Basra with the aim of controlling the

Figure 27. *Portrait of Gerald Leachman (RGS: frontispiece from Major Bray. 1936. A Paladin of Arabia).*

Figure 28. (opposite) *Leachman's pictures of the Great Mosque (RGS. Eid Al Yahya, 2006,* Travellers in Arabia, *48. London: Stacey International).*

Bedouin on the British left flank, and some observers believe that he ('Lijman') played a more important and less showy role than Lawrence ('Aurens'). His exploits in the First World War were never made public by himself or anyone else. Moreover, he behaved with great heroism at the disaster at Kut where besieged British troops were forced to surrender to the German and Turkish forces. Alas, he was killed, shot in the back, during a revolt near Fallujah in Iraq in August 1920, aged 40. Upright, cantankerous, irritable, brusque and ascetic, he served the British Empire with courage and devotion.

However, according to Lawrence he had 'an abiding contempt for everything native' and Lawrence (in Canton, *From Cairo to Baghdad. British Travellers in Arabia*, 2011, p. 68) described him as a 'ruffian' and as 'a long, lean, ugly jerking man, with deliberately bad manners, a yellow, jaundiced eye, harshtempered, screaming and violent'.

The magnificently named William Henry Irvine Shakespear (Figure 29) was born in Multan, in what is now Pakistan, in 1878. A creature of the Raj, he went to Sandhurst and thence to India, where he served as an officer in the Indian Army. Among his army activities in Bombay was the undertaking of a rat extermination programme. Winstone (1976, p. 34) refers to his impatient and bristling manner, his receding hairline and high forehead, his pomaded and waxed hair and moustache, and his aquiline nose and jutting chin, which gave him an appearance at once brooding and determined. In due course he was appointed to the political department of the Indian government, and served in Bandar Abbas (Persia) and then in Kuwait, where from 1909 he was a political agent. It was from Kuwait that he engaged in a series of journeys into the Arabian Desert. He also became an unswerving friend of Ibn Saud and was probably the first Englishman to meet him, in February 1910.

Figure 29. *Captain William Henry Irvine Shakespear (RGS: Photographed from Geographical Journal,* Volume LIX, No. 5, *May, 1922).*

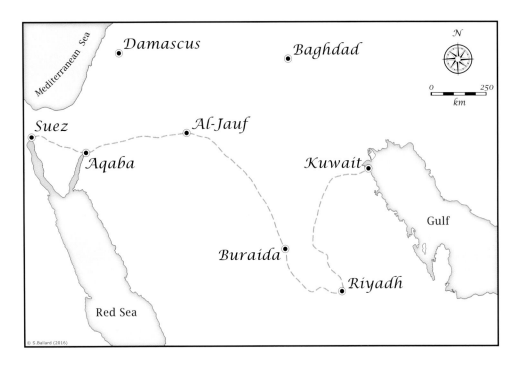

Armed with a sextant and a huge plate camera, a collapsible bathtub, and a supply of carefully concealed wine and whisky, Shakespear's longest journey was in 1914, from Kuwait to the Suez Canal via Riyadh (Figure 30), a distance of over 2,900 km, completed in 111 days and involving 87 different camps. About 1,930 km of the journey were through unknown country. He bathed in a special compartment of his tent, took his meals and Moselle in splendid isolation from his Arab co-travellers, and maintained his identity as a British officer. He was also an accomplished photographer. His maps and notebooks were models of accuracy and thoroughness, and his Arabic had a 'native perfection' (Winstone, *Captain Shakespear*, 1976, p. 135).

Figure 30. (above) *Shakespear's route 1914 (Map drawn by Sebastian Ballard).*

Figure 31. (right) *A picture by William Shakespear of Ibn Sa'ud's army on the march in 1914 (RGS: Eid Al Yahya, 2006,* Travellers in Arabia. *London: Stacey International).*

Fighting on the side of Ibn Saud (Figure 31) against the Rashids, he was killed in a tribal skirmish at Jarrab in 1915 and his head was cut off and hung on one of the main gates of Medina. Like Leachman, he never married, though he had a sweetheart, Dorothea Baird, but he was an intrepid, gallant and lone traveller. An early devotee of the motor car, in 1907 he took leave by driving back to England from the Middle East in his eight-horsepower Rover. Leachman and Shakespear appear never to have met and there may have been some antipathy between them. But they were both great patriots and both were great admirers of Ibn Saud the future king of Saudi Arabia. They helped him to establish his dynasty. When Ibn Saud was asked many years later who was the greatest Englishman he had ever met, he would answer, without hesitation, 'Shakespear'.

BIBLIOGRAPHIC REFERENCES AND FURTHER READING

Al Yahya, E. 2006. *Travellers in Arabia. British Explorers in Saudi Arabia.* London: Stacey International.

Brent, P. 1978. *Far Arabia. Explorers of the Myth.* Newton Abbot: Readers Union.

Canton, J. 2011. *From Cairo to Baghdad. British Travellers in Arabia.* London: I.B. Tauris.

Darlow, M. and Bray, B. 2010. *Ibn Saud. The Desert Warrior and his Legacy.* London: Quartet Books.

Goldberg, J. 1986. Captain Shakespear and Ibn Saud: a balanced reappraisal. *Middle Eastern Studies,* 22(1), 74–88.

Hogarth, D.G. Obituary. 1926, Lieut.–Colonel G.E. Leachman, C.I.E., D.S.O. *Geographical Journal,* 56, 325.

Sluglett, P. 2004. Leachman, Gerard Evelyn (1880–1920). *Oxford Dictionary of National Biography online.*

Sluglett, P. 2004. Shakespear, William Henry Irvine (1878–1915). *Oxford Dictionary of National Biography online.*

Winstone, H.V.F. 1976. *Captain Shakespear.* London: Jonathan Cape.

Winstone, H.V.F. 1982. *Leachman. O. C. Desert.* London: Quartet Books.

HARRY ST JOHN BRIDGER PHILBY

ST JOHN PHILBY (Figure 32), generally called Jack, born in Ceylon in 1885, was one of three great British explorers of the Great Southern Desert of Arabia, which is generally known as the Rub' al Khali or Empty Quarter. The other two were Bertram Thomas and Wilfred Thesiger. Educated at Westminster School and Cambridge University, he excelled at languages and was accepted into the Indian Civil Service. At his first marriage in 1910, his best man was distant cousin and young soldier Lieutenant Bernard Montgomery. In 1915 Philby was selected to go to Mesopotamia as a civilian administrator. In 1917 he contrived to approach, as head of mission, Ibn Saud, ruler of the Nejd in central Arabia, in the hope of seeking his support in the conflict against the Turks in the First World War. He travelled with a small group by camel from the Persian Gulf to Riyadh and then across to Jeddah on the Red Sea. It was on this trip that he developed an undying admiration for Ibn Saud. He also met the Hashemite ruler of the Hejaz, Sharif Hussein, whom he thought less suitable as a British ally. In 1917–18 he explored the southern province of the Nejd. For this and earlier journeys, he was awarded the RGS Founder's Medal in 1920. He reported the journey in *The Geographical Journal* for that year, and besides giving descriptions of the tribes, the settlements, irrigation systems and a wadi flood, he used it as an occasion to cast doubt on the veracity of Palgrave's accounts.

In 1922 Philby joined Major A.L. Holt, who had been investigating the possibilities of railway construction in Arabia on an expedition across from Amman, Jordan to Jouf and on to Karbala on the Mesopotamian border. What was significant about this expedition was that for part of the journey a small fleet of Ford motor cars was used, of the type that Dr John Ball and Claud Williams had utilised in Egypt in the Light Car Patrols in the Great War, though Philby maintained a personal preference for camels (*The Geographical Journal*, 1923).

Figure 32. (left and below) *Harry St John Bridger Philby, 1925 (RGS: from a series of glass lantern-slides entitled 'Dead Sea to Aquaba').*

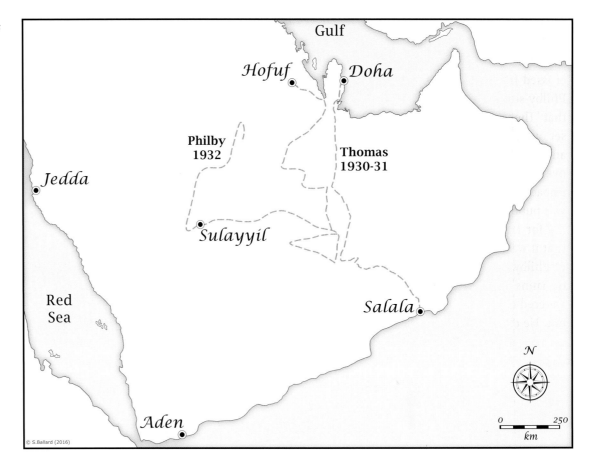

Figure 33. *The routes of Thomas and Philby (Map drawn by Sebastian Ballard).*

This did not stop him, however, from using cars in the 1930s to explore Arabia and to drive to and from England.

Never an easy man, and being obstinate and combative, seeing everything in terms of black and white, Philby left public service in 1925 and founded a trading company in Jeddah, where he became a close friend and adviser of Ibn Saud. In 1930 he converted to Islam and was known as Shaikh Abdullah by the Saudis. He made the hajj, or pilgrimage, to Mecca in 1931.

In the 1930s Philby travelled in the borderlands of the Yemen, but he is now known most of all for his attempt to be the first man to cross the Rub' al Khali. In the event he was beaten by Bertram Thomas, who, without seeking the permission from the authorities that delayed Philby, crossed from south to north in 1931 (Figure 33). However, it can be argued that Philby studied it more thoroughly. Notwithstanding his profound disappointment that 'The virgin charm of the Empty Quarter had been unveiled by another', Philby set out in January 1932 with food sufficient for three months of meandering travel and with 32 camels to carry his men and supplies. He travelled from north to south over a distance of 2,730 km. His journey, during which he came across the meteorite impact craters of Wabar (Figure 34), was described in *The Empty Quarter*, which was published in 1933. Thesiger, in his obituary of Philby in *The Geographical Journal* for 1960, argued that this journey was a greater one than that of Thomas, and that it was 'The greatest in the story of Arabian exploration'. Thesiger also spoke appreciatively of Philby's important collections of birds, mammals, plants and insects, and his scholarly work on ruins and inscriptions. Philby also found indications that the desert had once been better watered than today, causing rivers and human populations to expand, possibly in the Neolithic era. He experienced the phenomenon of 'singing sands' in the Rub' al Khali dunes, describing

'... a person whose life was dominated by two obsessions – the making of money and the winning of fame.'

Figure 34. *Wabar crater (RGS: Geographical Journal)*.

it as being like 'a siren or perhaps an aeroplane engine – quite a musical, pleasing, rhythmic sound of astonishing depth'. He also discovered fulgurites, sticks of sand that had been fused by lightning strikes.

During the Second World War Philby was a pacifist and appeaser. He attacked British policy (for which he was briefly imprisoned) and spent most of the remainder of his life living in Saudi Arabia (where he purchased a second wife) and Lebanon, where he died in 1960. At the time of his death he was staying with one of his sons, Kim, who gained notoriety as a Soviet spy during the Cold War. Overall Philby may have been an unpleasant individual and Middle-Eastern commentator Professor J.B. Kelly (1977) listed a series of failings that included: being a prig at school, a muddled communist, an admirer of Hitler, a philanderer, a bigamist, somebody who was negligent, capricious and moody towards his family, and a person whose life was dominated by two obsessions – the making of money and the winning of fame.

BIBLIOGRAPHIC REFERENCES AND FURTHER READING

Brent, P. 1978. *Far Arabia. Explorers of the Myth.* Newton Abbot: Readers Union.

Craig, J. 2008. Philby, Harry St John Bridger (1885–1960). *Oxford Dictionary of National Biography online.*

Kelly, J.B. 1977. Review of Philby of Araba by Elizabeth Monroe. *Middle Eastern Studies,* 13, 144–146.

Kiernan, R.H. 1937. *The Unveiling of Arabia.* London: Harrap.

Monroe, E. 1973a. Across the Rub 'Al Khali. *Saudi Aramco World,* 24, 6–13.

Monroe, E. 1973b. *Philby of Arabia.* London: Faber and Faber.

Philby, H. St J.B. 1933. *The Empty Quarter.* London: Constable.

Philby, H. St J.B. 1946. *A Pilgrim in Arabia.* London: Robert Hale.

Philby, H. St J.B. 1920. Southern Najd. *Geographical Journal,* 55, 161–185.

Philby, H. St J.B. 1923. Jauf and the North Arabian Desert. *Geographical Journal,* 62, 241–249.

Thesiger, W. 1960. Obituary. *Geographical Journal,* 126, 563–566.

Ure, J. 2010. Harry St John Philby. In R. Hanbury-Tenison (ed). *The Great Explorers.* London: Thames and Hudson. pp. 215–219.

BERTRAM SIDNEY THOMAS

BERTRAM THOMAS (Figure 35), born in England in 1892, was educated at Cambridge University and worked as an administrator in Transjordan and Oman, where he was financial adviser to the Sultan and given the title of wazir. He was the first European to cross the Rub' al Khali, a journey he described in *Arabia Felix* (1932) and for which he was awarded the RGS Founder's Medal. He outlined his main motive for this pioneering journey (p. xxiv):

> The remote recesses of the earth, Arctic and Antarctic, the sources of the Amazon, and the vast inner spaces of Asia and Africa, have one by one yielded their secrets to man's curiosity, until by a strange chance the Rub' al Khali remained almost the last considerable *terra incognita*.

Thomas made a preliminary journey northwards from Salalah in Dhofar on the Oman coast of the Arabian Sea to the edge of the Rub' al Khali in early 1930. He wore Bedouin clothing, spoke the local dialects, avoided the use of alcohol and tobacco, and became acclimatized physically. Under his Arab kerchief he wore a shallow RAF flying helmet with the brim removed. He made substantial collections en route of biological and other specimens for the British Museum, and undertook to measure the heads of the local

Figure 35a. *Bertram Thomas (RGS).*

Figure 35b. (opposite)
Bertram Thomas (RGS).

people for anthropological purposes. This was disagreeable work, since the people he measured in Dhofar were 'either Badawin with tousled hair full of sandy and other accumulations or sedentary townsmen whose locks were a mass of grease from applications of coco-nut oil'.

He recorded the nature of the men of the mountains (p. 53–4):

'Their heads are uncovered, except for a leather thong to keep their bushy curls in place...'

Of quite a peculiar type are these dark-looking men of the mountains, with their long rough head hair sometimes caught up and tied in a bun on top, but more often left wild and bushy, and practically no growth of hair on the face except a slight chin-tuft, many of them with refined non-Arab faces ... a leather girdle, looped as a cartridge belt, encircles the waist. Their heads are uncovered, except for a leather thong to keep their bushy curls in place; their black arms and legs below the knee are bare. Most of them wear a single ear-ring in the right ear and a single bracelet above the right elbow.

He described the circumcision rituals for boys and girls, and the way in which a strip of skin was removed from the centre of the head of recently married women so that the hair would never grow again – 'a scalping operation extremely painful and sometimes fatal'.

On 5 October 1930, Thomas set out from Muscat by sea and went once more to Salalah. As part of a caravan of 30 men and 40 camels, he suffered the usual deprivations of desert travel and was forever wary of tribal raids (Figure 36). He crossed the great dunes (Figure 37) of the Uruq-Adh-Dhahiya in Yemen (p. 170):

Very impressive is a great dune region at first sight – a vast ocean of billowing sands, here tilted into sudden frowning heights, and there falling to gentle valleys merciful for camels, though without a scrap of verdure in view. Dunes of all sizes, unsymmetrical in relation to one another, but with the exquisite roundness of a girl's breast, rise tier upon tier like a mighty mountain system.

The dunes were hard going, but they were also beautiful (p. 174):

Our toil had its compensations. There were moments when we came suddenly upon a picture of sublime grandeur, an immense and noble plastic architecture, an exquisite purity of colour, old rose-red, under the cloudless sky and brilliant light.

Figure 36. (left and below)
Images by Bertram Thomas
(RGS: Geographical Journal).

He also experienced the phenomenon of the 'singing sands', though he thought the term 'hardly appropriate to describe a sound indistinguishable from the siren of a moderate-sized steamship'.

Thomas reached the northern edge of the desert near Doha on 28 January 1931. A few days later he saw the waters of the Persian Gulf. He had stolen the prize of making the first crossing of the Rub' al Khali. Jack Philby had to take second place. Thomas eventually returned to England, where he died in 1950.

BIBLIOGRAPHIC REFERENCES AND FURTHER READING

Al-Hajri, H.S. 2003. *Oman through British Eyes: British Travel Writing on Oman from 1800 to 1970* (Doctoral dissertation, University of Warwick).

Brent, P. 1978. *Far Arabia. Explorers of the Myth.* Newton Abbot: Readers Union.

Hamilton, A. 2010. *An Arabian Utopia: the Western Discovery of Oman.* Oxford: Oxford University Press and Arcadian Library.

Kiernan, R.H. 1937. *The Unveiling of Arabia.* London: Harrap.

Thomas, B. 1932. *Arabia Felix: Across the Empty Quarter of Arabia.* London: Jonathan Cape.

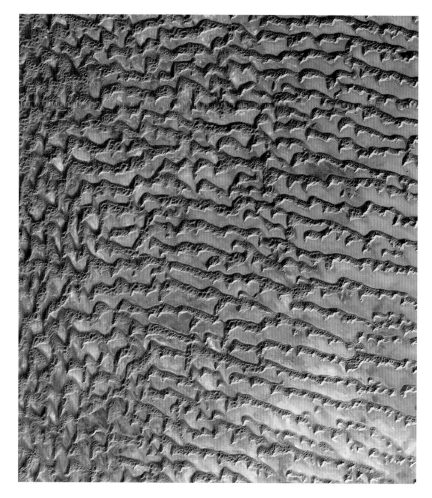

Figure 37. *Satellite image of the dunes of the Empty Quarter. The image was acquired December 2, 2005, covers an area of 54.8 Ê 61.9 km, and is located near 20.7° north latitude, 53.6° east longitude (*http://asterweb.jpl.nasa.gov/gallery/images/RubalKhali.jpg*) (NASA/GSFC/METI/Japan Space Systems, and U.S./Japan ASTER Science Team).*

SIR WILFRED PATRICK THESIGER

ALTHOUGH HE WAS SOMETHING of an anachronism, many observers have regarded Wilfred Thesiger (Figure 38) as the greatest desert explorer of the twentieth century. Whether this is true is debated, but he was certainly a great traveller, writer, and photographer and, more unusually, circumsiser. Born in Addis Ababa in 1910, Thesiger surmised that the 'perverse necessity' that drove him later in life to the deserts of the East may have lain in his childhood in Abyssinia (Ethiopia), and distant memories of such things as the smell of dust and acacias under a hot sun, and of camel herds at water holes. After prep school in Sussex, Thesiger was sent to Eton and then to Oxford University to read history and to box. In 1933–4, soon after going down from Oxford and only 23 years old, he traversed the Danakil Desert. His aim was to explore the Awash River and the Aussa Sultunate, which was peopled by nomads – the Dankali – who were noted for a tendency to kill men and carry off their testicles as trophies (*Geographical Journal*, 1935). Such practices, however, probably held little horror for Thesiger, who had survived fagging and flogging at school. It was also on this journey that he seems to have developed his an interest in circumcision, something at which he became a master in later life when he travelled in Iraq. After Danakil he joined the Sudan Political Service and travelled to Tibesti in the heart of the Sahara, a journey on which he discovered the motivation that drove him: (p. 22):

In the desert I found a freedom unattainable in civilization; a life unhampered by possessions, since everything that was not a necessity was an encumbrance. I had found, too, a comradeship inherent in the circumstances, and the belief that tranquillity was to be found there. I had learnt the satisfaction which comes from hardship and the pleasure which springs from abstinence.

Figure 38. *Wilfred Thesiger (centre) (RGS).*

However, he spent most of his time in the dry bush of Darfur, north-western Sudan. It was in Darfur that he first learnt to travel by fast-riding camel in the company of locals, dressing as they did, eating local food out of a shared bowl, and asking nothing of technology but a torch, a compass, and above all, a decent rifle. He acquired further desert experience in the Second World War, when he fought with the Special Air Service in Egypt's Western Desert, but there he felt that he was insulated from the desert by travelling in a jeep, something he regarded as an abomination. However, he considered all this desert experience a mere prelude to the five years of desert travel for which he is most famed – his journeys through the Empty Quarter of Arabia. This was made possible when he met O.B. Lean, a desert locust specialist working for the FAO (the United Nations Food and Agriculture Organization) in Addis Ababa towards the end of the war. Lean was looking for someone to travel in southern Arabia to collect information on locust movements. It provided Thesiger with the political permissions and the opportunity to enter an otherwise inaccessible land. As he wrote (*The Life of My Choice*, 1987, p. 397):

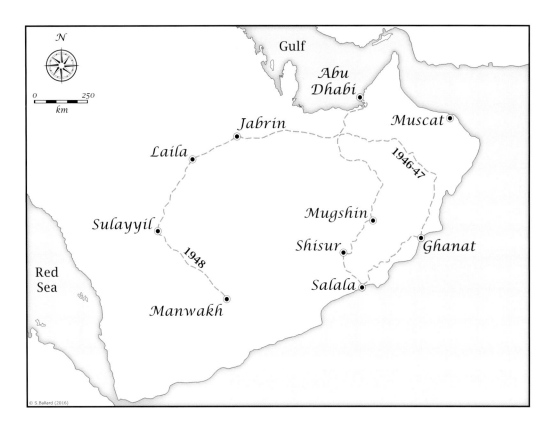

Only in Arabia did an enormous tract of desert, which even Arabs call Rub' al Khali, the Empty Quarter, remain largely inviolate, offering the final challenge of desert exploration.

Thomas and Philby had crossed the Empty Quarter in the early 1930s but no other European had been there since, no aeroplane had even flown over it, and no car had been nearer than the RAF camp at Salala, on the shore of the Indian Ocean, or the townships on the Trucial Coast. In contrast with the Sahara, vast areas of the Empty Quarter were still unexplored and it was surrounded by a no-mans-land of warring tribes.

Thesiger left Addis in March 1945 and stayed in Arabia, apart from brief periods of leave, until 1950. He made a

Figure 39. Thesiger's routes in Arabia (Map drawn by Sebastian Ballard).

series of journeys by camel (Figure 39) to Dhofar and the Hadramaut (Hadhramawt), to the southern Hejaz and to the Trucial Coast and Oman, where he described the quicksands of the Umm al Samim on the edge of the Empty Quarter. But, most importantly of all, he made two crossings of the Empty Quarter, one in 1946–7 and the other in 1948. The first of these journeys took him from Salala on the Arabian Sea across the Rub' al Khali to the oasis of Liwa, then back to Salala by the steppes of western Oman and the Jiddat al Harasis, and from there through the northern Mahra country to Al Mukala in Yemen. The second journey took him to more westerly parts of the sand sea. On these journeys with his Bedouin companions, he enjoyed various privations (*The Life of my Choice*, 1987, p. 398):

We endured almost incessant hunger and, worse still, thirst, sometimes for days on end rationing ourselves to a pint a day; there was the heat of a blazing sun in a shadeless land; the bitter cold of winter nights; incessant watchfulness for raiders, our rifles always at hand; anxiety that our camels, on which our lives depended, would collapse.

The compensations were the clean beauty of 'the sculptured shape of dunes that rose to seven hundred feet and extended for a hundred miles', and the generosity, honesty, pride and loyalty of his young companions. Thesiger's black and white photographs of both the landscapes and these people are breathtaking.

Thesiger regretted the modern world. As he lamented in the introduction to *Arabian Sands* (1959, p. xiii):

I went to Southern Arabia only just in time. Others will go there to study geology and archaeology, the birds and plants and animals, even to study the Arabs themselves, but they will move about in cars and will keep in touch with the outside world by wireless. They will bring back results far more interesting than mine, but they will never now the spirit of the land nor the greatness of the Arabs. … Today the desert where I travelled is scarred with the tracks of lorries and littered with discarded junk imported from Europe and America.

After Arabia, Thesiger continued his nomadic life, travelling inter alia in Iraq, Pakistan, Afghanistan, Morocco, Ladakh, Ethiopia and northern Kenya. Knighted in 1995, and a recipient of the RGS Founder's Medal in 1948, he died in Surrey aged 93 in 2003.

BIBLIOGRAPHIC REFERENCES AND FURTHER READING

Maitland, A. 2006. *Wilfred Thesiger. The Life of the Great Explorer*. London: Harper Press.
Thesiger, W. 1935. The Awash River and the Aussa Sultanate. *Geographical Journal*, 85, 1–19.
Thesiger, W. 1948. Across the Empty Quarter. *Geographical Journal*, 111, 1–19.
Thesiger, W. 1949. A further journey across the Empty Quarter. *Geographical Journal*, 113, 21–44.
Thesiger, W. 1950. Desert borderlands of Oman. *Geographical Journal*, 116, 137–168.
Thesiger, W. 1959. *Arabian Sands*. London: Longmans.
Thesiger, W. 1987. *The Life of my Choice*. London: Collins.

CHAPTER 2

SOUTH AMERICA

TO THE WEST OF THE Andean Cordillera in South America, between latitudes 5° and 30°S, lies the largest west-coast desert in the world – the Atacama Desert (Figure 40). It is also the world's driest desert and Quillagua (mean rainfall 0.05 mm per year) is probably the driest place on Earth. There are fogs (the *garuá* of Peru and the *camanchaca* of Chile) and occasional high rainfall years associated with conditions caused by El Niño that result in great floods, but in general the aridity is intense. This condition has persisted for a long time and, like the Namib, the Atacama has an extended history that goes back tens of millions of years. This long persistent, intense aridity is the reason that the Atacama contains the most famous and important caliche (sodium nitrate fertilizer) deposits in the world. The nitrates mantle the landscape, break up the underlying bedrock and are largely derived from the atmospheric sources that have formed old, desert surfaces. Nitrate, being highly soluble, can only accumulate under very dry conditions.

Diego de Almagro was one of the first Spanish explorers to visit Chile and he crossed the Atacama in the early sixteenth century, as did Pedro de Valdivia. The coastal cities of the Atacama, such as Iquique and Arica, were established in the sixteenth, seventeenth and eighteenth centuries during the time of the Spanish Empire, when they emerged as shipping ports for silver produced in Potosí, in what is now Bolivia, and in other mining centres. During the nineteenth century the desert came under the control of Bolivia, Chile and Peru. However, with the discovery of the sodium nitrate deposits and as a result of unclear borders, the area soon became a zone of conflict and resulted in the War of the Pacific, in which Chile gained a great deal of territory at the expense of Peru and Bolivia. The nitrates were extensively exploited in the nineteenth century, not least by the British. William Bollaert was one of those who took an interest in the deposits, as did J. Harding (1877) (see The Desert of Atacama (Bolivia) in the *Journal of the Royal Geographical Society of London*, pp. 250–253).

The Andes Mountains have a major influence on the landscape of the Atacama. Over a distance of no more than 300 km, the land rises from the Peru-Chile Trench (at some 7,620 m below sea-level) to Andean peaks over 6,100 m above sea level. There is much evidence of volcanic activity. The grain of the land runs approximately north to south, with a very narrow or non-existent coastal plain, a coastal mountain range (Cordillera de la Costa), a longitudinal Central Valley and then, to the east, the higher level Andes and Altiplano. Inland, the Altiplano is a high plateau composed of the sedimentary infill of a series of intermontane tectonic trenches. It is characterised by some large basins (*salars*), which in the past have contained large bodies of water. One of these is the dazzling Salar de Uyuni in Bolivia.

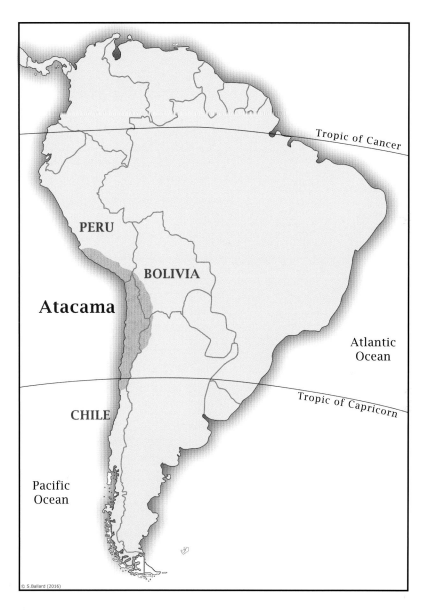

Figure 40. *The Atacama desert*
(Map drawn by Sebastian Ballard).

WILLIAM BOLLAERT

WILLIAM BOLLAERT was born into a large family in Lymington, southern England, in 1807. His father was a Dutch emigrant who had served in the British army and practised as an unregistered apothecary in London. Between the ages of 14 and 18, Bollaert worked as a chemical assistant at the laboratory of the Royal Institution in London, but this came to an end when his father's sudden blindness forced him to relinquish his position and to seek a better salary elsewhere. William went to Peru where he used his chemical skills to work as an assayer and chemist at the silver mines of Guantajaya. He was also commissioned by the Peruvian government to make a survey of the province of Tarapacá, and it was while he was engaged on this that he made a transect across the Atacama Desert with a nitrate refiner, George Smith. They were perhaps the first Europeans to undertake such a journey.

Bollaert published accounts of his work in the Atacama in the *Journal of the Royal Geographical Society of London.* These accounts tend to read like a list of facts rather than providing an engaging narrative, but they contain much valuable new information on southern Peru and northern Chile, parts of which were then Peruvian territory. His papers contain valuable cross sections from the Pacific shore ('perhaps the most barren coast in the world') across the coastal ranges and the Pampa del Tamarugal to the Andes (Figure 41) and the high Puna plateau. He also refers to the *médanos*, moving barchan dunes, which ranged in size 'from anthills to hundreds of feet' and caused travellers to be 'overwhelmed and lost in them'. He recorded the occurrence of sandstorms (*Journal of the Royal Geographical Society of London*, 1851, p. 113):

In 1830 there was a terrible sand-storm, the gale blowing from the S.: the sand was lifted up more than 100 yards into the air; the sun was obscured; the people in the little villages were

Figure 41. *The Atacama Desert and the snow-capped Andes (author's image).*

greatly terrified, and hurried to the chapels to embrace the statues of the saints and pay to them for protection.

Bollaert also provided a great deal of historical data on the severe earthquakes that afflict towns like Arequipa and played an important role in drawing attention to the nitrate-rich caliche deposits which were to be extensively exploited in the region during the nineteenth century as a source of fertilizer. He also made some fascinating observations on the settlements along the coast (*Journal of the Royal Geographical Society of London*, 1851, p. 106):

> Iquique is the only village on the coast of the province; the other places named in the charts are merely headlands, beaches, islands, &c., visited by the fishermen from Iquique in search of congrio, seals, and sea otters, in their ingeniously constructed balsas, or floats made of sea-skins, inflated with air. During their stay at such places they live in caves or wretched cabins built of whales' ribs covered with sea-skins, and subsist on water, maize, and fish which they take with them.

He noted that in some areas there were 'some rude Indian works of art' ('Pintados de los Indios') representing animals such as the llama, created by removing the dark, varnished, stones from the surface of the desert, thereby exposing the lighter coloured material beneath.

Bollaert described the Indians of the region in sympathetic terms (p. 122):

'The Indians are of a brown colour, straight black hair, sparsely made and may be called a small race of people.'

The Indians are of a brown colour, straight black hair, sparsely made and may be called a small race of people. They have been so subdued that they now pass for an inoffensive and quiet race. …The Indian is slow in his movements, but most patient and persevering, performing long journeys with troops of mules and asses … with a little toasted Indian corn and some coca they will travel for many days over the most desert countries. The coca is masticated with llucta or llipta, composed of an alkaline ash, generally mixed with boiled potato.

During the course of the nineteenth century the growth of the nitrate industry caused a radical transformation of the area. When he first visited Iquique in 1826, there were seldom more than a hundred people there and he noted it was very healthy. By the time Bollaert was writing in the *Proceedings of the Royal Geographical Society of London* in 1867–8, Iquique had developed into a town with over 5,000 people (p. 128):

The streets are lined with well-built houses; there are several moles, a lighthouse, two churches, hospital, theatre, club, newspaper, and the place is lit with gas; indeed, all the comforts of life are had at this barren spot where there is neither vegetation nor water; the last most necessary article is distilled from that of the ocean.

On the other hand, the town had ceased to be healthy, being visited by *peste* 'of a bad bilious and yellow fever character'. Whether this had come from Panama by ship was not clear, but he recorded that the town was afflicted by the ordure of the thousands of animals that brought the nitrate from the refineries to the port, and also by the heaps of bones of the horses, mules and asses that had died there.

Bollaert returned to London in 1830 and then worked in various capacities in Portugal in 1833, where he fought as a volunteer in the civil war, and Spain, before going to the independent

Republic of Texas to prepare a report for the British Admiralty. He made further journeys to South America in the 1850s from Britain and became an expert on the Incas. Not only did Bollaert make major studies himself, he also brought the work of others to the attention of scientific bodies in Britain, including that of the German–Chilean naturalist, Rodolfo Amando Philippi, who, in 1853 explored the Atacama Desert and recorded its flora and fauna. However, after suffering from great ill health, Bollaert died in relative obscurity and apparently straitened circumstances in London in 1876, having run a private boarding house in the city's Hanover Square.

BIBLIOGRAPHIC REFERENCES AND FURTHER READING

Bermudez, O. 1975. Esbozo biografico de William Bolleart. *Norte Grande*, 1, 313–318.

Bollaert, W. 1851, Observations on the Geography of Southern Peru, including survey of the Province of Tarapaca, and route to Chile by the coast of the Desert of Atacama. *Journal of the Royal Geographical Society*, 21, 99–130.

Bollaert, W. 1854, Observations on the history of the Incas of Peru, on the Indians of South Peru, and on some Indian remains in the Province of Tarapaca. *Journal of the Ethnological Society of London*, 3, 132–164.

Bollaert, W. 1867/8, Additional notes on the Geography of southern Peru. *Proceedings of the Royal Geographical Society of London*, 12, 126–134.

Harding, J. 1877. The Desert of Atacama (Bolivia). *Journal of the Royal Geographical Society*, 47.

Roeckell, L.M. 2010. Bollaert, William (1807–1876). *Oxford Dictionary of National Biography online*.

Tate, M.L. 2011. Bollaert, William. *Handbook of Texas online*.

CHAPTER 3
AUSTRALIA

Figure 42. (opposite) *The immense size of Australia (Map drawn by Sebastian Ballard).*

AUSTRALIA IS THE WORLD'S second driest continent, but the aridity is not especially intense and nowhere does mean annual rainfall drop below 100–125 mm. This enormous landmass (Figure 42) is also for the most part at low altitude, with about 40 per cent of its area standing less than about 200 m above sea level. Much drainage water flows towards Lake Eyre, the fifth largest terminal lake in the world. Australia is also dominated by large plains, many covered with a lag of stone pavement. It is also an ancient continent with extensive venerable shield areas and land surfaces that have been exposed to sub-aerial processes for hundreds of millions for years. It is geomorphologically comatose and a museum of relict features, with some of the lowest denudation rates of any land surface in the world. Other distinctive phenomena include a massive anticlockwise whirl of sand deserts, composed very largely of linear dunes, great networks of complexly branching rivers created by intense tropical storms, and numerous salt lakes or clay pans that were filled by large bodies of water at various times in the Pleistocene era.

Although the first people reached Australia some 50,000 years ago, European settlement did not start until the late eighteenth century. Moreover, in the early decades, settlement was concentrated on the perimeter. The interior was an enigma and its area huge – greater than Europe. However, particularly from the 1840s onwards, there was a boom period of exploration of the dry heart of Australia. The aim was to extend the frontier of settlement, to seek minerals and to establish possible routes for transcontinental communication. Some exploration was also spurred on as a result of the competition between the different colonies that existed prior to the establishment of federation. It took some time, however, for large tracts of central Australia to be discovered by the Europeans, and it was only in 1873, for example, that William Gosse reached Ayers Rock (Uluru) and Ernest Giles reached the Olgas (Kata Tjuta). Giles was much struck by Mount Olga (*Australia Twice Traversed*, 1889, chapter 2.3), which he described in a somewhat overblown way:

The appearance of Mount Olga from this camp is truly wonderful; it displayed to our astonished eyes rounded minarets, giant cupolas, and monstrous domes. There they have stood as huge memorials of the ancient times of earth, for ages, countless eons of ages, since its creation

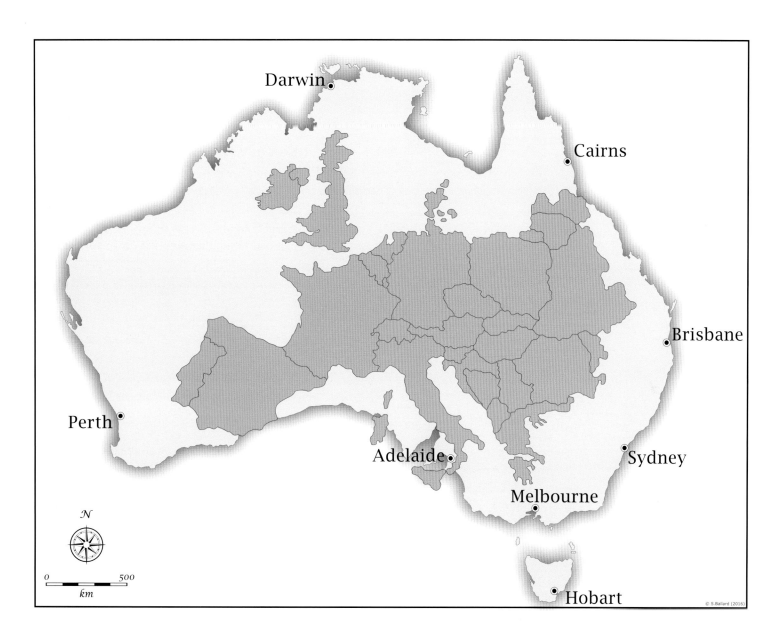

Darwin

Cairns

Brisbane

Perth

Adelaide

Sydney

Melbourne

Hobart

N

0   500
        km

© S.Ballard (2016)

first had birth. The rocks are smoothed with the attrition of the alchemy of years. Time, the old, the dim magician, has ineffectually laboured here, although with all the powers of ocean at his command; Mount Olga has remained as it was born; doubtless by the agency of submarine commotion of former days, beyond even the epoch of far-back history's phantom dream.

Indeed, Giles traversed immense tracts of Western Austalia and South Australia on a range of expeditions in the 1870s, including one on which his young companion, Alfred Gibson, lost his life. The Gibson Desert is named after him.

The Royal Geographic Society awarded its gold medals to eleven explorers: Edward Eyre, Pawel Strzelecki, Charles Sturt, Ludwig Leichardt, Robert Burke, John McDouall Stuart, Augustus Charles and Francis Thomas Gregory, Peter Warburton, John Forrest and Ernest Giles. Exploration continued into the twentieth century, but then, as Michael Terry, Francis Birtles and Cecil Thomas Madigan showed, the use of the horse and the camel could be supplemented by the car and the aeroplane.

Pioneer Europeans found Australia odd. Alan Moorehead (*Cooper's Creek*, 1963, p. 1) wrote:

Nothing in this strange country seemed to bear the slightest resemblance to the outside world: it was so primitive, so lacking in greenness, so silent, so old. It was not a measurable man-made antiquity, but at appearance of exhaustion and weariness in the land itself. … Everything was the wrong way about. Midwinter fell in July, and in January summer was at its height; in the bush there were giant birds that never flew, and queer, antediluvian animals that hopped instead of walked or sat munching mutely in the trees.

This section of the book selects some of those explorers who made lengthy journeys with horses or camels across the obdurate heart of Australia, sometimes termed 'the Ghastly Blank', and struggled with this unfamiliar land, drought, spinifex, the lack of established trade routes and sometimes hostile local people. Compared with Africa, it was difficult to recruit porters and the explorers often had to bring along almost all the food they expected to consume during their journeys – food that was monotonous and provided a diet similar to that which made sailors so susceptible to scurvy on long voyages. Camels and their handlers, imported from Afghanistan and Pakistan, were much used, by Burke and Wills (see p. 119) and by Gosse. Dane Kennedy (2013) describes some of these distinguishing features of Australian exploration in his *The Last Blank Spaces. Exploring Africa and Australia*.

CHARLES STURT

CHARLES STURT (Figure 43), one of the greatest explorers of the interior of Australia, was born in India in 1795, one of 13 children. After being educated at Harrow, he joined the British Army, and in 1827 made the voyage to Sydney in charge of a group of convicts. Soon he was appointed to military positions there, but appears to have become smitten by the idea of searching for a supposed great inland sea.

In 1828 (Figure 44) Sturt started his first expedition, assisted by explorer Hamilton Hume and accompanied by three soldiers and eight convicts. They discovered 'a noble river' flowing to the west, which Sturt named Darling in honour of the governor of New South Wales, Sir Ralph Darling. On a second expedition he took a whaleboat down the Murrumbidgee and reached another great river in January 1830, which he named the Murray in honour of Sir George Murray, secretary of state for the colonies. Sturt had discovered the great river system of south-eastern Australia.

Sturt suffered from poor health and lost his sight for a time. He settled down, bought property, married and had children. He also got embroiled in various disputes regarding his administrative career. However, in August 1844, he embarked on his third expedition, the one for which he is best remembered and on which his second in command, James Poole, would die of scurvy.

Figure 43. *Charles Sturt (RGS).*

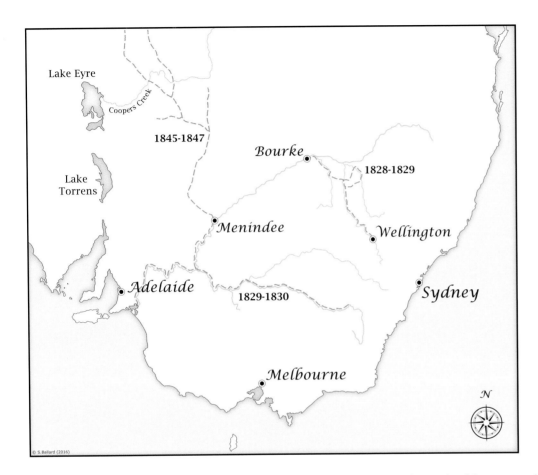

Figure 44. *Map of Sturt's expeditions (Map drawn by Sebastian Ballard).*

Sturt left Adelaide with 15 men, 6 drays, a boat and 200 sheep (Figure 45). He would not return until January 1846. He failed by a mere 240 km, to reach the centre of the continent, but he trekked through and mapped thoroughly and meticulously more than a hundred thousand square miles of very desolate territory. He had to contend with the sand dunes and spinifex tussocks of the Simpson Desert and with Sturt's Stony Desert. It was also a particularly dry year.

On their departure, Sturt told his team (*Journal of the Royal Geographical Society*, 1847, p. 85) that they would be required to render mutual assistance to each other, 'that disputes and quarrelling would be discountenanced, and all intercourse with the natives, but more particularly the native women, was positively forbidden'. The expedition headed to Lake Bonney and the Murray River, and 'the sheep travelled admirably'. They then continued on to the Darling River and to Cooper's Creek, suffering extreme heat during the day and coldness at night. On 2 January 1845 Sturt reported (p. 106):

The men stated that the heat had been so intense that, when they stopped, the poor animals pawed the ground away from the surface to get at a cooler bottom. Mack's boots were so burnt that they cracked, and Lewis, who foolishly exposed his back to the sun, got severely punished. The dogs lost all the skin off the soles of their feet, and could hardly crawl: one of them indeed, fell in the rear and must have inevitably perished.

Remarkably, the sheep, 'their fleeces as white as snow', continued to be 'in excellent condition'. On some days they could not travel until the evening, for otherwise 'the iron bows of the bullocks were so hot that they would have burnt the animals' necks'.

On 12 February 1845 Sturt recorded the nature of dune country (p. 110):

We are now, I believe, in the most gloomy desert man ever trod; all the sand-ridges are covered with tussocks of spinifex, a thick wiry grass generally found near the sea-coast and only in the most barren situations. The character of the country continues the same, small flats surrounded by sandhills. The sandhills are covered with hakea bushes, all, or the majority of them, dead; and the only shelter was under the cart. These deserts are as silent as the grave. No living creatures save ants are here, even the fly is absent: we have not seen a bird or heard an insect all day, yet the tracks of wild dogs are everywhere visible. How they subsist I am at a loss to imagine.

Later in the year, having lived largely off salted meat, the expedition began to suffer from scurvy (p. 114):

We were attacked with swollen and ulcerated gums, violent headaches, pains in the limbs, &c. In my own case, the limbs were free from pain, but I had constant, though not profuse, bleeding from the nose. … Mr Poole became worse and worse: ultimately the skin over the principal muscles became black, and he lost the use of his lower extremities.

'We were attacked with swollen and ulcerated gums, violent headaches, pains in the limbs...'

Poole died in July 1845 and was buried at the Depot Glen campsite. In due course the party reached the Stony Desert (p. 117):

The plain spread out before us like a gloomy sea. … It was so thickly covered with stones as wholly to exclude the growth of vegetation; the stones, composed of fragments of quartz rounded by attrition, lay evenly over the surface, and being thickly coated with oxide of iron, gave a reddish-brown and purple tinge to the whole plain. Our horses left no track behind them, nor was there an object on the visible horizon to direct us in our course; like a ship at sea, we were obliged to steer by compass, and to depend on our own correctness for the chance of retracing our steps.

Figure 45. *Captain Sturt leaving Adelaide in 1844 (Drawing by S.T. Gill).*

Beyond Cooper's Creek (p. 121) they 'had the mortification to see once more the sandy ridges rising before us'. The 'sterile and inhospitable character' of the parallel dunes which ran just west of north was noted, as was 'the hopelessness of the prospect before us'. Just short of the centre of the continent they prudently decided to turn back in November 1845, Sturt feeling that he had 'done all a man could do'. He also felt that God wanted to save him (p. 123) 'from that destruction in which my own impulses would otherwise have involved me'. The return journey was itself gruelling and the ground surface was so hot that 'any matches accidentally dropped immediately ignited'. They reached the Darling on 20 December 'without the loss of a single sheep'.

On the way back Sturt encountered a large group of local people (p. 126):

No people could have received strangers with more kindness that did these receive us: the fact is that, we had so completely overrun the interior, that our presence was known far and wide. We had, in our excursions, fallen in with many straggling parties of natives, and had frequent opportunities for relieving them when pressed by thirst, and had ever treated them with kindness.

So, in contrast to others of his time, Sturt was impeccable in his treatment of the indigenous people, had an unshakable faith in God and behaved like an English gentleman. He also observed the birds of the Australian interior, and collected many plants and geological specimens, the latter leading to some later mining discoveries at Broken Hill and elsewhere.

Sturt was a polished writer, though he tended towards having a depressing view of the landscape of the Australian interior. Sir Roderick Murchison, president of the Geographical Society, described him as modest, brave, most kind hearted and 'compassionate almost as a woman'. Sturt was, however, financially naive. He received the society's Founder's Medal in 1847, and returned to England in 1853, never having found the great inland sea. He died in genteel poverty in Cheltenham, a stylish magnet for retired colonials, in 1869.

BIBLIOGRAPHIC REFERENCES AND FURTHER READING

Beale, E. 1979. *Chipped Idol. A Study of Charles Sturt the Explorer*. Sydney: Sydney University Press.

Cumpston, J.H.L. 1951. *Charles Sturt. His Life and Journeys of Exploration*. Melbourne: Georgian House.

Gammage, B. 2004. Sturt, Charles (1795–1869). *Oxford Dictionary of National Biography online*.

Gibbney, H.J. 'Sturt, Charles (1795–1869)', Australian Dictionary of Biography, National Centre of Biography, Australian National University, http://adb.anu.edu.au/biography/sturt-charles-2712/text3811, published in hardcopy 1967, accessed online 22 April 2014.

Kennedy, Dane. 2013. *The Last Blank Spaces. Exploring Africa and Australia*. Cambridge, Massachusetts: Harvard University Press.

Mitchell, A. 2000. 'Amid th'encircling gloom': the moral geography of Charles Sturt's narratives. *Journal of Australian Studies*, 24, 85–94.

Moorehead, A. 1963. *Cooper's Creek*. London: Hamish Hamilton.

Ross, J. 2010. Charles Sturt. In R. Hanbury-Tenison (ed). *The Great Explorers*. London: Thames and Hudson. pp. 204–208.

Sturt, C. 1847. A condensed account of an exploration in the interior of Australia. *Journal of the Royal Geographical Society of London*, 17, 85–129.

Sturt, C. 1848–49. *Narrative of an expedition into central Australia, performed under the authority of Her Majesty's Government, during the years 1844, 5, and 6: together with a notice of the province of South Australia, in 1847*. London: T. and W. Boone, 2 vols.

Figure 46. (opposite) *Percy Warburton (RGS).*

PETER EGERTON WARBURTON

PETER EGERTON WARBURTON (Figure 46) was born in Cheshire, England, in 1813. He joined the Royal Navy at the age of 12 and later served in the Bombay Army, where he attained the rank of major. In 1853 he went to Australia, where he had a brother, and joined the police in Adelaide. In the course of the years that followed he travelled to parts of the interior and began a notable career of Australian desert exploration. In 1857 he visited Lake Gairdner and the Gawler Ranges, and the next year Lake Eyre and South Lake Torrens. During the 1860s he travelled again, including the area around the northern shores of Lake Eyre. Bearded, gaunt and with deeply set yet penetrating eyes, he searched unsuccessfully for Cooper's Creek, but found a large river, subsequently named the Warburton, which he traced towards the Queensland border. In 1873–4 he made his name by undertaking the first great east-to-west trek from Alice Springs across the Great Sandy Desert to the Oakover River, in the far west of Western Australia. This took him across some of the driest and most difficult areas of the continent (Figure 47).

In his account in the *Proceedings of the Royal Geographical Society,* 1874–5, p. 41) Warburton started by saying:

> I hope that I shall not be accused of boasting, when I assure you that the journey we went through was well nigh proving too hard for us. It was by the merciful interposition of providence alone that our lives were saved – but there was nothing whatever to spare. We got off with our lives, and our lives only; and therefore all boasting or vain-glory would be absurd.

He and two companions, his eldest son and J.W. Lewis, an experienced bushman, travelled by horse and used camels to carry their provisions. The journey from Adelaide to Alice Springs was itself over 1,770 km. Waiting in Alice for the cooler season to set in, they finally departed in April 1873, but once clear of the MacDonnell Ranges their troubles started. As Tim Flannery (1998, p. 291) recounts:

> Fly-blown camels whose sores had to be emptied of maggots with a pint-pot, constipated camels which had to be relieved by enemas administered through double-barrelled shotguns, demented Afghan camel-drivers, and festering scorpion bites were just a few of the expedition's tribulations.

Also, being Europeans, they found it difficult to find water and when they did encounter small amounts in the holes made by the local people in the sand, they were insufficient to water their camels. The locals were not helpful (*Proceedings of the Royal Geographical Society,* 1874–5, p. 43):

> The natives gave us very much trouble, because they did not like us; they were afraid of us, and we never could succeed in catching one, which we wanted to do, in order that by keeping him without water he might be compelled to show us where it was to be got. They were, however, too clever for us, and too quick for us. They saw us before we could see them, and they escaped.

On one occasion, however, they captured an 'urchin' who proved to be too frightened to be of use, while on another occasion they caught a young girl and tied her by a rope to a tree, but she gnawed through it and fled, on her toes so that she could not be tracked. 'A terrible old witch' proved to be no more

useful. The camels met with greater respect from Warburton, for they seemed to cope when other animals would have expired and proved to be patient and easily managed. This did not, however, stop Warburton from eating seven of them (p. 45):

> I daresay that when the animal is fat and well fed on oilcake and other things, it cannot be very bad, but when he has been worked to that extent that he is unable to stand, and is shot only because he is unable to stand, and is shot only because it would be a pity to leave him to rot, his meat is not very good, and it is interlaced with large sheets of parchment. He looks a very large animal, but there is very little meat on him. … The head is somewhat of a delicacy, and the feet are really very good, for his condition does not affect his feet very much. In our distress, however, we were obliged to eat him, inside and outside too; and his hide is pretty good when you cannot get anything else; but if anybody here has the boldness to taste the contents of a carpenter's glue pot, it comes to very much the same thing.

It was just as well that Warburton had with him a 'black fellow' called Charley, who found water when they were on the point of dying from thirst. On one occasion Charley was speared and clubbed by other local people. They rescued him and he recovered, a fact that Warburton attributed to the thickness of his skull, which he stated was five times that of a European. Warburton was awarded the Royal Geographical Society's Patron's medal in 1874. He died near Adelaide in 1889.

Figure 47. (opposite) *Warburton sheltering from a dust storm (RGS: (engraving by Ulick J. Burke. From Peter Egerton Warburton. 1875.* Journey across the Western Interior of Australia, *facing 194. London).*

BIBLIOGRAPHIC REFERENCES AND FURTHER READING

Deasey, D. Warburton, Peter Egerton (1813–1889), *Australian Dictionary of Biography*, National Centre of Biography, Australian National University, http://adb.anu.edu.au/biography/warburton-peter-egerton-4798/text7993, published in hardcopy 1976, accessed online 22 April 2014.

Flannery, T. (1998). *The Explorers. Stories of Discovery and Adventure from the Australian Frontier.* New York: Grove Press.

Harris, C.A. 2004. Warburton, Peter Egerton (1813–1889). *Oxford Dictionary of National Biography online.*

Warburton, P.E. 1874–5. Journey across the Western Interior of Australia. *Proceedings of the Royal Geographical Society*, 19, 41–51.

Warburton, P.E. 1875. *Journey Across the Western Interior of Australia.* London: Sampson Low.

EDWARD JOHN EYRE

EDWARD JOHN EYRE (1815–1901) (Figure 48) was born in England and migrated to Australia in 1833. He is notable for the journeys he made inland and to Western Australia from Adelaide. He was also a staunch supporter of the rights of the indigenous people.

In 1839 he undertook two expeditions northwards from Adelaide, the first of which took him to a huge salt lake that he named Lake Torrens, in honour of Sir Robert Torrens, one of the South Australian Colonization Commissioners. In 1840 he attempted to move further north, but was thwarted by the terrain and so decided to make a journey westwards, around the north of the Great Australian Bight towards Western Australia (Figure 49). His journeys were described in his book, *Journals of Expeditions of Discovery into Central Australia*, which was published in 1845, and his feats were recognised by the Royal Geographical Society, which awarded him one of its Gold Medals in 1847.

Eyre's progressive views on the inhabitants were clearly expressed in his *Journals*:

For the account given of the Aborigines the author deems it unnecessary to offer any apology; a long experience among them, and an intimate knowledge of their character, habits, and position with regard to Europeans, have induced in him a deep interest on behalf of a people, who are fast fading away before the progress of a civilization, which ought only to have added to their improvement and prosperity. Gladly would the author wish to see attention awakened on their behalf, and an effort at least made to stay the torrent which is overwhelming them.

It is most lamentable to think that the progress and prosperity of one race should conduce to the downfall and decay of another; it is still more so to observe the apathy and indifference with which this result is contemplated by mankind in general, and which either leads to no investigation being made as to the cause of this desolating influence, or if it is, terminates, to use the language of the Count Strzelecki, "in the inquiry, like an inquest of the one race upon the corpse of the other, ending for the most part with the verdict of 'died by the visitation of God.'"

Discovering Lake Torrens, Eyre viewed it as a severe barrier to northward exploration:

I found Lake Torrens completely girded by a steep sandy ridge, exactly like the sandy ridges bounding the sea shore, no rocks or stones were visible anywhere, but many saline coasts peeped out in the outer ridge, and upon descending westerly to its basin, I found the dry bed of the lake coated completely over with a crust of salt, forming one unbroken sheet of pure white, and glittering brilliantly in the sun. On stepping upon this I found that it yielded to the foot, and that below the surface the bed of the lake consisted of a soft mud, and the further we advanced to the westward the more boggy it got, so that at last it became quite impossible to proceed, and I was obliged to return to the outer margin of the lake without ascertaining whether there was water on the surface of its bed further west or not.

Foiled in the hope of reaching the water, I stood gazing on the dismal prospect before me with feelings of chagrin and gloom. I can hardly say I felt disappointed, for my expectations in this quarter had never been sanguine; but I could not view unmoved, a scene which from its character and extent, I well knew must exercise a great influence over my future plans and hopes: the vast area of the lake was before me interminable as far as the eye could see to the northward, and the country upon its shore, was desolate and forbidding.

'I stood gazing on the dismal prospect before me with feelings of chagrin and gloom.'

Figure 48. (opposite) *Edward John Eyre (RGS).*

Eyre suffered many privations on his final great westward journey. Halfway across, his European companion, John Baxter, was murdered by two of the local people in the party, leaving Warburton and his local guide Wylie in dire straits:

> Upon raising the body of my faithful, but ill-fated follower, I found that he was beyond all human aid; he had been shot through the left breast with a ball, the last convulsions of death were upon him, and he expired almost immediately after our arrival. The frightful, the appalling truth now burst upon me, that I was alone in the desert. He who had faithfully served me for many years, who had followed my fortunes in adversity and in prosperity, who had accompanied me in all my wanderings, and whose attachment to me had been his sole inducement to remain with me in this last, and to him alas, fatal journey, was now no more. For an instant, I was almost tempted to wish that it had been my own fate instead of his. The horrors of my situation glared upon me in such startling reality, as for an instant almost to paralyse the mind. At the dead hour of night, in the wildest and most inhospitable wastes of Australia, with the fierce wind raging in unison with the scene of violence before me, I was left, with a single native, whose fidelity I could not rely upon, and who for aught I knew might be in league with the other two, who perhaps were even now, lurking about with the view of taking away my life as they had done that of the overseer. Three days had passed away since we left the last water, and it was very doubtful when we might find any more. Six hundred miles of country had to be traversed, before I could hope to obtain the slightest aid or assistance of any kind, whilst I knew not that a single drop of water or an ounce of flour had been left by these murderers, from a stock that had previously been so small.

Figure 49. Map of Eyre's explorations (Map drawn by Sebastian Ballard).

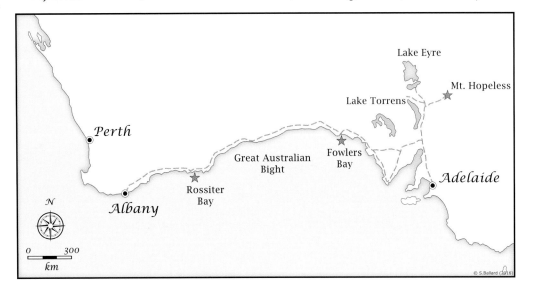

For over two months, Eyre and Wylie struggled on to the west, until, at Rossiter Bay near what is now the coastal town of Esperance, they were able providentially to obtain stores thanks to a chance encounter with a French whaler, the *Mississippi*. They then proceeded to Albany further west along the coast. As Warburton's obituary notice in the *The Geographical Journal* (1902, p. 100) remarked: 'The hardships encountered by Mr Eyre in this first plunge into the unknown deserts between South and Western Australia have had few parallels in the history of exploration.'

After his journey, Eyre debated whether or not the centre of Australia was occupied by a great inland sea (*Journal of the Royal Geographical Society*, 1846). He believed that 'the fiery and withering blasts' of wind that came from the interior made it unlikely that they could have 'wafted over a large expanse of water'. He also reported that conversations with the locals had not suggested that a sea was present in the interior. This was to be an issue that occupied many later explorers.

In 1846 Eyre became lieutenant governor of New Zealand and subsequently held similar posts in various parts of the West Indies. In Jamaica his handling of a rebellion caused major controversy. As Governor of the Colony, Eyre, fearful of an island wide uprising, brutally suppressed the Morant Bay Rebellion. He died in Devon in 1901.

> 'The frightful, the appalling truth now burst upon me, that I was alone in the desert.'

BIBLIOGRAPHIC REFERENCES AND FURTHER READING

Anon. 1902. Obituary: Edward John Eyre. *Geographical Journal*, 19, 99–100.

Dutton G. 'Eyre, Edward John (1815–1901)', Australian Dictionary of Biography, National Centre of Biography, Australian National University, http://adb.anu.edu.au/biography/eyre-edward-john-2032/text2507, published in hardcopy 1966, accessed online 22 April 2014.

Eyre, E.J. 1845. *Journals of Expeditions of Discovery into Central Australia and Overland from Adelaide to King George's Sound in the year 1840–1*. London: T. and W. Boone.

Eyre, E.J. 1846. Considerations against the supposed existence of a Great Sea in the interior of Australia. *Journal of the Royal Geographical Society of London*, 16, 200–211.

JOHN MCDOUALL STUART

Figure 50. *John McDouall Stuart*
(RGS: c.1860, photographer unknown).

JOHN McDOUALL STUART (Figure 50) was a Scot, born in the Kingdom of Fife in 1815. A young man of slight build with a very slim waist, he decided to migrate to South Australia and took passage in 1838. Experienced in the art of surveying, he joined Charles Sturt on the latter's great expedition of 1844 to the Simpson Desert. Stuart headed his first expedition in 1858, with financial backing from William Finke. Its aim was to find new pasturelands and minerals and they got as far as Coober Pedy. Stuart also discovered Chambers Creek, naming it after early settler John Chambers, (Figure 51).

In 1859 and 1860 Stuart undertook two more expeditions. For the second, he was awarded £2,500 by the government of South Australia with the aim of establishing a route for the new overland telegraph. A race was on, for the government of Victoria had also dispatched Burke and Wills to cross the continent. It was during this second journey that Stuart discovered and named some more notable South Australian features: the Finke River, named after his earlier backer; the MacDonnell Ranges, named after Sir Richard MacDonnell, then governor of South Australia; and Tennant Creek, which he named after John Tennant, who also helped finance the 1860 expedition. Stuart contracted scurvy and lost the sight of one eye. However, he became the first European to reach the heart of the continent, planting his British flag on a hill he generously named Central Mount Sturt (later changed to Stuart) after his great predecessor and friend.

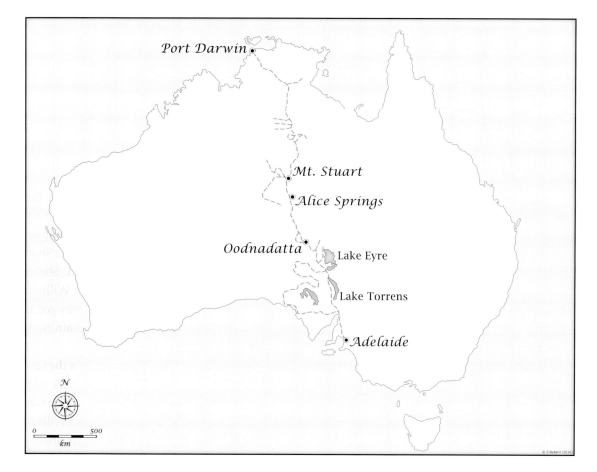

Figure 51. *Stuart's routes 1856–1862 (Map drawn by Sebastian Ballard).*

In 1861, therefore, he headed north from Chambers Creek but was forced to turn back by a shortage of water, scurvy, problems with the aborigines and the deteriorating health of their horses. However, undaunted, he set off again later in the year, accompanied by the botanist Frederick Waterhouse, with the goal of reaching the Indian Ocean. Stuart's account of his journey at the Royal Geographic Society, which awarded him a Gold Medal, one of the 11 medals it awarded in the nineteenth century to explorers of Australia, was published in the *Journal of the Royal*

Geographical Society in 1863. As an account it tends to be rather a catalogue and lacks some of the colour provided by, for example, Sturt and Warburton. Perhaps not surprisingly, given the environment, it spends much time discussing water holes and the burning of the bush by the indigenous people. There is relatively little on the landscapes or the peoples that he encountered. 'Through the instrumentality of Divine providence' he reached the waters of the Indian Ocean in Van Diemen Gulf where he fixed his Union Jack – his name sewn in the centre – to a tall tree. He also buried an airtight tin case in which he placed the following notice:

South Australian Great Northern Exploring Expedition

The exploring party under the command of John M'Douall Stuart, arrived at this spot on the 25th day of July, 1862, having crossed the entire Continent of Australia from the Southern to the Indian Ocean, passing through the centre. They left the city of Adelaide on the 26th day of October, 1861, and the most northern station of the colony on the 21st day of January, 1862. To commemorate this happy event, they have raised this flag bearing his name. All well. God Save the Queen!

During the return journey Stuart suffered two strokes and was at death's door. He had to be transported on a litter between two horses. Half blind and partially crippled, he returned to London where he died in poverty in 1866 at the age of 50. He was the first European to make a successful return crossing of Australia, and his route was to form the backbone of the telegraph route, the railway line from Adelaide to Darwin and the eponymous Stuart Highway. Well-liked and generous, on the expeditions of which he was leader he never lost a man.

BIBLIOGRAPHIC REFERENCES AND FURTHER READING

Morris, D. 'Stuart, John McDouall (1815–1866)', Australian Dictionary of Biography, National Centre of Biography, Australian National University, http://adb.anu.edu.au/biography/stuart-john-mcdouall-4662/text7707, published in hardcopy 1976, accessed online 22 April 2014.

Stuart, J.M. 1863. Explorations from Adelaide across the continent of Australia, 1861–2. *Journal of the Royal Geographical Society of London*, 33, 276–321.

ROBERT O'HARA BURKE AND WILLIAM JOHN WILLS

BURKE AND WILLS (Figures 52a and b) both perished on the return portion of their great south-to-north crossing of Australia. Robert O'Hara Burke, the elder of the two, was born in County Galway in the far west of Ireland, in 1821. He migrated to Australia in 1853 and became a policeman in Victoria. In 1860 he was given leave to take command of the 3,220-km transcontinental expedition being organized by the Royal Society of Victoria and supported by the colony's government. He was impulsive, quick-tempered, inflexible, brave and charming, but he had very limited experience of either Australia, or of bush craft and exploration. He was said to be a 'death or glory' type of man. He achieved both.

William John Wills, who was born in 1834 in Devon, England, migrated to Victoria in 1853 and studied surveying and astronomy under Professor Georg Balthasar von Neumayer. It was Neumayer, a member of the very inexperienced exploration committee of the Royal Society of Victoria, who encouraged Wills to join the expedition planned for the Gulf of Carpentaria. When Burke was made leader, he selected Wills as surveyor, astronomer and third in command (he later became

Figure 52a. *Portrait of William John Wills (RGS).*

Figure 52b. *Portrait of Robert O'Hara Burke (RGS).*

Burke's deputy). Wills, a serious-minded young man, served Burke faithfully through thick and thin, even though Burke's leadership left a great deal to be desired.

The Burke and Wills expedition was the result of the newly gold-rich colony of Victoria wanting to show that in exploration it was at least the equal of the adjacent colony of South Australia, where people like Warburton, Sturt and Stuart had already completed great journeys. The objectives of the Burke and Wills journey, known as the Victorian Exploring Expedition, were hazy, with the route between Cooper's Creek and the Gulf of Carpentaria being selected in haste and Burke's instructions incoherent.

By the standards of the age, the expedition (Figure 53) which left Melbourne on 20 August 1860 was costly but well equipped. It included camels imported from India, horses and wagons, abundant food for two years, and large amounts of equipment, perhaps as much as 20 tonnes. In addition to Burke and Wills, there was a camel master called George James Landells, two German scientific officers named Ludwig Becker and Hermann Beckler, a foreman called Charles Ferguson and nine assistants, and three Indian cameleers. Burke would have preferred to travel fast and light without excess impedimenta, and early on dumped his supplies of lemon juice, with the consequence that four of his party died of scurvy. He also restricted his team's personal baggage amount and to lessen the burden on the horses ordered the men to walk.

The expedition set off from Royal Park in Melbourne under the watchful eye of some 15,000 cheering spectators, heading for the settlement of Swan Hill and the Darling River. Burke's deputy, Landells did not approve of some of Burke's decisions regarding alcohol, and at Kinchega on the Darling he resigned from the expedition. Wills took his place. By the time they reached the settlement of Menindee, a stretch that took them a very leisurely two months, other changes in the team had occurred. Dr Beckler resigned, 13 members of the expedition had been sacked, and eight new men had been hired. From Menindee they headed to Cooper's Creek, and set up a depot, leaving William Brahe in charge. Rather than waiting for cooler weather, Burke set off for the Gulf of Carpentaria with Wills, John King, Charles Gray, six camels, one horse, and enough food for just three months. The journey from the creek to the mangrove swamps of the Gulf of Carpentaria was relatively easy but took longer than anticipated – 59 days. As a consequence they only had enough food for 27 days to see them through the entire return journey.

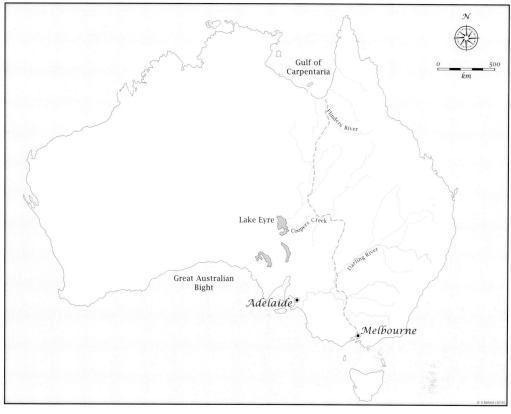

Figure 53. *The route of Burke and Wills (Map drawn by Sebastian Ballard).*

The return journey proved horrific (Figure 54). Gray died of dysentery, having been beaten by Burke for purloining food, and four camels and the horse had to be shot. They reached the depot on Cooper's Creek on 21 April, but found that Brahe had already left. Rather than going back to Menindee, Burke ordered that they should head out into the Strzelecki Desert towards Mount Hopeless, in the Flinders mountain range north of Adelaide. This was an error, and Burke and Wills both died, probably of starvation, in late June or early July 1861. King, with the help of a tribe of Yandruwandha, managed to survive for six months until rescued by a relief expedition, but he died some years later at the age of 33, having never recovered his health.

Burke had beaten John McDouall Stuart in the race to the north, but at great cost. He had kept no very informative journal, finding that there was no time for serious scientific observation, although the scientific results of the expedition proved greater than has often been assumed.. He had employed a route that subsequently proved to be less useful than that of his South Australian competitor. He could not bring himself to associate with the indigenous people, who might well have saved him, and in this was very different from Charles Sturt. Nonetheless, the remains of Burke and Wills were taken to Melbourne, where they were accorded Victoria's first state funeral. The Royal Geographical Society awarded Burke its Founder's Medal posthumously, in 1862.

BIBLIOGRAPHIC REFERENCES AND FURTHER READING

Fitzpatrick, K. 1969. Burke, Robert O'Hara (1821–1861). *Australian Dictionary of Biography*, Volume 3, Melbourne University Press, pp. 301–303.

Garnett, R. 2004. Burke, Robert O'Hara (1820–1861). *Oxford Dictionary of National Biography online*.

Joyce, E.B. and McCann, D.A. 2011. *Burke and Wills: the Scientific Legacy of the Victorian Exploring Expedition*. Collingwood, Victoria: CSIRO.

McLaren, I.F. 1976. Wills, William John (1834–1861). *Australian Dictionary of Biography*, Volume 6, Melbourne University Press, 410–411.

Moorehead, A. 1963. *Cooper's Creek*. London: Hamish Hamilton.

Figure 54. (opposite) Close to death
(The arrival of Burke, Wills and King at the deserted camp at Cooper's Creek, Sunday evening, April 21, 1861, painting by John Longstaff, 1907, held at National Gallery of Victoria, Australia).

JOHN FORREST

U NLIKE STURT, WARBURTON, Stuart, and Burke and Wills, John Forrest (Figure 55), was a native-born Australian. Of Scottish stock, he was born near Bunbury in Western Australia, in 1847. He became a surveyor in the colony's government service.

In 1869, between April and August, (Figure 56) Forrest led an expedition from Perth in the hope of finding clues as to what had happened to another explorer, Ludwig Leichardt, a Prussian naturalist who had disappeared many years before without trace. Forrest and his team of six men and sixteen horses travelled around 3,220 km in the vicinity of lakes Moore and Barlee, and reached as far inland as the town now known as Laverton. He undertook systematic surveying and brought back geological and botanical specimens. On this and other expeditions he was greatly appreciative of the help rendered – especially in finding water, the provision of meat, the collecting of horses and communication with the indigenous inhabitants – by a local named Tommy Windich.

Later in the same year, the governor of Western Australia asked Forrest to retrace – though in reverse – Edward John Eyre's journey along the coastline of the Great Australian Bight from Perth, through Eucla, to Adelaide. This journey was carried out in 1870 and was the first west-to-east crossing of Western Australia by land. Some of the coastline encountered on 6 June was terrifying (*Journal of the Royal Geographical Society of London*, 1871, p. 365):

> Continuing for 4 miles, we reached the sea-cliffs, which fell perpendicularly into the sea, and although grand in the extreme, were terrible to gaze upon. After looking very cautiously over the precipice, we all ran back quite terror-stricken by the dreadful view.

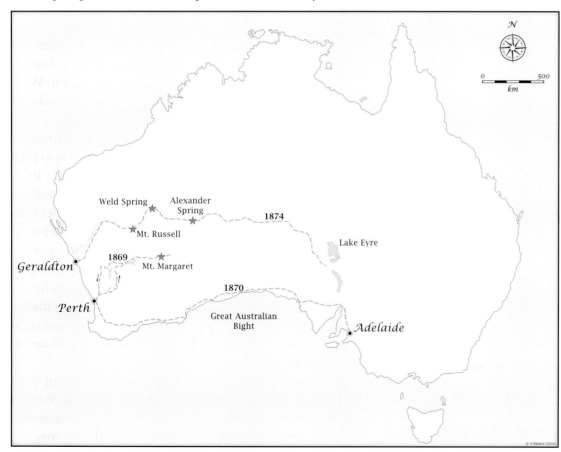

Figure 55. (opposite) *John Forrest (RGS).*

Figure 56. (left) *John Forrest's routes (Map drawn by Sebastian Ballard).*

On June 24 they encountered some indigenous people (p. 369):

> 'Tommy heard a coo-ey, and after answering it a good many times, we were surprised to see two natives walking up towards us, unarmed.'

Tommy heard a coo-ey, and after answering it a good many times, we were surprised to see two natives walking up towards us, unarmed. I approached and met them; they did not appear very frightened, and at once began to eat the damper I gave them. We could not understand anything they said. I beckoned them to come with us, which they did at once, and followed so closely after me as to tramp on my spurs. They pointed to water further ahead. After walking behind me about a mile, we saw four more running after us, who on joining us made a great noise, singing and appearing very pleased. Shortly afterwards two more joined us, making eight in all. They were all entirely naked, and circumcised. ... The eight natives slept at the fire. We gave them as much damper as they could eat. They had not the least particle of clothing, and made pillows of each other's bodies, resembling pigs more than human beings.

Forrest's greatest expedition was in 1874 when he led a team of six men and 20 horses from the coastal town of Geraldton, to the source of the Murchison River, then on to the settlement of Peak Hill on the north–south overland telegraph line, before heading down to Adelaide, where they arrived after six months of travelling. This was the first west-to-east crossing through the western centre of Australia. In the process, he encountered hostile local people (Figure 57), some of whom his party shot at, was threatened with death from thirst and lost 16 of his horses. In 1875 he published an account of his three expeditions under the title *Explorations in Australia* [this is in the list at the end]. It is for the most part a tedious read, being largely a day-by-day account of looking for water, with very little about the landscape or the people. It also is characterised by the rather immodest amount of space given to the adulatory receptions Forrest received in Adelaide and Perth, and brings out very clearly the limitations of the horse compared with the camel for desert exploration (*Journal of the Royal Geographical Society of London*, 1875, p. 297):

> When it is remembered that a horse in poor condition and in warm weather cannot go much over a day without water, and when the sterility of the country is considered, it will be readily seen what a disadvantage one labours under without camels, which can go ten days without water ... horses are the noblest and most useful animals in the world, but they must have

food and water regularly. The camel, on the other hand, is physically formed to travel over these desolate regions, and in Australia has been known to go 12 and 14 days without water, carrying 300 lbs. and sometimes 400 lbs. in weight.

In 1876 Forrest was awarded the Royal Geographical Society's Founder's Medal. He went on to become a great political figure in Western Australia, was knighted and became the first premier of the colony. After federation, he engaged in federal politics and held various high offices, which culminated in his appointment as acting prime minister. He was also a great figure physically, in his later years weighing almost 127 kg and having a 137-cm waist. He died in 1918, on board a ship off Sierra Leone that was bound for London.

Figure 57. *The native attack of 1874 (From Forrest, J., 1875, Explorations in Australia, 3 volumes. London: Sampson Low).*

BIBLIOGRAPHIC REFERENCES AND FURTHER READING

Crowley, F.K. 'Forrest, Sir John (1847–1918)', Australian Dictionary of Biography, National Centre of Biography, Australian National University, http://adb.anu.edu.au/biography/forrest-sir-john-6211/text10677, published in hardcopy 1981, accessed online 22 April 2014.

Forrest, J. 1871. Journal of an expedition to explore the country from West Australia to Port Eucla, and thence to Adelaide, South Australia. *Journal of the Royal Geographical Society of London*, 41, 361–372.

Forrest, J. 1875. Explorations in Australia. 3 volumes. London: Sampson Low.

Forrest, J., Weld, F.A. and Fraser, M. 1875. Journal of the Western Australian Exploring Expedition through the centre of Australia from Champion Bay to the Overland Telegraph Line between Adelaide and Port Darwin. *Journal of the Royal Geographical Society of London*, 45, 249–299.

CHAPTER 4
CHINA AND CENTRAL ASIA

THE DESERTS OF CHINA and its neighbours range in altitude from the Turfan (Turpan) Depression at −150 m below sea level to the high mountains of the Kunlun and Karakoram, where altitudes exceed 5,000 m, and are all characterized by very low winter temperatures and very high summer ones. The annual temperature range in parts of the Gobi Desert is −40°C to +50°C. Taklamakan, 'the place from which there is no return', is China's largest desert and is very dry, with mean annual precipitation dropping to as low as 10 mm. It lies within the Tarim Basin, which, with an area of 530,000 km², is one of the largest closed basins on Earth. Lop Nor, 'the wandering lake' is also within the basin, at its eastern end, and is just 780 m above sea level. The Tarim Basin is bounded to the south by the Kunlun Mountains and to the north by the Tian Shan mountain range. The Taklamakan Desert is a major sand sea. At 337,600 km² it is indeed huge, with a diverse range of dune types, many of which are 80–200 m high.

There are also some other deserts to consider. The Turpan-Hami Basin (the same as the Turfan/Turpan Depression), which covers well over 50,000 km², is separated from the Tarim Basin by the Kuruk Mountains. It contains the Ayding salt lake, which, at around 158 m below sea level, is the lowest place in China. The Qaidam Basin – 850 km long from east to west, and 250 km wide from north to south – lies at an altitude of 2,600–3,000 m above sea level and is surrounded by the Kunlun, Altun and Qilian mountains. As in the Tarim Basin, alluvial fans and river deposits occur on the margins, but the sand dunes are more scattered and less extensive, and saline lakes occupy the basin centre. The Gansu (Hexi) Corridor runs from the eastern end of the Tarim Basin for about 1,000 km to the Yellow River, about 130 km north of Lanzhou. It is bounded to the north by the Mongolian Plateau and the Gobi steppes and to the south by the Qilian Mountains. Alluvial fans and gravels dominate the surface, most of which lies at between around 1,000 m and 1,500 m above sea level. Some of the dunes in the Badain Jaran Desert of Inner Mongolia are enormous mega dunes that may be as much as 450 m high, making them amongst the world's tallest. Towards the east of the Chinese arid zone, and lying within the big bend of the Yellow River, is the Ordos Plateau. The northern section is known as the Hobq Desert and contains extensive areas of mobile dunes. The more southern sector, which is moister, is the Mu Us Desert.

In the nineteenth and twentieth centuries, there was a great deal of interest in the deserts of China, and during the Great Game, Britain and Russia vied to gain influence in the area. There was also great interest in the Silk Road and in the many imposing archaeological remains that existed.

Figure 58. *A dune field in the Alashan District of north west China (author's image).*

Figure 59. *Portrait of Nikolay Przhevalsky (RGS).*

NIKOLAY PRZHEVALSKY (Figure 59) was the greatest Russian explorer of Central Asia and a ruthless advocate of Russia's part in the Great Game, gathering vast amounts of intelligence over an enormous area of territory. He was born in 1839 into a noble Polish family in the Russian city of Smolensk, and died of typhus in 1888 on the lakeshores of Issyk-Kul, in present day Kyrgyzstan, whilst engaged on an attempt to reach Lhasa in Tibet. Donald Rayfield in *The Dream of Lhasa* has succinctly summarised what makes his subject an intriguing figure (p. xi):

Przhevalsky's image in history and science is heroic, but his personality is enigmatic. A man of ruthless determination and of shy tenderness, an apostle of European superiority who loathed European society, an explorer of China who despised the Chinese, a big-game hunter on an epic scale who mourned the death of his dogs, a major-general who disliked the army, a materialist and a Byronic materialist, he had the paradoxical temperament and universality of genius.

In 1855, towards the end of the Crimean War, Przhevalsky joined the army and studied hard for entry into the Military Academy of the General Staff in St Petersburg. He then taught cadets in Warsaw, where he studied zoology, ornithology and botany in preparation for his hoped-for career as an explorer. Finally, he was allowed to leave Warsaw and went off to Eastern Siberia on the two-year-long expedition on which he was to make his name.

Thereafter, he made four Central Asian expeditions. The first, which took place between 1870 and 1873, funded by the Russian War Department, the Imperial Russian Geographical Society and the St Petersburg Botanical Gardens, took him from Siberia across the Gobi to Beijing, the upper Yangtze Basin and into Tibet. The second, between 1876 and 1877, took him through East Turkestan, Lop Nor and the Tian Shan Mountains. The third (1879–80) took him through Hami and the Qaidam Basin, Koko Nor (the Blue Lake) and to within 260 km (160 miles) of Lhasa in Tibet. On this expedition he was probably the first European to see the Cave of a Thousand Buddhas, at Dunhuang, which Aurel Stein would later explore. The fourth (1883–85), took Przhevalsky across the Gobi to the Alashan and the eastern Tian Shan Mountains, returning via Koko Nor towards the ancient city of Khotan and Issyk Kul Lake. He travelled, as he liked to say, 'with a carbine in one hand and a whip in the other'.

An account of Przhevalsky's 1876 journey was published in England, in 1879, entitled *From Kulja, Across the Tian Shan to Lob-Nor*. He wrote scathingly about the people of the Tarim River Valley (p.70–71):

'The wife is mistress of her household, but at the same time her husband's slave...'

With regard to the moral side of the inhabitants of the Tarim, their chief characteristic, as with Asiatics in general, is laziness; and, next to this, dissimulation and suspicion; fanaticism does not run high here, and their family life is probably the same as that of other Turkestanis. The wife is mistress of her household, but at the same time her husband's slave, and he may turn her out whenever he chooses and take another, or keep several wives at a time. Marriage may be contracted for the shortest period, even though only for a few days. Their most peculiar habit is that of talking loudly, and with great rapidity of utterance; so much so, that on hearing them conversing with one another, a stranger might suppose that they were quarrelling.

He was especially dismissive of the women (p. 112):

Externally the women are very unattractive; the old women are especially hideous, and one of those I saw at Lob-nor, emaciated, wrinkled, clad in rags, with matted hair, and shivering from ague, presented a most sorry likeness of humanity.

On the other hand (p. 90–91), he was impressed by the many wild camels he encountered:

> Unlike the domesticated animal, whose chief characteristics are cowardice, stupidity, and apathy, the wild variety is remarkable for its sagacity and admirably developed senses. Its sight is marvellously keen, hearing exceedingly acute, and sense of smell wonderfully perfect. The hunters told us that a camel could scent a man several versts (c.1 km) off, see him, however cautiously he might approach, from a great distance, and hear the slightest rustle of his footsteps. Once aware of its danger, it instantly takes to flight and never stops for some dozens, or even hundreds. … One would suppose that so uncouth an animal would be incapable of climbing mountains; the contrary, however, is actually the case, for we often saw the tracks and droppings of camels in the narrowest gorges, and on slopes steep enough to baffle the hunter.

'… we often saw the tracks and droppings of camels in the narrowest gorges, and on slopes steep enough to baffle the hunter.'

Przhevalsky also noted that Lop Nor had formerly possibly been of greater extent that when he visited it:

> Beyond the salt marshes, at all events on the south where I surveyed them, a narrow belt of tamarisk-trees follows the shore line, and beyond this again a pebbly plain rising considerably though gradually to the foot of Altyn-tagh. This was probably in remote times the border of Lake Lob itself, which at that period overflowed its shores, and was therefore far more extensive, and probably deeper and less obstructed by reeds than at present. What caused the diminution of the lake, and whether this phenomenon was periodical or not, I cannot say. But the fact that almost all the lakes of Central Asia show signs of desiccation is well known.

He observed that this large body of water in the middle of the desert attracted huge numbers of birds (p. 104):

> In spring, however, especially at its commencement, Lob-nor is literally alive with water-fowl. Situated in the very midst of a wild and barren desert, half-way between north and south, it serves without doubt as an admirable resting-place for birds of passage, belonging to the web-footed and wading orders.

Przhevalsky's popular fame is associated with the discovery of the Mongolian wild horse (*Equus przewalskii*) (Figure 60), which is named after him, but he should in reality be remembered for being the first explorer to make a systematic study of the deserts and mountain chains of Central Asia and for being the second European in modern times to reach the lake Lop Nor (the Swede Johan Gustaf Renat was the first). He is also notable for the collections he made of plants and animals, bringing back some 16,000 specimens of 1,700 botanical species, including over 700 mammals, some 1,200 reptiles and amphibians, and over 5,000 bird skins. It has often been noted that his appearance was similar to that of the great Russian tyrant, Joseph Stalin. Like Hedin and Stein he never married. He was probably homosexual and groomed a succession of young male assistants. He was contemptuous of Asian peoples and an exponent of Russian imperialism in Asia. He achieved great fame in his lifetime, rose to the rank of major general, was awarded the Royal Geographic Society's Founder's Medal in 1879, and is commemorated by a large statue in St Petersburg, with a camel kneeling at its base.

Figure 60. *Mongolian wild horse (Rayfield, 1976).*

BIBLIOGRAPHIC REFERENCES AND FURTHER READING

Brower, D. 1994. Imperial Russia and its orient: the renown of Nikolai Przhevalsky. *Russian Review*, 53, 367–381.

Meyer, K.E. and Brysac, S.B. 1999. *Tournament of Shadows*. Washington, D.C.: Counterpoint.

Przhevalsky, N. 1879. *From Kulja, Across the Tian Shan to Lob-Nor*. London: Sampson Low.

Rayfield, D. 1976. *The Dream of Lhasa. The Life of Nikolay Przhevalsky (1839–1888) Explorer of Central Asia*. London: Paul Elek.

Ure, J. 2010. Nikolai Przhevalsky. In R. Hanbury-Tenison (ed). *The Great Explorers*. London: Thames and Hudson. pp. 93–97.

SIR MARC AUREL STEIN

AUREL STEIN (Figure 61) was born in Hungary in 1862 to a Jewish bourgeois family, but he was brought up a Lutheran. He studied at the universities of Vienna, Leipzig and Tübingen and also at the British Museum and the Oriental Institute in Woking. In 1887 he left for India, where, with the help of Sir Henry Rawlinson, he held various university and government posts. In 1900, after his experience of traveling in Kashmir, stimulated by the findings of Sven Hedin and with the support of Lord Curzon, the viceroy, he set out on the first of various expeditions to East Turkestan, now Xinjiang, though later in life he also worked in the parched terrains of Persia, the Thar Desert, Balochistan, Seistan, Makran and elsewhere. He died of a stroke while at the US Legation in Kabul, Afghanistan, in 1943, and after an Anglican service was buried in the Christian cemetery in the city.

Stein, in common with many men of his generation, had little contact with women. His mother had little to do with his upbringing, his sister was already adult when he was born, and he attended all-male schools. On his expeditions he spent most of him time in exclusively male company. There is no suggestion that he was homosexual, and it was once said that he had chosen Central Asia as his bride. He also lavished affection on

Figure 61. (opposite) *Sir Aurel Stein (RGS: from a contemporary lithograph in Rayfield, D. 1976. The Dream of Lhasa, plate 12).*

Figure 62. (left) *Sir Aurel Stein (seated) with one of his dogs in the Tarim Basin (from Stein, On Central-Asian Tracks, Vol I).*

a succession of seven fox terriers, all of which were named 'Dash'. They accompanied him every-where (Figure 62).

Stein's biographer, Annabel Walker, said that he was a boring man who led an exciting life. One reviewer commented that Stein had 'all the allure of an Edwardian chartered accountant'. He focussed relentlessly on his aims, seeking to work in wild places and to be supported finan-cially for doing so. He was phenomenally well organised and diligent, wrote extensively and well, was a gifted linguist, and took many thousands of superb landscape photographs. Stein was also a very serious scholar and for a time held a fellowship at Merton College, Oxford, where he was awarded a D.Litt (doctor of letters). Cambridge University, for its part, gave him an honorary degree. He was also given the Founder's Medal by the Royal Geographical Society in 1909, was made a fellow of the British Academy, and received a knighthood, having acquired British nationality in 1904.

Only 1.6 m tall, Stein was sparely built but had broad shoulders and an iron constitution. He enjoyed good health, kept fit, was very energetic and seems to have been largely indifferent to food and to extreme physical hardship.

In Turkestan, the epicentre of his 55 years of unremitting travel and research, this little terrier of a man travelled huge distances (over 16,000 km by camel or on foot) and established the existence of otherwise forgotten civilizations along the Silk Road. He discovered and excavated over 1,000 archaeological sites and routes, and delved deep into the Taklamakan and Lop deserts, from Keriya in the south to Turfan in the north, and from Kashgar in the west to Dunhuang in the east. It was at this last location that in 1907 he reached the Caves of the Thousand Buddhas and discovered manuscripts, textiles and paintings in huge profusion. He was greatly excited (*The Geographical Journal*, 1909, p. 243):

'There were hundreds of grottoes, large and small, honeycombing in irregular tiers the sombre rock-faces...'

There were hundreds of grottoes, large and small, honeycombing in irregular tiers the sombre rock-faces, and my first hurried inspection showed that almost all of them had on their plastered walls a profusion of beautiful and more or less well preserved frescoes.

Stein bribed Wang, the caretaker, to open a sealed door and discovered more than 9,000 manuscripts in Sogdian, runic, Sanskrit, Tibetan, Khotanese, Saka and Toacharian, some of which are still being translated today. It was a momentous find.

Stein received great help from the surveyors of the Survey of India, which he regularly and warmly acknowledged. His maps were of a very high quality and provided a great deal of important strategic information to the Indian government.

One remarkable feature of Stein was his consideration for men and beasts. No member of his four Turkestan expeditions was buried on a mountaintop or left to die of thirst in a desert. He also showed great concern for his camels. As he remarked of one day in the Taklamakan Desert on his 1913–16 Turkestan expedition (*Geographical Journal*, 1916, p. 113–4):

Next morning I ascended the highest dune near our camp, and carefully scanning the horizon saw nothing but the same expanse of formidable sand ridges like huge waves of an angry ocean suddenly arrested in movement. There was a strange allurement is this vista suggesting nature in the contortions of death. But hard as it seemed to resist the Syren voices of the desert which called me onwards, I felt forced to turn northwards. Though we men might have struggled through, I should probably have had to incur the needless sacrifice of some of our brave camels.

In the Lop Desert he describes how he and his men treated the lacerated feet of his camels (*Geographical Review,* 1920, p. 28):

It was a painful process for the poor beasts, however, beneficial in its results, this sewing on of small pieces of thick oxhide to the live skin as to protect the sore places. Then came in the evening the almost equally troublesome business of giving the camels their draft of rapeseed oil, which Hassan considered it requisite to administer now every second night in order to keep up their stamina. He called it "the camel's tea", and I knew well from previous desert journeys what excellent effect this provision of oil had on camels when subjected to prolonged deprivation of grazing and water. But it was not easy to make the poor beasts swallow it.

The dryness of the desert contributed to the preservation of the great masses of material he discovered and collected. Following his 1906–8 expedition, he wrote (*The Geographical Journal,* 1909, p. 34):

So it was natural enough that the hundreds of inscribed pieces of wood, bamboo, silk, the remains of clothing, furniture, and equipment, etc., all the miscellaneous articles of antiquarian interest, which the successive occupants of these desolate posts had left behind as of no value, should have survived practically uninjured. Sometimes a mere scraping on the surface of what looked like an ordinary gravel slope adjoining the ruined watch –station sufficed to disclose rubbish heaps in which files of wooden records, thrown out from the office of some military commander before the time of Christ, lay amongst the most perishable materials. Straw, bits of clothing, etc, all looking perfectly fresh.

Stein has been criticised in the modern era, not least by the Chinese, who regarded him as one of the worst of 'the foreign devils' for his collection of such archaeological materials and their dispatch to Britain and Europe. However, his aim was to take the materials to a safe place and to make them available to scholars, most of whom worked in the West.

As his obituary in the *Proceedings of the British Academy* put it: 'As Marco Polo is regarded as the greatest traveller of medieval times, so Marc Aurel Stein is likely to be considered in many respects the greatest traveller and explorer of modern times. In him we can see an outstanding, if not unique, example of the combination of a great scholar and a great man of action.'

BIBLIOGRAPHIC REFERENCES AND FURTHER READING

Hopkirk, P. 1980. *Foreign Devils on the Silk Road.* Oxford: Oxford University Press.

Ikle, F.W. 1968. Sir Aurel Stein. A Victorian Geographer in the tracks of Alexander. *Isis*, 59, 144–155.

Meyer, K.E. and Brysac, S.B. 1999. *Tournament of Shadows.* Washington, D.C.: Counterpoint.

Oldham, C.E.A. W. 1943. Sir Aurel Stein – obituary. *Proceedings of the British Academy*, 29, 453–465.

Stein, M.A. 1909. Explorations in Central Asia, 1906–8. *Geographical Journal*, 34, 5–36, 241–264.

Stein, M.A. 1916. A third journey of exploration in Central Asia. *Geographical Journal*, 48, 97–130.

Stein, M.A. 1920. Explorations in the Lop Desert. *Geographical Review*, 9, 1–34.

Stein, M.A. 1925. Innermost Asia: its geography as a factor in history. *Geographical Journal*, 65, 377–403.

Walker, A. 1995. *Aurel Stein. Pioneer of the Silk Road.* London: John Murray.

Whitfield, S. 2010. Marc Aurel Stein. In R. Hanbury-Tenison (ed). *The Great Explorers*. London: Thames and Hudson. pp. 106–111.

SIR FRANCIS EDWARD YOUNGHUSBAND

FRANCIS YOUNGHUSBAND was born in 1863 in Murree in British India to a military family; one of his uncles was Robert Shaw, a noted explorer of Central Asia and the first Englishman to visit Kashgar and Yarkand in 1868. At the age of 13 Francis was sent to Clifton College, Bristol, an institution which, like Cheltenham and Wellington, turned out Christian gentlemen who were destined for the Army. One of his contemporaries there was Douglas Haig, who became British commander in chief in France in the First World War. After Clifton College, where stern athleticism was favoured, Younghusband went to Sandhurst, and then in 1882 was commissioned as a subaltern in the 1st King's Dragoon Guards, stationed at Meerut in India. In 1886 he was sent to Manchuria on a seven-month expedition of exploration, where, in Beijing, he met a great figure in British military intelligence, Colonel Mark Sever Bell, VC. Bell is now largely forgotten, but Curzon remarked: 'His extraordinary travels over almost the whole Asian continent ... entitle him to be considered the territorial Ulysses of his age.' It was the brave, brisk and blunt Bell who encouraged Younghusband to make the enormous trek across the Gobi from Beijing to Kashmir and who helped get the necessary permissions for him to do so.

One reason why Younghusband was keen on this opportunity was that he was worried by the threat that Russia posed to the Indian Empire. As he expressed it in *The Heart of a Continent*, p. xiii:

> As a glacier under the pull of gravitation moves from higher to lower regions, so did the Russian Empire move from the colder to the warmer regions of Asia. Towards Persia, towards Afghanistan, towards India, towards China the Russians were moving under some seemingly natural impulse. We in India had anxiously to watch their progress. The question was, "Could the Chinese Empire act as a buffer?"

Figure 63. *Younghusband as a young soldier (RGS: From Younghusband, F., 1937. The Heart of a Continent, 1. London: John Murray.*

Great Russian explorers were already operating in the area, including Nikolay Przhevalsky.

The other prime motive was the sheer exhilaration of solitary exploration. He wrote (*The Heart of a Continent*, p. 2):

The project before me was a journey in length nearly as great as one across Central Africa and back again, and, to me at least, far more interesting than any African travel – a journey through countries varying from the level wastes of the Gobi Desert to the snow-clad masses of the Himalaya; passing, moreover, through the entire length of an empire with a history of three thousand years and still fresh in interest to the present day. And with the chance of making such a journey, who could help feeling all the ardent excitement of travel rising in him, and long to be started on it.

On 4 April 1887 the 23-year-old Younghusband (Figure 63) set off from Beijing on his seven-month-march across the Mongolian steppe, through the Gobi and Turfan deserts, and on to Kashgar and the Yarkand River, through the Muztagh Pass across the Karakorams, and thence to Srinagar in the Vale of Kashmir. Covering 4,000 miles, it was longer than the journey from New York to San Francisco and involved crossing mountains higher than the Rockies. Much of the time he travelled alone except for guides, although he was accompanied throughout by a general factotum, Liu San, to whom he felt a strong debt of gratitude (even though he appears to have been repeatedly duped), but in his *The Heart of the Continent*, Younghusband dismisses Liu San as somebody who was 'A Chinaman, and therefore not a perfect animal.' They travelled on camel and by foot, frequently in the late afternoon and early night, when temperatures were cooler. The expedition was scourged by a series of sand and dust storms, and Younghusband frequently referred to the dreariness of the landscape, but he was also spiritually moved by the vast vistas and the clarity of the night skies. His descent of the uncharted Muztagh Pass, at an altitude of around 5,800 m, through the Karakoram Range was a major achievement and served to cement Younghusband's reputation not only as a desert explorer but as a mountaineer.

He appears to have been particularly exercised by high winds (*The Heart of a Continent*, p. 44):

> The darkness was so great that we could not see a yard in front of us, a regular hurricane was blowing, and heavy bursts of drenching rain kept falling at intervals. The lantern could not be lighted, on account of the violence of the wind, and we had to grope about amongst the camels, get the loads off, feel for the tent, and then get that up as best we could – which was no easy matter, for the wind blowing against it nearly blew us off our legs, and it was all we could do to prevent the whole thing from being carried away.

On the other hand, his travels had a mystical significance that moulded his future views on religion (p. 220):

> There, far away in the desert, there was little to disturb the outward flow of feeling towards Nature. There, before me, was nothing *but* Nature. The boundless plain beneath and the starry skies above. … In those pure skies the stars shone out in unrivalled brilliancy, and hour after hour, through the long nights, I would watch them in their courses over the heavens, and think of what they are and what they represent and try to realize the place we men hold in the universe stretched out before me.

At the end of his journey, Younghusband arrived in Srinagar 'Dressed in a Yarkand sheepskin coat and long Yarkand boots, and with a round Tam-o'-Shanter cap as the only European article of dress about me, and with a rough beard, and my face burnt by exposure in the desert and cut and reddened by the cold on the glaciers.' He was told by the political agent to take a bath. Going on to Rawalpindi one of his own corporals failed to recognise him. 'I beg your pardon, sir, but you looked so black.'

> 'There, before me, was nothing *but* Nature. The boundless plain beneath and the starry skies above…'

One significant fact about the expedition is that Younghusband made no systematic observations at all. He himself was saddened by this and felt an inadequate recipient of the Royal Geographical Society's Patron's Medal in 1890. He had not collected rocks, plants or antiquities, made maps, measured people or studied languages. He remarked that he must have appeared 'a miserably ill-equipped and thoughtless traveller, who had simply thrown away his

Figure 64. *Younghusband in maturity (RGS).*

golden opportunities' (Seaver, 1952, p. 96). His was not a scientific expedition but an act of military intelligence gathering.

Younghusband was a complex individual. His family and school background instilled in him ideas of duty and diligence. They also made him religious and guilt-ridden. He was stubborn and impetuous, politically naive and fond of solitude. He detested regimental and cantonment life and was socially inept. Although small in stature, he had huge reserves of stamina. On the other hand, moulded in what Curzon later termed 'the frontier school of character' he possessed many of the virtues required by a romantic hero at that time. Indeed, as Peter Hopkirk, 1990 (p. 447) remarked, 'he might almost have been a model for such John Buchan heroes as Richard Hannay and Sandy Arbuthnot – men who pitted themselves single-handed and in lonely places against those threatening the British Empire.' This mix of qualities marked him out for his great explorations as well as for his role in the Jameson Raid in the Transvaal and the British invasion of Tibet in 1903. However, between the end of the First World War and the beginning of the second his attitude to India changed. Once a noted Curzonian imperialist, he became a supporter of the Indian National Congress and Gandhi, and an advocate of British withdrawal from India. He died in 1942 in Dorset, in the arms of his passionate young mistress rather than in the arms of his wife to whom he had been married since 1897. In his later years (Figure 64) he had come to believe in free love.

BIBLIOGRAPHIC REFERENCES AND FURTHER READING

Hopkirk, P. 1990. *The Great Game*. Oxford: Oxford University Press.
French, P. 1994. *Younghusband. The Last Great Imperial Adventurer*. London: Harper Collins.
Matless, D. 2004. Younghusband, Sir Francis Edward (1863–1942). *Oxford Dictionary of National Biography.*
Meyer, K.E. and Brysac, S.B. 1999. *Tournament of Shadows*. Washington, D.C.: Counterpoint.
Seaver, G. 1952. *Francis Younghusband, Explorer and Mystic*. London: John Murray.
Verrier, A. 1991. *Francis Younghusband and the Great Game*. London: Jonathan Cape.
Younghusband, F. 1937. *The Heart of a Continent*. London: John Murray.

SVEN ANDERS HEDIN

Figure 65. *Dr Sven Hedin and a prize Kerghiz camel (RGS).*

SVEN HEDIN (Figure 65), born in Stockholm in 1865, wanted to become an explorer from an early age. As he wrote in *My Life as an Explorer* (p. 1):

At the early age of twelve my goal was fairly clear. My closest friends were Fenimore Cooper and Jules Verne, Livingstone and Stanley, Franklin, Payer and Nordenskiöld, particularly the long line of heroes and martyrs of Arctic exploration.

When he was 15, Hedin witnessed the triumphal return home from the Arctic of Adolf Nordenskiöld in the *Vega*, after making the first successful navigation of the Northeast Passage. Hedin vowed that one day he too would like to return home to such acclaim. However, the Arctic was not to be his sphere of activity, for, aged 20, it was arranged for him to take up a position as a private tutor in Baku on the Caspian Sea. During that time he was able to traverse much of Persia, and remarked that 'the glamour of the whole Orient was to unfold before me'.

After studying at Uppsala in Sweden and in Berlin under the great German physical geographer Ferdinand von Richthofen, who coined the term the 'Silk Road', Hedin made two trips to Persia, and then between 1894 and 1908 (Figure 66) conducted three great expeditions by camel and on foot through the deserts and mountains of Central Asia. His mapping activity was prodigious,

© S.Ballard (2016)

RUSSIA

N

Orenburg

Novosibirsk

Irkutsk

Ulan Bator

Black
Sea

Caspian
Sea

Aral
Sea

TURKEY

MONGOLIA

Baku

Urumqi

Beijing

Tashkent

Baghdad • *Tehran*

Khasgar

TIBET

Xian

IRAN

AFGHANISTAN

CHINA

ARABIA

Arabian Sea

PAKISTAN

NEPAL

Figure 66. *Hedin's routes (Map drawn by Sebastian Ballard).*

but he also unearthed the ruins of ancient Buddhist towns, which was to prove a stimulus to Aurel Stein (see p. 136), who often followed in his footsteps. Like Stein, Hedin was of small stature and never married, though he had women friends. About 20 years later, in the 1920s and 1930s, he returned to Mongolia and Turkestan. This time he was also able to experiment with motor transport, most notably between 1927 and 1935, with financial support from the governments of Sweden and Germany and from the German national airline Deutsche Lufthansa, and led a large interdisciplinary and international Sino–Swedish scientific programme. Just as Roy Chapman Andrews (see p. 159) was to demonstrate the value of big interdisciplinary expeditions through his projects in Mongolia, so did Hedin in the Gobi. He also started to employ the motor car with a view to using it to revive the ancient Silk Road. It was, however, to be his last expedition. He died in Stockholm in 1952, aged 87. He left his entire scientific and personal estate to the Royal Swedish Academy of Sciences for the formation of the Sven Hedin Foundation.

Hedin was a prolific author and wrote nearly 50 books based on his own best-selling recipe (Meyer and Breysac, 1999, p. 316):

> A generous helping of descriptive writing, add a spattering of derring-dos, pepper with historical asides, baste liberally with meetings with the high and mighty, finally, top off with one near-death experience.

His books and lectures were used to finance his expeditions, for he held no public or academic positions.

It was in 1895, in the dunes of the Taklamakan, that one of these near-death experiences occurred, largely as a result of his impetuosity and lack of careful planning. Tall dunes, searing, deafening, hurricane-force dust storms and a shortage of water and fuel placed the expedition in severe, and for some, fatal difficulties. Dogs expired, camels died and men were abandoned. He described all this graphically in *My Life as an Explorer* (p. 123):

> Countless dune-waves rose all the way to the eastern horizon, where the sand disappeared in the haze of distance. We had to get over them, and all those beyond the horizon! Impossible! We had not the strength! Both men and animals grew weaker with every day that passed.

Hedin drank the Chinese spirits for his Primus stove with disastrous results. Members of his team also drank the blood from a rooster and camel urine, mixed with sugar and vinegar. 'They were overcome with violent cramps and vomiting, and lay writhing and groaning on the sand.' (p. 130). Eventually, alone, Hedin made it to the dry bed of the Khotan River (now Hotan River) and, almost dead, found a pool of water (p. 140–1):

> I sat down calmly on the bank and felt my pulse. It was so weak it was hardly noticeable. … Then I drank, and drank again. I drank without restraint. … I drank again, and sat caressing the water in this blessed pool. Later on, I christened this pool Khoda-verdi-kol, or "The Pool of God's gift".

'Countless dune-waves rose all the way to the eastern horizon, where the sand disappeared in the haze of distance.'

Hedin could also describe landscapes with graphic prose, as when he wrote of the wind-eroded yardangs he had to cross near Lop Nor (the 'wandering lake', p. 64):

> They assumed more and more fantastic shapes, resembling tables, projecting roofs and mould-ings with deep shadows underneath. Sometimes they had a deceptive resemblance to towers, walls, old houses and fortifications built by men's hands. They assumed the shapes of lions in ambush, recumbent dragons, inscrutable sphinxes and sleeping dogs.

In his later years and after his death, his reputation suffered greatly on account of his many links with the Nazi regime in Germany (Figure 67) and his many personal contacts with Hitler and other members of the German High Command. The British, who, at Curzon's behest, had given Hedin

Figure 67. (right) *Hedin and Hitler (http://www.sydsvenskan. se/kultur--nojen/aventyraren-som-gick-vilse/).*

Figure 68. (opposite) *Portrait of Sven Hedin (RGS).*

honorary degrees from Britain's best universities, a knighthood and a Royal Geographical Society's Gold Medal in 1898, were also not impressed by his support for Kaiser Wilhelm during the First World War. This is evident from his obituary, written by Sir Clarmont Skrine, former British consul general in Kashgar, for the *The Geographical Journal* (1953, p. 252–3), which pulled no punches:

> By temperament Hedin was a Nazi, to whom exploration was a *Kampf*, a struggle not only against the forces of nature but also on paper, against rival explorers. It is not surprising that he espoused in turn the causes of Kaiser Wilhelm II and Hitler.

Some of his claims and methods had also provoked adverse comment from Sir Thomas Holdich, surveyor general of India, and from various Royal Geographical Society stalwarts, including the mountaineer Tom Longstaff. At times Hedin showed European arrogance (Figure 68). He was also criticised for the fact that, unlike Aurel Stein, he was willing all too often, as in 1895, to callously sacrifice both his animals and his men in pursuit of his goals. Rare was an expedition in which more than a handful on his pack train came back alive. His obituary in the *The Geographical Journal* lamented:

> Once he had made up his mind to attain a particular object, no consideration of other people's feelings, convenience or even safety was ever allowed to deflect him. Not only did he sacrifice ruthlessly his faithful riding and pack animals when crossing desolate wastes, but he deliberately exposed his native companions as well as himself to the risk of a horrible death.

Hedin's willingness, like Amundsen, to sacrifice his dogs was especially unpalatable to the British, and was in marked contrast to the devotion that Stein showed to his fox terriers. In his defence it has to be said that, unlike Younghusband, Hedin made very extensive collections of rocks, plants, animals and antiquities. Even though he was not a great academic archaeologist like Stein, Hedin stimulated the scientific and archaeological work of others. His work on Lop Nor was notable, as was his navigation of the Tarim (Yarkand) River, and his discussion of wind-eroded features – yardangs – establishing the term in scientific literature. However, it was his topographic mapping of the Pamirs, the Taklamakan, Tibet, the Silk Road and the Himalayas that was his greatest, and perhaps most lasting, contribution, and the amount of territory in central Asia that he explored was truly amazing, even if, as Sir Thomas Holdich maintained, his surveying methods were not as good as those of Aurel Stein.

BIBLIOGRAPHIC REFERENCES AND FURTHER READING

Hedin, S. 1926. *My Life as an Explorer*. London: Cassell and Company.
Hedin, S., 1914. *From Pole to Pole*. London: Macmillan.
Hedin, S., 1940. *The Wandering Lake*. London: George Routledge and Sons.
Hopkirk, P. 1980. *Foreign Devils on the Silk Road*. Oxford: Oxford University Press.
Meyer, K.E. and Brysac, S.B. 1999. *Tournament of Shadows*. Washington, D.C.: Counterpoint.
Montell, G. 1954. Sven Hedin the explorer. *Geografiska Annaler*, 36, 1–8.
Skrine, C. 1953. Obituary: Sven Hedin. *Geographical Journal*, 119, 252–253.

ELLSWORTH HUNTINGTON

ELLSWORTH HUNTINGTON, who was born in Illinois, USA, in 1876, and, like another great explorer of central Asia, Roy Chapman Andrews, attended Beloit College in Wisconsin, was not only one of the greatest, most well-known and controversial academic geographers of his generation, but also made major contributions to our knowledge of the geography and history of large tracts of dry Asia. He was rather unpromising material as an explorer. As a child he had been very slight of build and his mother had great trouble buying him underwear and gloves that would fit.

After Beloit, Huntington obtained a position as a missionary at Euphrates College in Harput, a hill town on a great bend of the Euphrates, located in present-day Turkey. Apart from teaching English and Christianity, he took the opportunity to travel in Anatolia, to make meteorological observations and, in 1901, to travel down the Euphrates River on a raft made of saplings buoyed up by inflated sheepskins. After that he received a scholarship to study physiography at Harvard under the great William Morris Davis. On his journey back to America he read James Geikie's *The Great Ice Age and its relations to the Antiquity of Man*, which stimulated his life-long effort to link climate change to the history of human societies. It sowed the seeds of the environmental determinism for which Huntington became famous, or, depending on your point of view, notorious. He was also noted in his later years for his espousal of the cause of eugenics.

Davis took Huntington on a field trip to the arid south-west of the USA in 1902, and in 1903, accompanied again by Davis, Huntington participated in a three-month Central Asian expedition led by Raphael Welles Pumpelly and supported by the Carnegie Institution in Washington. This expedition took him to Kashgar at the western end of the Tarim Basin. During the winter of 1903–4 he worked in the Seistan Basin (which he described as 'a hell'), at the borders of Persia and

Figure 69. (opposite)
*Huntington in middle age,
taken in 1920 (Yale Manuscripts
and Archives).*

Afghanistan. He then made a trip with Robert Le Moyne Barrett in 1905–6, which was sponsored by the newly formed Association of American Geographers (AAG). He fell out with Barrett, who felt that Huntington had claimed the credit for the expedition of which Barrett was leader. This expedition took Huntington first to Kashmir and Peshawar (where he met Aurel Stein) and then over the Karakorams to the Lop Nor basin in East Turkestan and on to Turfan. Upon his return, Huntington wrote his great *The Pulse of Asia*, in which he argued that the climatic factor was crucial for understanding the history of the peoples whose regions he had been through. He speculated that pulsations of climate had served as a driving force in the history of Eurasia, impelling nomadic invaders in dry periods to overrun the civilizations that surrounded them (p. 385):

> With every throb of the climatic pulse which we have felt in Central Asia, the centre of civilization has moved this way or that. Each throb has sent pain and decay to lands whose day was done, life and vigor to those whose day was yet to be.

As he explained (p. 14):

'Each throb has sent pain and decay to lands whose day was done, life and vigor to those whose day was yet to be.'

> In relatively dry regions increasing aridity is a dire calamity, giving rise to famine and distress. These in turn are fruitful causes of wars and migrations, which engender the fall of dynasties and empires, the rise of new nations, and the growth of new civilizations. If, on the contrary, a country becomes less arid, and the conditions of life improve, prosperity and contentment are the rule. There is less temptation to war, and men's attention is left more free for the gentler arts and sciences which make for higher civilization.

Huntington was especially struck by the information about past climates that could be provided by lake deposits and old strandlines in arid regions (*Geographical Journal*, 1910, p. 406):

> There are numerous salt lakes, all of which act as rain-gauges, expanding or contracting in response to variations in rainfall or evaporation. The deposits laid down in and around such lakes vary greatly, in accordance with the degree of aridity and the amount of vegetation in the regions whence the waters of the lake are derived. The deposits of one phase cover those

of another, and there is little loss by erosion. Thus a complete record is preserved, which can easily be read, provided we know the effect of specific climatic conditions upon the nature of deposits, and provided the buried records can be observed.

He was also struck by the relic shorelines of Lop Nor, which rose to up to around 180 m above the present lake and indicated to him a lake that was formerly 480–640 km long and 160 km wide.

The other major impact that the Central Asian experience made on Huntington was his realisation that ethnic characteristics owed much to their physical environment. Examples of this are his contrasting descriptions of the Chanto agriculturalists of the oases and the Khirghiz (Kirghiz) nomads of the steppes (*The Pulse of Asia*, p.223):

> The environment of the Khirghiz compels him to travel continually, and to become a self-reliant, hardy, adventurous nomad; that of the Chanto limits him to one place, where patience and steady work bring success, and where timidity is no special disadvantage.

His willingness to stereotype ethnic groups is demonstrated by his description of the Chantos (p. 225):

> Among the good qualities, the chief are gentleness, good temper, hospitality, courtesy, patience, contentment, democracy, religious tolerance, and industry; among the bad are timidity, dishonesty, stupidity, provincialism, childishness, lack of initiative, lack of curiosity, indifference to the suffering of others, and immorality. ... It is noticeable that strong characteristics, whether good or bad, are absent

By contrast, he concluded (p. 385) that in some parts of the world, such as Western Europe and North America, climatic conditions led to races who possessed 'a high degree of will-power and energy, and a capacity for making progress and for dominating other races'.

Bald and bespectacled, short, round headed and with big lips (Figure 69), Huntington wore starched collars in the field and was a prolific writer, often for a popular audience, eschewing esoteric jargon. He wrote or co-wrote 29 volumes. He was also a man of great industry and perseverance, who found that deafness increased his concentration and discouraged interruptions. According to one biographer, 'He worked like an ant attempting the labours of Hercules'. He was supportive of other scholars, but his desire to arrive at big truths with insufficient proof was disturbing to those of a cautious bent. Huntington died from a heart attack, after a checkered career, mainly spent at Yale, in New Haven, Connecticut, in 1947. He was remembered for his firmly held and increasingly unfashionable views on determinism and eugenics, encapsulated in his penultimate book, *Mainsprings of Civilization* (1945), rather than for his pioneering and prescient work on the importance of climate change.

BIBLIOGRAPHIC REFERENCES AND FURTHER READING

Chappell, J.E. 1970. Climate change reconsidered: another look at "The Pulse of Asia". *Geographical Review*, 60, 347–373.

Davidson, K. 2000. Huntington, Ellsworth. *American National Biography online*.

Geikie, James. 1874. *The Great Ice Age and its relations to the Antiquity of Man*. London, W. Ibister & Co.

Huntington, E. 1905. The depression of Sistan in eastern Persia. *Scottish Geographical Magazine*, 21, 379–385.

Huntington, E. 1907. *The Pulse of Asia*. Boston and New York: Houghton, Mifflin and Company.

Huntington, E. 1910. Problems in exploration: Central Asia. *Geographical Journal*, 35, 395–419.

Huntington, E. 1945. *Mainsprings of Civilization*. New York: Wiley.

Kreutzmann, H. 2004, Ellswoth Huntington and his perspective on Central Asia. Great Game experiences and their influence on development thought. *GeoJournal*, 59, 27–31.

Martin, G.J. 1973. *Ellsworth Huntington: His Life and Thought*. Hamden, CT: Archon Books.

Visher, S.S. 1948. Memoir to Ellsworth Huntington, 1876–1947. *Annals of the Association of American Geographers*, 38, 38–50.

EVANGELINE AND FRANCESCA FRENCH AND MILDRED CABLE

THE SISTERS EVA and Francesca French, together with Mildred Cable, were three extraordinarily intrepid British evangelical women missionaries (Figure 70). As members of the China Inland Mission (CIM), in the 1920s they travelled in the Gobi Desert to take the gospel to the Muslim regions of north-western China.

Eva French was born in 1869 in Algeria to English parents and was educated in Switzerland. She joined the CIM in 1893. Francesca, who was born in Belgium, was four years younger than her sister and joined her in China in 1908. Mildred Cable was born in 1878 to a prosperous Guildford family, studied pharmacy and human sciences at London University, suffered a broken engagement, and joined the CIM in 1901.

In 1923 the trio decided to establish a mission in Gansu Province, north-west China, and apart from periods of furlough in England, they spent the years until 1936 travelling across the Gobi. Though not members of the Salvation Army, they adopted many of its methods: music and taking the gospel to the people was the basis of their mission. All three were fluent in spoken and written Chinese, wore Chinese dress and adopted the customs of the local population. They also mastered Uighur, the Turkic language of the region, and ate no pork, in order to evangelise more effectively. Basing themselves in Jiuquan, they travelled out from the city in the summer months. The hardships and dangers they endured made them pioneer women explorers, and they were the first British women to visit the city of Urumchi, in East Turkestan, now Xinjiang.

Cable, though the youngest of the trio, established herself as its dominant member, and was responsible for much of their writing. She was a formidable and rather intimidating individual, nicknamed Napoleon by activists in the British and Foreign Bible Society. She had dark rings around her eyes, which made her look like a panda.

Mildred Cable spoke graphically to the Royal Geographical Society (*The Geographical Journal*, 1942, p. 200-201) about the terrible changes that occurred in the Gobi in the 1930s as a result of political instability and Soviet influence:

'Travel permits, secret police interrogations, and registration forms were the order of the day...'

Outside the towns peaceful Gobi homes were left desolate, farmsteads were burnt, the trees of the oases hewn down, and young men were recruited for brigand bands. Many of the oasis wells were filled up with sand. ... The inns were untenable because men's bones and dead men's clothes littered the rooms and lay about in courtyard enclosures. The palaces of Hami were destroyed and nothing but rubble remained where once a medieval court held sway. ... Travel permits, secret police interrogations, and registration forms were the order of the day. ... The spirit of Gobi culture was replaced by fear, suspicion and treachery.

She also lamented the use of motor lorries. The women travelled for the most part by mule cart in the company of normally disreputable carters.

However, she also spoke of the Gobi's allure (p. 195):

The Gobi lured me from place to place, disciplining me by its spirit of austerity, strengthening me to endure its hardships, and then, as if in compensation for its rigours, it took me to see some of its hidden treasures. I found its singing sands, the marvel of which I had read but never heard, I saw the great horns of its wild sheep and measured them with astonishment; I visited its caves of the Thousand Buddhas, whose frescoed walls had been preserved for more than a millennium by the desert sand, and I rested in the Lake of the Crescent Moon.

The trio had a great liking and respect for the desert dwellers, though they were not flattering about innkeepers (*The Gobi Desert*, p. 119–20:

The intense isolation of the inhabitant of a small oasis, and the extraordinarily low standard of life imposed upon him, produce a strange mentality. His normal condition is torpor. He sits or lies on his mud bed and thinks of nothing. Only when a traveller arrives does he experience the discomfort of rousing himself, but then, though it may be cold or windy, he must leave the pleasant stuffiness of his bed-living-room, throw of the greasy coverlet which he has drawn over his crossed legs, come into the open and give the service which is demanded of him as innkeeper.

They also had views on Bactrian camels (p. 162–3):

The strength of the camel varies according to its size and age, but the driver has an unfailing test by which he knows if each beast's burden is suitable to its capacity. When it kneels to be laden it always grumbles, growls and shows resentment, but of this the driver takes no notice. He goes on loading up until the moment when the beast suddenly becomes silent; then he knows that it is enough, and nothing more is added.

It is a slow, heavy beast, but with muscles like steel and amazing powers of endurance which carry it through extremes of heat, cold, hunger and thirst such as no other beast of burden could stand. Its weak point is *morale*, and it is here that so much depends on its human master. Discouragement is fatal, and it cannot react against over-pressure. When exhausted it loses heart, sinks by the wayside and dies. It is not a clever animal.

Figure 70. *The trio: Eva French, Francesca French, Mildred Cable, 1930s (Cable and French 1942).*

The women were greatly intrigued by the great Turfan Depression, one of the lowest places on Earth, which contained an oasis whose fertility and luxuriance contrasted with the sterility and desiccation of the desert in which it lay. They drew attention to its *karez* irrigation systems, its handsome mosques, its dried fruit market ('one of the most varied and certainly the cheapest in the world'), the cotton sellers, herbalists, silk and leather merchants, storytellers and letter writers, musicians and vineyards. They were also thrilled by the Caves of the Thousand Buddhas of Dunhuang. (p.48):

> We looked up at the great façade, pierced with innumerable openings, each one of which was the entrance to a temple or shrine. These openings lay in irregular lines, rising to three or four tiers; the doorways of the lower caves were generally blocked by sand-drift, but we could look straight into the upper shrines and see frescoed walls and carved figures. The warm-tinted sand underfoot, the grey face of the cliff and the gay tints of the old frescoes were in joyous harmony with the deep tone of the blue sky and the tender green of young poplar trees.

In 1936, along with other 'foreign devils', they were ordered out of China and the trio retired to Dorset. In 1925 the women adopted a deaf and dumb Tibetan Mongol beggar girl, Ailian Gai (Eileen Guy), who was nicknamed Topsy and died in London in 1998. Mildred Cable died in 1952, while the French sisters died within a month of each other in 1960.

BIBLIOGRAPHIC REFERENCES AND FURTHER READING

Benson, L.K. 2008. *Across China's Gobi*. Norwalk, CT: EastBridge.
Cable, M. and French, E. 1942. *The Gobi Desert*. London: Hodder and Stoughton.
Cable, M. 1942. A new era in the Gobi. *Geographical Journal*, 100, 193–205.

ROY CHAPMAN ANDREWS

ROY CHAPMAN ANDREWS (Figures 71a and 71b) was an American explorer of the Gobi Desert, known for his pioneering use of motor transport and for his collections of dinosaur remains. He was born in 1884, in the green and forested state of Wisconsin, where he was also brought up. On graduation from Beloit College (also attended by Huntington), he moved to New York to seek work at the American Museum of Natural History. He started as a janitor and floor scrubber in the taxidermy department, but while working there also earned an MA in mammalogy from Columbia University. In due course he went on collecting trips to Alaska, British Columbia, the East Indies and the Yunnan Province of China. He became a leading authority on whales.

Andrews is best known for his expeditions to the Gobi Desert in Outer Mongolia, made between 1922 and 1930. One feature of the expeditions was that they were orchestrated,

Figure 71a. *Roy Chapman Andrews (RGS: 1928, photograph: AP/American Museum of Natural History).*

multi-disciplinary affairs in which an increasing range of scientists were brought together to tackle specific problems in the field. Another was that the expeditions were made possible by successfully raising large sums of money, which in turn was facilitated by courting publicity and approaching financiers such as John D. Rockefeller, Jr, Cleveland Dodge and J.P. Morgan, Jr. A third characteristic was that these large complex expeditions required a new style of efficient management, while a fourth was that Andrews made use of motor vehicles – Dodge cars and Fulton trucks. Finally, Andrews's camps were relatively comfortable. He did not believe that an army can fight if not well fed and argued that hardships should be avoided for they lessen effectiveness. In other words, he modernised the approach to field expeditions. His expedition was very different from that of Younghusband three or four decades earlier, who had travelled more or less alone, made no major collections and did not even carry a camera. Younghusband somewhat ruefully acknowledged this when he generously congratulated Andrews on his achievements at a meeting at the Royal Geographical Society.

Among the team that Andrews assembled were the palaeontologist Walter Granger, the geologists Charles Berkey and George Olson, and the archaeologists Nels Nelson and Pierre Teilhard de Chardin. In keeping with the age he also had a cinematographer, James B. Shackelford. By 1925 the expedition involved 40 people, 7 vehicles, and 125 camels. The American flag flew proudly and ostentatiously from the vehicles as they sped across the desert, and Andrews himself (Figure 72) was a striking figure, with his large hat, field glasses and guns. He even had a machine gun mounted on one of the cars in the hope that it would deter bandits.

The greatest achievement of the expeditions was the discovery in 1923 of remarkable dinosaur bones and eggs in Cretaceous beds in the snake infested 'Flaming Cliffs of Shabarrakh Usu'. These were the first dinosaur eggs ever to have been found. There were also important archaeological discoveries and the expedition also led to

Figure 71b. (opposite) *Roy Chapman Andrews (seated, second from left) (RGS: 1928, photograph: AP/American Museum of Natural History).*

Figure 72. (below) *An armed Roy Chapman Andrews on horseback (Andrews, R.C. 1921. Across Mongolian Plains).*

Figure 73. *A camel and a motor car tyre (Andrews, R.C., Granger, W., Pope, C.H., Nelson, N.C., 1932.* The new conquest of central Asia: a narrative of the explorations of the Central Asiatic expeditions in Mongolia and China, 1921–1930, *plate 22. New York: American Museum of Natural History).*

a major account of the geology and geomorphology of Mongolia by Charles Berkey and Frederick Morris. Andrews described his philosophy of exploration to the Royal Geographical Society in 1926 (*Geographical Journal*, 1927, p. 1):

> I realized that we could obtain satisfactory results only by bringing to bear upon the problem every branch of science which could assist in its solution. A group of highly trained specialists must be taken into the field *together*. Thus the work of each man could assist all the others.
>
> The value of such correlated work was demonstrated continually. As we sat in the mess tent at night discussing the day's work, it was most interesting to see how puzzling situations in geology would be clarified by the palaeontologist; how the topographer brought out important features which gave the key to physiographic difficulties; and how the palaeontologist would be assisted by the palaeobotanist or geologist solving stratigraphic problems.

Andrews believed that this was the first expedition of such magnitude to employ such methods and predicted that it would become the recognised type of scientific exploration in the future. The various projects launched by the RGS and other bodies in the decades after the Second World War demonstrated that his prediction was correct.

He also championed the value of motor vehicles (p. 2):

The success of the motor transport is shown by the fact that in the first two seasons with the same fleet we travelled 10,000 miles in a region where there were no roads, and that at the end the cars were sold as they stood, with no repairs, for more than they cost in America when new. A camel caravan averages 10 miles a day, but in the motors we could do 100 miles daily. Thus the expedition had the advantage of speed over the previous explorers who had crossed the desert with camels only and we were able to do virtually ten years of work in a single season.

'A camel caravan averages 10 miles a day, but in the motors we could do 100 miles daily.'

He still had to use camels however (Figure 73). One hundred and twenty-five of them were employed in a supporting caravan that acted as a movable base; carrying supplies of petrol and food for five months, it was sent many weeks in advance of the motor party.

In 1934 Andrews became director of the American Museum of Natural History. He retired from the museum in 1942 and died in California in 1960.

BIBLIOGRAPHIC REFERENCES AND FURTHER READING

Andrews, R.C. 1927. Explorations in Mongolia: a review of the Central Asiatic Expeditions of the American Museum of Natural History. *Geographical Journal*, 69, 1–19.

Ballard, J.S. 2000. Andrews, Roy Chapman. *American National Biography online.*

Kroll, G. 2000. Roy Chapman Andrews and the business of exploring: cetology and conservation in progressive America. *Endeavour*, 24, 79–84.

CHAPTER 5
ETHIOPIA AND ERITREA

T HE DANAKIL DESERT (an area with probably the world's highest mean annual temperature) occupies the northern end of the East African Rift Valley at its junction with the Red Sea Rift. It has active volcanoes and tectonism and includes two areas that extend below sea level. One lies to the west of Djibouti and contains a sump, Lake Assal Hayk, whose surface is around 150 m below sea level and is the lowest point in Africa. It is also reputed to be the saltiest body of water in the world. The other area, the Dallol salt flats, lie in Tigray and Eritrea and extend to 116 m below sea level. The Awash River flows into the Danakil; its course was traversed in the 1930s by Wilfrid Thesiger. The reputation of the indigenous people of the area struck fear into the hearts of potential explorers, and Werner Munzinger regarded the Afars as the most barbarous people in Africa. They killed the Italian explorer, Giuseppe M. Giulietti and his colleagues in 1881.

Between the travels of Munzinger and Ludovico Nesbitt, two pioneer motorists made the journey from Djibouti to Addis Ababa via this region. They were Bede Bentley, who later claimed to have invented the tank, and Arnold Holtz. The two men, one Brtish and one German, raced each other in motor cars across the southern part of the Danakil in 1907–8. The idea was to be the first to present a car to Emperor Menilek II of Abyssinia. Bentley, who got there first, drove a Siddeley and Arnold Holtz a Nacke. Bentley's brand-new Siddeley was picked out in light and dark green stripes. He was accompanied by a taciturn chauffeur called Reginald Wells, a Somali known as George and a brindled bulldog called Bully. They had a very hard crossing of the southern Danakil, were attacked several times by armed Issas and Afars, and were wracked by hunger and dehydration – at one point drinking rusty water from the Siddeley's radiator and licking the grease from its gearbox. But they made it.

WERNER MUNZINGER

Figure 74. *Portrait of Werner Munzinger (RGS).*

WERNER MUNZINGER (Figure 74) was born in Switzerland in 1832. He had a varied career as linguist, mercenary, consul, imperial agent and desert explorer, and was best known for his work in eastern Africa, especially in what is now known as Eritrea. After studying natural science, oriental languages and history at Bern, Munich and the Sorbonne, he went to Cairo, where he perfected his Arabic. He then entered a French mercantile house with dealings in the Red Sea region and was based at the port of Massawa. In 1855 he moved to Keren in north-east Abyssinia, the principal town of the Bogos, where he married a local woman and also took a concubine. This area became the subject of his first major publication *Über die Sitten und das Recht der Bogos* (*The Laws and Customs of the People of Bogos*) in 1859. He explored the region over the next six years, and in 1861 travelled via the Gash and Atbara rivers to Kordofan and other parts of Sudan. In 1865 the Egyptians annexed Massawa, and Munzinger was appointed British consul and also French consul. He assisted British forces during their foray into Abyssinia in 1867. In that year, he also explored the southern parts of Eritrea and traversed parts of the Danakil from the north. In 1870, with Captain S.B. Miles, he explored parts of Yemen and described this brief journey in the

Journal of the Royal Geographical Society of London (1871). After that, appointed governor of Massawa by the Khedive of Egypt, he annexed the disputed Bogos and Hamasen provinces for Egypt and is credited with instigating the separation of Eritrea from the Ethiopian state. He was an advocate of the need for the Egyptians to have control of the lands drained by the White and Blue Niles. Finally, he was selected in to command a small expedition that was intended to take him through the country of the Afars to Ankober on the edge of the Abyssinian plateau, with the intention of opening up communication with Menelik, king of Shoa and later Menilek II of Abyssinia, who had shown some sympathy with the Egyptian expansion in the region. It was on this expedition that Munzinger, his wife and nearly all his followers were killed by a large group of Gallas in the Aussa Sultunate.

Munzinger's most important expedition was conducted in 1867. He had eight men with him, all armed with muskets, and they travelled from Amphilla Bay on the Red Sea coast across 'The Great Salt Desert' of the Danakil to Ala on the edge of the Abyssinian Highlands, before turning north to Annesley Bay.

On the edge of the great salt plain of Danakil, Munzinger encountered the Woyta tribe, who had no tents or houses and lived under the palm trees. He recounted that they seemed to live off palm wine, which ferments very quickly and seemed like 'milk-and-water, very frothy and tasting like cider' (*Journal of the Royal Geographical Society of London*, 1869, p. 200). Although afflicted by the heat and strong sirocco winds, he found the salt plain to be a 'terrific' piece of scenery and remarked, 'The illusion of snow and ice would have been complete but for the heat.' The expedition also encountered salt caravans heading for the interior and gave details of how the salt was cut up, carried and sold. Munzinger believed that the salt plain had formerly been linked to the sea, evidence for which was provided by the presence of shells. He also believed that volcanic uplift was responsible for isolating the lake from the sea. Munzinger described the different ethnic groups that made up the Danakils and wrote of the Afars (p. 217):

> The dress of the Afars is very simple: the men wear a piece of calico forming a mantle, another covering the loins, and a strong belt; rich people wear coloured stuffs and silks. The only luxuries are in the way of weapons, which consist of a curved cutlass, which they fasten on the right side, and enormously long and heavy spear, and a large round shield of buffalo-hide. Many add an English sword: no one has firearms. Even little children of ten or twelve years old carry at least the cutlass, which is never taken off except in bed.

> '... they are considered by their husbands as very inferior beings, and often ill-treated, and even beaten...'

Of their women, he wrote (p. 218):

The women hardly hold the same position as in Mussulman society. They do not hide their faces, talk with whom the like, salute strangers without shyness, and work much both indoors and out; but they are considered by their husbands as very inferior beings, and often ill-treated, and even beaten, although they are good companions and very active.

As to the character of the Afars (p. 220):

From what I have seen, I should say that the intelligence of the Afars was very mediocre, although they are not wanting in animal instincts. The Afars have many bad qualities: they are very avaricious, liars, obstinate, and cruel. ... They also have some fine qualities: one is the respect they pay to old age ... another is the profound disgust they have for stealing; this crime is, therefore unknown here – an extraordinary virtue for such avaricious people ... in the whole of barbarous Africa there is not a race more barbarous than the Afars.

BIBLIOGRAPHIC REFERENCES AND FURTHER READING

Cox, F.J. 1952. Munzinger's observations on the Sudan, 1871. *Sudan Notes and Records*, 33, 189–201.

Halle, C. 1913. *To Menelek in a Motor-Car.* London: Hurst and Blackett.

Munzinger, W. 1859. *Über die Sitten und das Recht der Bogos* (*The Laws and Customs of the People of Bogos*). J. Wurster: Winterthur.

Munzinger, W. 1868–1869. Journey across the Great Salt Desert from Hanfila to the foot of the Abyssinian Alps. *Proceedings of the Royal Geographical Society*, 13, 219–224.

Munzinger, W. 1869. Narrative of a journey through the Afar Country. *Journal of the Royal Geographical Society*, 39, 188–232.

Munzinger, W. and Miles, S.B. 1871. Account of an excursion into the interior of southern Arabia. *Journal of the Royal Geographical Society of London*, 41, 210–245.

Nicholson, T.R. (1965). *A Toy for the Lion.* London: W. Kimber.

Rawlinson, H.C. 1875–1876. Address to the Royal Geographical Society. *Proceedings of the Royal Geographical Society of London*, 20, 377–448.

LUDOVICO MARIANO NESBITT

Figure 75. *Ludovico Marcello Nesbitt (photo Eva Barrett 1930, taken from Nesbitt, L.M. 1930. La dancalia explorata. Florence).*

LUDOVICO (LEWIS) MARIANO NESBITT (Figure 75) was a British explorer and mining engineer, who was the first European to traverse the Danakil Desert of eastern Africa and to survive. Born to Scottish and Italian parents and raised in Italy, he packed a great of travel into his life before dying in 1935, at the age of 44, when a Dutch airliner on which he was flying crashed in the Swiss Alps.

Trained as a mining engineer at the Technical Institute in Rome, the Camborne School of Mines in Cornwall, and the South African Institute of Mining and Metallurgy in the Witwatersrand, he worked first in the South African gold mines, after which he went to Cuba, Venezuela and the Llanos of Venezuela. In 1927 he left Sudan, where he had been prospecting, for Abyssinia. His ambition was to explore Danakil, that stretch of torrid terrain that is situated between the Ethiopian Plateau and the Red Sea.

Before Nesbitt's expedition, there had been three others to the region: those of Werner Munzinger in 1875, Giuseppe Giulietti in 1881, and Gustavo Bianchi in 1884, all of which ended in disaster and no European member of any of them ever returned. Notwithstanding this, Nesbitt, with two Italian companions, Giuseppe Rosina and Tullio Pastori, set off on an 1300-km march (Figure 76) that was to last three and a half months. Pastori was a self-confessed spy for Mussolini, who was already seeking to gain intelligence to aid the subsequent Italian invasion of Abyssinia. Travelling from south to north, much of it down the Awash River valley, Nesbitt's team made compass traverses covering some 52,000 km². They had with them 15 Abyssinians and Eritreans, and a caravan consisting of 25 camels and 4 mules. Three of their 'native

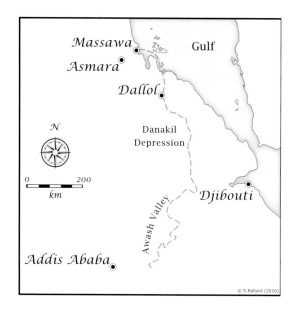

attendants' were killed by the Danakils, whose reputation for ferocity was legendary, while 10 camels and 3 mules died of thirst, starvation and fatigue.

The journey was made in secret, without the permission of the Abyssinian government and without informing the British or Italian legations. They feared official opposition. Setting out from a location on the railway line called Awash Station, they soon encountered the Madima tribe (Hell-hole of Creation, p. 135):

Many of these Madima men had bracelets, worn between the elbow and the shoulder. These ornaments indicated that the wearer had slain a man or men, each bracelet representing one victim. Every grown man also had a hole pierced in the lobe of each ear, a sign that a year had elapsed since he had killed his first victim. The younger ones wore instead a feather stuck in their long woolly hair, to show that though they had nevertheless already been successfully engaged in the honourable pastime. The feather is worn during the twelve months immediately following the first kill. All these men looked savage and bloodthirsty.

Figure 76. *Nesbitt's route 1928 (Map drawn by Sebastian Ballard).*

Nesbitt was not fond of the Danakils (p. 164):

There is no more slothful race of men than the Danakil. They are indeed more like wild animals than men, sleeping on the ground, living almost exclusively on raw meat and milk. No work spoils the elegance of their supple feline bodies. … The lines of their faces are clean-cut, angular, chiselled, and somewhat effeminate.

The expedition encountered camel caravans transporting salt from French Somaliland to the Ethiopian Plateau. They were also beset by ticks, wriggle-worms and pestilential horseflies. One of the worst problems was the extreme heat, with temperatures regularly exceeding 60°C (p. 249):

As soon as the sun rose, the heat became torrid. We were soon in motion on the burning desert, which was here intersected by walls of basalt. These stood out in sharp lines of metallic blackness against the white dazzling plain. Not a sign of life was visible; there was no animate thing besides ourselves in the whole glistening wilderness.

At one water hole they encountered nature at its most cruel (p. 270):

> We were awakened at dawn by the cries of partridges, and the hissing of snakes. ... At sunset, the reptiles creep out of their hiding-places, and prepare to prey upon the birds as they alight to drink. At night, the despairing cries of the victims, and the mad flapping of their wings, are continually heard.

Towards the end of their journey they reached the saline lake of Egogi (Afrera), the first Europeans ever to do so, and a group of five smoking volcanic cones at Hertale (Erta Ale), the greatest reward for the privations they had undergone. They also saw Lake Assale, with its huge salt deposits and one of the lowest spots on Earth. Eventually they reached the Red Sea port of Massawa, and their journey was over. Some years later, another extraordinary explorer, Wilfred Thesiger, was also to brave Danakil. Thesiger (*Geographical Journal*, 1934, p. 527), though critical of some of Nesbett's statements and expressing misgivings about the scientific exactitude of his observations, admired his 'vivid and distinctive prose', but most of all was struck by his 'unshakeable patience, courage, and determination'.

BIBLIOGRAPHIC REFERENCES AND FURTHER READING

Nesbitt, L.M. 1934. *Hell-hole of Creation. The Exploration of Abyssinian Danakil*. New York: Knopf.
Thesiger, W. 1934. Review. *Geographical Journal*, 84, 527–528.

CHAPTER 6
INDIA AND PAKISTAN

The Thar Desert of India and Pakistan (Figure 77) is not an area of profound aridity and very little of the area receives less than 100 mm of mean annual rainfall. However, it shows great diversity, for there is a striking contrast in relief between the arid foothills and valleys of the Karakorams and Ladakh in the north, the enormous alluvial plain and delta of the Indus River, the salty sabkha of the Rann of Kutch in the south, and the ancient mountain stumps of the Aravallis in the east.

The flood-prone Indus, explored by Alexander Burnes, which derives its waters from Asia's high mountains, is a dominant influence on the desert, but in the past the mountains also provided the discharge of a whole series of 'lost rivers' that are a feature of the Punjab and which had lost their discharges either because of climate changes or because their courses had shifted. Other rivers, such as the Luni, flow from the Aravallis, which are notable because they are one of the oldest remaining mountain systems in the world.

The Thar is a relatively moist and low velocity wind environment, but it has large expanses of dunes. Uniquely in the world, many of the dunes are rake-like parabolics, which have formed transverse to the dominant early summer south-westerly monsoon winds. Dunes were, however, much more extensive under past, more arid conditions. The Thar contains some lake basins, created in part by the damming of of drainage lines by dunes, and these provide evidence for former wetter conditions between about 9000 and 4000 years ago.

In the nineteenth century the British sought to extend their control over the Indian Empire. One of their ambitions was to explore the Indus and to assess its suitability as a way into the interior. Another was to seek basic information on the landscapes and people of the Thar Desert itself, something at which James Tod excelled. Many great explorers went through the area en route to Afghanistan and Central Asia, while Sir Richard Burton described the peoples and landscapes of Sind.

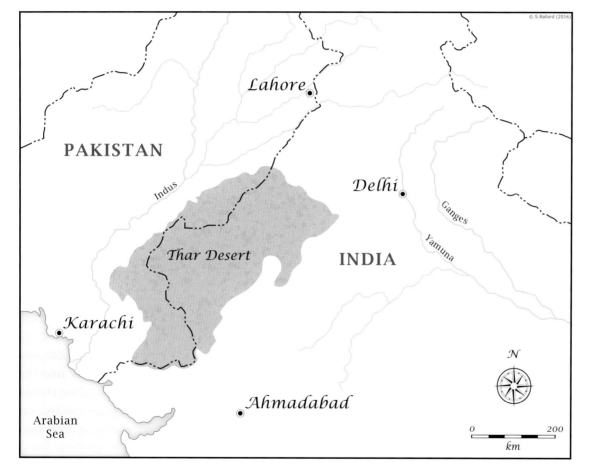

Figure 77. *The Thar Desert*
(*Map drawn by Sebastian Ballard*).

JAMES TOD

Figure 78. *James Tod (Photograph of painting of Lt Col James Tod from frontispiece of 1920 edition of his* Annals and antiquities of Rajasthan, *volume 2 edited by William Crooke, Oxford University Press, 1920).*

JAMES TOD, A BRITISH SOLDIER and political officer for the British East India Company (Figure 78), was, along with Alexander Burnes, one of the greatest early-nineteenth century explorers of the Thar. Born in London in 1782, at the age of 17 he was sent to India as a cadet in the Bengal army. In 1818 he was appointed political agent or 'resident' for various princely states in the western part of Rajasthan, also called Rajputana. Though based in Udaipur, he travelled widely through the region, sometimes by elephant (Figure 79), and took the opportunity to make a detailed study of its history. He amassed a collection of religious and historical manuscripts, along with coins, miniature paintings and commissioned drawings of the many sites he visited. Many of these he donated to the Royal Asiatic Society. His ostensible role, however, was to try and bring peace and stability to the area, to reconstruct the framework of society in the disorganised states, and to strengthen the area as a buffer zone against possible Russian advances.

Although Tod's historical analysis of the Rajput clans has proved to be controversial, partly because it contains inaccuracies and partly because of its romantic view of the Rajputs, there is no doubt that he made a massive contribution to our understanding of the geography and landscape of the Thar – the *maroosthali* (*marusthali*) 'the region of death'. Prior to the mapping work that he undertook, the best existing maps showed cities like Udaipur and Chitor in the wrong place and rivers were shown flowing in the wrong direction. Tod filled in the blanks and made available the first useful and relatively reliable maps of Rajasthan. He did this partly through his own labours, but he also employed able Indian assistants: Sheikh Abul

Birkat and Madarri Lall. The sheikh, who went to Sind, the Indus and Jaisalmer 'was a fearless and enterprising character, and moreover a man with some tincture of learning'. Tod describes Lall as 'a perfect adept in these expeditions of geographical discovery and other knowledge resulting therefrom', but records that though 'ardent, persevering and generally well-informed', he eventually died, suddenly, 'the victim of depressed spirits'. Tod remarked that 'geography has been destructive to all who have pursued it with ardour in the east'.

Some of Tod's writing shows his combination of scientific and historical interests. This is made clear in his description of the beautiful holy town and sacred Pushkar Lake (Figure 80) (*Annals and Antiquities*, volume 1, p. 814):

> We again crossed the Sarasvati, at the entrance of the valley of Poshkur, which comes from Old (*boora*) Poshkur. … The sand drifted from the plains by the currents of air have formed a complete bar at the mouth of the valley, which is about one mile in breadth; occasionally the *teebas*, or sand hills, are of considerable elevation. The summits of the mountains to the left were sparkling with a deep rose-coloured quartz.
>
> Poshkur is the most sacred lake in India; that of Mansurwar in Thibet may alone compete with it in this respect. It is placed in the centre of the valley, which here becomes wider, and affords abundant space for the numerous shrines and cenotaphs with which the hopes and fears of the virtuous and wicked amongst the magnates of India have studded its margin.

He also visited the neighbouring city of Ajmer, which he remarked (p. 819) 'had been too long the haunt of Moguls and Pathans, the Goths and Vandals of Rajasthan, to afford much scope to the antiquary'.

In the heart of the Thar, Tod visited the town of Bikaner, where he was struck by the deterioration that had taken place over the previous three centuries as a result of the attentions of organised bands of robbers and the never-ending demands of a rapacious government. On the other hand, he was sufficiently perspicacious to see that the Thar was far from useless

Figure 79. *Tod travelling by elephant, October 1922 (Edwin Binney 3rd Collection, San Diego Museum of Art, author unknown).*

terrain and that it was possible to grow large crops of pulses, cotton and cereals. He was especially impressed by the gigantic watermelons that were produced in great plenty (*Annals and Antiquities*, volume 2, p. 219):

> The latter is most valuable; for being cut in slices and dried in the sun, it is stored up for future use when vegetables are scarce, or in times of famine, on which they always calculate. … The copious mucilage of the dried melon is extremely nourishing.

Unfortunately, his immediate superior, Major General Sir David Ochterlony, who allegedly kept a harem of 13 concubines drawn from the local women in Delhi, was upset by Tod's rapid rise in authority and his unwillingness to consult him or to follow orders.

'The copious mucilage of the dried melon is extremely nourishing.'

Figure 80. *Pushkar, Rajasthan (author's image).*

People were also concerned that Tod, a great champion of the Rajput princes, might have become corrupt. As his responsibilities and authority had been undermined and his health had deteriorated, Tod decided to leave India, which he did in 1823. He died in Regent's Park, London, in 1835, having suffered an apoplectic stroke.

BIBLIOGRAPHIC REFERENCES AND FURTHER READING

Cotton, H.E.A. (1921). Tod's Rajasthan Annals and Antiquities of Rajasthan, or the Central and Western Rajput States of India. By Lieut.-Col. James Tod, late Political Agent to the Western Rajput States. Edited, with an introduction and notes, by William Crooke. *Bulletin of the School of Oriental and African Studies*, 2, 139–145.

Freitag, J. 2009. *Serving Empire, Serving Nation: James Tod and the Rajputs of Rajasthan*. Leiden and Boston: Brill.

Tillotson, G. (ed.). 2007. *James Tod's Rajasthan. The Historian and His Collections*. Mumbai: Marg Publications.

Tod, J. 1829–1832. *Annals and Antiquities of Rajasthan*. London: Smith Elder.

Tod, J. 1839. *Travels in Western India, Embracing a Visit to the Sacred Mounts of the Jains, and the Most Celebrated Shrines of Hindu Faith Between Rajpootana and the Indus: With an Account of the Ancient City of Nehrwalla*. London: W.H. Allen and Company.

Wheeler, S. 2004. Tod, James (1782–1835). *Oxford Dictionary of National Biography online*.

SIR ALEXANDER BURNES

ORN IN MONTROSE on the rocky shores of Angus in eastern Scotland, in 1805, Alexander Burnes, a kinsman of Robert Burns (who spelled his name differently), was a soldier and political officer, and an early player in the Great Game, as well as an explorer who undertook remarkable investigations in India, Afghanistan and Central Asia, before being slaughtered in Kabul in 1841. An angular, wiry man, 1.75 m tall, he was described as having a broad face, high forehead, deeply inset eyes and a quizzical set to his mouth.

In 1821, at the age of 16, Burnes was offered a cadetship in the Bombay Native Infantry. He soon showed himself to be an outstanding linguist and writer. By the age of 18 he had been promoted to lieutenant and was soon posted to Cutch on the coast of north-west India. In 1829 he was transferred to the prestigious political branch of the colonial government. Burnes was given the task of travelling via Sind and the Indus River (Figure 81) to Lahore, a journey of over 1,600 km, where he was to deliver a gift of five great English dray horses and a state carriage to Maharajah Ranjit Singh. He was also expected to conduct a detailed survey of the river and the countries bordering it. No European had fully explored Sind and navigated the lower Indus since Alexander the Great. In 1832 he crossed into Afghan territory from India and travelled to Bokhara, in present-day Uzbekistan, the Turkmen Desert, the Caspian Sea and Teheran, the Persian capital. His account of that journey, *Travels into Bokhara*, published in three volumes, made him a celebrity. Dubbed 'Bokhara Burnes', when back in London he was granted an audience with King William IV and given the Founder's Medal by the Geographical Society in 1835.

In spite of his relatively brief education, thanks to the admirable Scottish system combined with his own innate ability, Burnes was a considerable scholar, a very fluent writer, a shrewd diplomat and a highly competent observer of the landscape and environment of the deserts through which he passed. He also possessed great charm, which enabled him to strike up strong relationships with some of the rulers and officials that he met. Later in his short life, he also appears to have been active in the pursuit of Afghan women.

Burnes (Figure 82) wrote a series of informative and detailed papers and books about the territories he surveyed. For example, he wrote about the role that the Great Cutch Earthquake of 1819 played in the throwing up of the great Allah Band, a long ridge of high ground, and the effect this had on the course of the Indus. He described how the landscape had evolved since 'this memorable convulsion of nature'. He also provided intelligence on the salty waste of the Rann of Cutch (1834):

Figure 81. *The Indus River in Sind (author's image).*

> The whole tract may be truly said to be a "terra hospitibus ferox". Fresh water is never to be had any where but on its islands, and there it is scarce; it is without herbage on all parts, and vegetable life is only discernible in the shape of a tamarisk bush, which thrives by its suction of the rain water that falls near it. It is, I believe, a space without a counterpart on the globe.

Burnes described its mirages, its salt crusts and its wild asses, and speculated on its formation and whether it was an ancient course of the Indus and had once been an ancient sea.

Burnes gave a detailed report on the Indus, full of valuable military and commercial intelligence, to the RGS (*Journal of the Royal Geographical Society of London*, 1833). He argued (p. 113): 'There are few rivers in the world where steam might be used with better effect than on the Indus. It has no rocks or rapids to obstruct the ascent, and the current does not exceed two and a half miles per hour.' Even without steam he felt it would be possible to travel down from Lahore to the sea in just 15 days. He recognised, however, that there were obstacles to using the Indus as a channel of commerce, for 'the people and princes are ignorant and barbarous'. Burnes outlined the history, characteristics and navigability of the Indus River Delta distributaries and believed that this valuable tract of fertility was greatly underdeveloped, attributing this to an evil government and oppressive taxation system. He also was of the opinion that on account of the

sultry and disagreeable climate it was 'in every respect a trying country to the human constitution' (p. 125). As he ascended the river he described the main settlements, recording their history and assessing the strength of their fortifications. Finally, he sailed up the Ravee (Ravi), 'a foul river, much studded with sand-banks, many of which are dangerous quicksands' (p. 153). He was impressed by the Seiks (Sikhs) (p. 155):

> There are few Asiatics more brave, - they are individually brave, and will attack a tiger or a lion on foot with a sword. Their physical powers, also surpass much those of the natives of Hindoostan. … Their religion is not so strict in its observances of caste and food as that of the Hindoos; and the Seiks are provisioned like a European army, and eat in messes, like English soldiers. They undergo great fatigue, and the length of their marches is incredible.

The Indus did indeed prove navigable for steam vessels, and the first commercial steamship, the *Indus*, commanded by Lieutenant John Wood, set sail in October 1835. Burnes calculated the flow of the Indus at 80,000 ft^3 (2,265 m^3) of water a second, which he believed exceeded by four times the flow of the Ganges in the dry season and nearly equalled the flow of the Mississippi.

Burnes also wrote an equally informative account of the Thar and produced a detailed map. Again his paper (*Journal of the Royal Geographical Society of London*, 1834) is full of military and geographical information. He described the Parkur area, noting that its inhabitants were addicted to opium, and observed the problems of traversing the dunes that develop as the Thar is approached. He remarked of the dunes (p. 100): 'Hill and valley alternate, as if the surface had been troubled like the sea in a tempest, and left stationary in its fury.' He made some observations on their form (p. 114) that were far in advance of anything else that had been written up to that time, noting the positions and angles of their lee and windward sides and relating this to the prevailing wind directions. He also noted that though they appeared stable, their crests were active during the dry, hot months of the pre-monsoon season.

Burnes noted that by contrast Jaysulmeer (Jaisalmer) was very rocky rather than sandy, and barren and unproductive, but he was greatly impressed by the city itself and by its complex fortifications (p. 109):

> The fort, or castle, of Jaysulmeer, which crowns a rocky hill on the south-western angle of the city, has a most commanding and magnificent appearance. … It is a mass of towers, built of hard, squared stone, tapering to the top, and which are studded over every acclivity of the hill almost to the exclusion of the curtain. In all places, the mass of fortification is double, and in some places treble, and even quadruple. It is built on a rock about eighty or a hundred feet higher than the city. There is but one entrance … altogether it is a place of considerable strength.

As to the people of the region, Burnes described (p. 121) the Rajputs as 'proud, haughty, vindictive, tyrannical, dissolute, indolent, and inattentive to business, not from want of capacity, but generally from intoxication'.

On his great expedition to Bokhara, he threw away his European clothes, adopted the flowing robe of the Afghans, wore swords and a cummerbund, had his head shaved, and 'groaning under ponderous turbans' strutted about slipshod. On his way to Kabul, Burnes encountered the simoon or dust storm (*Travels into Bokhara*, vol.1, p. 120):

> The natives of this country describe the simoon as generally fatal. Travellers, who have recovered, say that it attacks them like a cold wind, which makes them senseless. Water poured with great violence into the mouth sometimes recovers the patient; and a fire kindled near him has a good effect. Sugar and the dried plums of Bokhara are also given with advantage. Horses and animals are subject to the simoon as well as man; and the flesh of those who fall victim to it is said to become so soft and putrid, that the limbs separate from each other, and the hair may be pulled out with the least force.

He had views on the Afghans of Kabul (*Travels into Bokhara*, vol.1, p. 144):

Figure 82. (opposite) *Alexander Burnes (RGS: Originally published in Burnes, Alexander. 1842. Cabool: Being a personal narrative of a journey to, and residence in that city, 1836–38. London: John Murray).*

'... the flesh of those who fall victim to it is said to become so soft and putrid, that the limbs separate from each other, and the hair may be pulled out with the least force.'

Figure 83. *Bamian (From Burnes, Alexander. 1834).*

The Afghans are a nation of children; in their quarrels they fight, and become friends without ceremony. … If they themselves are to be believed, their ruling vice is envy, which besets even the nearest and dearest relations. … I was particularly struck with their idleness; they seem to sit listlessly for the whole day, staring at each other; how they live it would be difficult to discover, yet they dress well, and are healthy and happy. I imbibed a very favourable impression of their national character.

Burnes was also struck by Kabul itself, 'a most bustling and populous city', and noted the excellence of its grapes. As a place of defence he remarked that it was 'contemptible' (vol. 2, p. 335). He also visited the rock cut statues, the 'gigantic idols' of Bamian (Figure 83), since demolished by the Taliban, and encountered the Uzbeks (*Travels into Bokhara*, vol. 1, p. 262):

A grave, broad-faced peaceable people with a Tartar expression of countenance. They are fair, and some of them are handsome; but the great bulk of the people, the men at least, are without personal beauty.

In Bokhara he witnessed the slave bazaar (p. 280), and, as in Kabul, was struck by the moving mass of human beings in the great fruit market. Between Bokhara and the Oxus River (Amu Darya) he marvelled at the horseshoe shaped dunes (vol. 2, p. 2). He was struck by the bright clothes of the Turkmens, and particularly by the headdress of the women, which would 'do honour to the galaxy of an English ball-room' (p. 29). He described the Turkmen thus (p. 58):

The Toorkmuns have no mosques; they say their prayers in the tent or in the desert, without ablution and without a carpet. They have few Moollahs or priests, for the church has little honour among them, and they are but poor followers of the prophet. They have no education to assuage their fiercer passions, which renders the men unsusceptible of pity, and the women indifferent to chastity.

The Turkmen horses also attracted his attention (*Travels in Bokhara*, vol. 2, p. 271):

> The Toorkman horse is a large and bony animal, more remarkable for strength and bottom that symmetry and beauty. Its crest is nobly erect, but the length of body detracts from its appearance in the eye of an European; nor is its head so small or its coat so sleek as the brood of Arabia.

From the Oxus, Burnes proceeded via the ancient cities of Merv and Meshid to the Caspian Sea and thence to Tehran and the Persian coast, before returning to India. By 1835 he was back in Cutch and was then sent once again to Kabul. In 1838 he was knighted and promoted to lieutenant colonel, and returned to Kabul for the last time in 1839. He was involved with, though disapproved of, a British invasion of Afghanistan, which proved to be highly unpopular among the Afghans and he was murdered by a mob in 1841, along with his younger brother Charles and Lieutenant William Broadfoot. The trunk of his headless body was left in the street to be chewed over by the dogs of the city. The subsequent disastrous retreat of the British Army was an ignominious chapter in imperial history.

BIBLIOGRAPHIC REFERENCES AND FURTHER READING

Burnes, A. 1833. Substance of a geographical memoir on the Indus. *Journal of the Royal Geographical Society*, 3, 113–156.

Burnes, A. 1834. Papers descriptive of the countries on the North-West Frontier of India: The Thurr, or Desert: Joodpoor and Jaysulmeer. *Journal of the Royal Geographical Society*, 4, 88–129.

Burnes, A. 1834. *Travels into Bokhara 1831–33*. London: John Murray.

Burnes, A. 1834. Memoir on the Eastern Branch of the River Indus, giving an account of the alterations produced on it by an earthquake, also a theory of the formation of the Runn, and some conjectures on the route of Alexander the Great; drawn up in the years 1827–1828. *Transactions of the Royal Asiatic Society of Great Britain and Ireland*, 3, 550–588.

Burnes, A. 1837. On Sind. *Journal of the Royal Geographical Society*, 7, 11–20.

Hopkirk, P. 1990. *The Great Game*. Oxford: Oxford University Press.

Omrani, B., 2006, "Will we make it to Jalalabad?" 19th century travels in Afghanistan. *Asian Affairs*, 37, 161–174.

Prior, K. 2004. Burnes, Sir Alexander (1805–1841). *Oxford Dictionary of National Biography*.

CHAPTER 7
LIBYA AND EGYPT

THE LIBYAN DESERT is bounded to the east by the Nile Valley and grades into the Sahara in the west. In the early nineteenth century there was a spate of exploration upriver in search of antiquities. Most memorable among the explorers were Johann Burckhardt, William Bankes, Giovanni Belzoni and his courageous wife, the scholars Edward Lane and Sir Gardner Wilkinson, and various others who were encouraged by Henry Salt, the British consul general in Cairo. To the west of the Nile, the Libyan Desert, or Western Desert where it extends into Egypt, which is also the eastern part of the great Sahara, is the world's largest tract of aridity. Its dunes, salt flats, gravel plains and occasional mountains contrast with the startling green of the Nile Valley. Michael Mason, who travelled the Libyan Desert in the 1930s, summed up its character in this way (*The Paradise of Fools*, p. 13):

> The Libyan Desert lies immense and idle, scorching and stewing in the dancing mirage of noon; pale and ghostly beneath the cold moon of night; vast as India; sterile and barren as India is teeming with life; the skeleton of a great land dead of drought, crumbling beneath the sand-blast.

At its centre the mean annual rainfall is no more than 1 mm and rain may not fall for years on end. The Libyan Desert is not, however, the driest place on Earth. That record is held by the Atacama Desert in Chile. The Atacama, however, is relatively small and narrow, squeezed between the snow-capped Andes and the cold waters of the Pacific Ocean. The Libyan Desert, by contrast, is a huge stretch of territory that extends hundreds of kilometres from the Mediterranean Sea to Sudan and from the Nile to the mountains of the central Sahara: the Ennedi Plateau, Erdi, the Tibesti range, Tummo mountain and the mountainous region of Fezzan. In shape and extent it resembles the Indian subcontinent (Figure 84).

In terms of scenic diversity, the Libyan Desert is not perhaps the most alluring of the world's great deserts. It does not, for example, have the great backdrop of snow-capped volcanic mountains that makes the Atacama so special. Nor does it have enormous canyons and mountains like some of the deserts of North America. For the most part the Libyan Desert is rather flat and only limited areas reach altitudes greater than a few hundred metres above sea level. Much of it is underlain by relatively gently dipping sedimentary rocks that create low escarpments and gently sloping plateaux. High land tends only to occur in the south-west of the region in the Gilf Kebir, a huge erosional remnant of sandstone attaining heights of more than 1,000 m above sea level, and at the crystalline Jebel Uweinat which rises to over 1,900 m. The Gilf Kebir plateau, discovered only in the 1920s, roughly equals Switzerland in size, its south-eastern section edged with sheer cliffs.

Desert winds have moulded sand into fields of dunes – sand seas or ergs, the main enthusiasm of one of the pioneers of desert exploration, Ralph Bagnold (see p. 232). The greatest of these sand tracts is appropriately called the Great Sand Sea. Beginning just south of Siwa Oasis, it continues almost uninterrupted for 600 km to the Gilf Kebir and covers some 150,000 km^2 of eastern Libya and western Egypt. Most of the dunes are great ridges called whale-backs, upon which long parallel ridges or *seifs* run more or less north to south in response to the trend of the dominant winds. Because of their height, width (often 1 km or more), steepness and instability, they pose a formidable barrier to travel from Egypt to Libya (from east to west), for a large proportion of the dune summits attain heights of more than 100 m above the underlying plains.

The dune sands and other parts of the desert surface can be whipped up into dust storms and sandstorms, known locally as a khamsin or haboob, both of which pose problems for travellers.

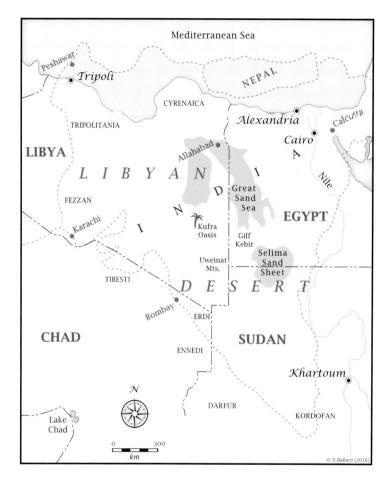

Figure 84. *The Libyan Desert – the size of India*
(map re-drawn by Sebastian Ballard, from Goudie, A. 2008).

Figure 85. *Dakhla: Western Desert of Egypt (author's image).*

The desert also contains some major depressions (Figure 85), often bounded by steep cliffs, which have been excavated in part by millennia of wind erosion. This has also moulded the ground into aerodynamically shaped landforms called yardangs or mud lions, named thus because of their supposed resemblance in shape to those beasts in recline. The depressions – Fayum, Qattara, Farafra, Bahariya, Dakhla, Kurkur, Kharga and Siwa – are places where underground groundwater reservoirs approach the surface and allow oases of date palms to occur. These have long been points from which explorers set off, and the only places where people can settle for any extended period. They form splashes of greenery, some with fields of alfalfa and date groves, many with swaying doum palms, and some with blue lakes and gushing springs. Some of the depressions are excavated below sea level, most notably Qattara, the base of which lies 133 m lower than the surface of the Mediterranean, though this was not known until the 1920s.

Even as late as the 1920s and 1930s, large tracts of the desert had only recently come under colonial control, and were still largely terra incognita, with boundaries that were imperfectly delimited. This was especially true in the vicinity of Uweinat, a vital source of water inconveniently located at the borders of Egypt, Sudan and Libya. Uweinat was far from the centres of colonial power: 1,750 km as the crow flies from Tripoli, 1,350 km from Cairo, 1,250 km from Fort Lamy and almost 1,000 km from Khartoum. Notwithstanding the barren nature of the terrain and the paucity of human population, the colonial powers were nervous about their distant boundaries and suspicious of the strategic ambitions of each other. The gathering of intelligence was a major priority and the motor car provided the means by which this might be acquired by figures like Ralph Bagnold and 'Teddy' Almásy (see p. 228).

Prior to the motor car there had nonetheless been a number of important explorations of the Western Desert by camel. Particularly notable was Gerhard Rohlfs (1831–1896), 'who mounted an expedition from Dakhla Oasis in the Western Desert to Kufra in south-eastern Libya. He could not reach his objective and was forced to head towards Siwa though the Great Sand Sea. His grim account of this journey and of his privations were not such as to encourage future explorers. Nonetheless, subsequently, men like William Joseph Harding King ranged widely in the northern parts of the Libyan Desert, as did Wilfred ('Wiffy') Jennings-Bramly, who entered the walled city of Siwa in 1897.

The Egyptian explorer Ahmed Hassanein (see p. 220), who travelled with the dashing Rosita Forbes, captured the essence of the desert in his beautiful book *The Lost Oases* (1925). He appreciated its perils and its allure. (p. 25):

'The desert smiles and there is no place on earth worth living in but the desert.'

It is as though a man were deeply in love with a very fascinating but cruel woman. She treats him badly, and the world crumples in his hand; at night she smiles on him and the whole world is a paradise. The desert smiles and there is no place on earth worth living in but the desert.

WILLIAM GEORGE BROWNE

WILLIAM GEORGE BROWNE, born in London in 1768 and educated at Oriel College, Oxford, was one of the earliest and most tenacious British explorers of Egypt, Sinai and Sudan. He is, however, largely forgotten.

He was described as thin, rather above middle size, of a dark countenance, with a grave and pensive look. Left a moderate inheritance by his father, and inspired by the travels of James Bruce in pursuit of the source of the Nile, this well-educated man determined to become an African explorer and arrived in Alexandria, Egypt, in 1792. In that same year he visited the Siwa Oasis, the first European known to have done so since antiquity. Early in 1793 Browne went to Sinai and then in May of that year he set off on his greatest journey to Darfur and Kordofan, reaching Darfur by caravan in July. There he had a tough time – he contracted dysentery, was robbed of most of his property and was detained by the sultan for three years. He again travelled to Egypt in 1796, and then visited Syria, finally returning to London in 1798. He described his journeys in 1799, in *Travels in Africa, Egypt and Syria, from the Years 1792 to 1798*.

This book has been rightly praised for its level of information, but it has also been criticised for its abruptness and dryness of style, described as 'solid rather than shining'. In 1820 Reverend Robert Walpole, rector of Christ Church, St Marylebone, remarked, 'it contains some passages offensive to good taste, and a few that are more seriously objectionable.' It is indeed full of material that would not perhaps have been written about in more puritanical Victorian times. Browne does, for example, discuss venereal diseases, aphrodisiacs and circumcision. It is also immensely valuable as an early and detailed account of Darfur, where Browne was forcibly detained by the sultan, robbed of most of his property and suffered from dysentery.

In Egypt he spent some time in Kahira (Cairo) where he noted the women:

In general, the women of Kahira are not tall, but well formed. The upper ranks tolerably fair, in which and in fatness, consist the chief praises of beauty in the Egyptian climate. They marry at fourteen or fifteen, and at twenty are passed their prime. For what reason the natives of hot climates ordinarily prefer women of large persons, I have not been able to discover. Nevertheless, the Coptic women have interesting features, large black eyes, and a genteel form.

Browne vsited many parts of Egypt, including the lakes in the Wadi Natrun depression, Siwa, Fayum and the oases of the Western Desert. He described his descent down the great escarpment above Kharga:

It forms the Western side of the ridge, which constitutes, as it were, the wall of Egypt, and the Eastern boundary of the low desert, in which lie the *Oases*. It consists of a coarse *tufa*, and is of rugged and difficult descent. The road seems in many places to have been opened by art.

Figure 86. *Luxor Temple (author's image).*

We were a full hour in reaching the bottom. The camels not without great pain carrying their loads on the steep declivity, and being often in danger of falling. From the summit of this rock the view lost itself in an extensive valley, consisting chiefly of rocks and sand, but diversified by small bushes of the date tree, and other marks of vegetation, near the spring where we designed to repose. Nothing could exceed the sterility of the mountain we had passed.

He was impressed by Thebes (Luxor) (Figure 86):

The massy and magnificent forms of the ruins that remain of antient Thebes, the capital of Egypt, the city of Jove, the city with a hundred gates, must inspire every intelligent spectator with awe and admiration. Diffused on both sides of the Nile, their extent confirms the classical observations, and Homer's animated description rushes into the memory.

In Darfur Browne gave full descriptions of the countryside, the people and the animals. Of the local camels he wrote:

There are few countries where the animal abounds more than in Dar-Fur. They are remarkable for enduring thirst, but not for bearing great burthens. The camels in this country are particularly subject to the mange, (*Gcraby*) which attacks them chiefly in winter, and in some pastures much more than in others. This malady is very contagious. It is cured by the application of a kind of tar, procured by distillation per deliquium, from the feeds of the water-melon. When the male camel is found unruly, they sometimes deprive him of one or both testicles. It is a cruel operation, as immediately after having incided with an ordinary knife, they sear the wound with an hot iron till the hemorrhage be stopped.

He also had some interesting observations on lions:

The Arabs hunt them, strip off the skin, which they sell, and often eat the flesh, which they conceive generates courage and a warlike disposition. They occasionally take them young, and bring them for sale to the Jelabs, who sometimes carry them as presents to the great men in Egypt. I purchased two lions: the one was only four months old when I bought him. By degrees,

'I purchased two lions: the one was only four months old when I bought him.'

having little else to employ me, I had rendered him so tame, that he had acquired most of the habits of a dog. He satiated himself twice a week with the offal of the butchers, and then commonly slept for several hours successively. When food was given them they both grew ferocious towards each other, and towards any one who approached them. Except at that time, though both were males, I never saw them disagree, nor shew any sign of ferocity towards the human race. Even lambs passed them unmolested. The largest had grown to the height of thirty inches and a half over the shoulders.

The *ennui* of a painful detention, devoid of books and rational society, was softened by the company of these animals.

Browne's most interesting observations, however, were with respect to the peoples and their customs. He noted the consumption of alcohol was prevalent:

Prone to inebriation, but unprovided with materials or ingenuity to prepare any other fermented liquor than *buza*, with this alone their convivial excesses are committed. But though the Sultan hath just published an ordinance (March 1795) forbidding the use of that liquor under pain of death, the plurality, though less publicly than before, still indulge themselves in it. A company often sits from sun-rise to sun-set drinking and conversing, till a single man sometimes carries off near two gallons of that liquor. The buza has however a diuretic and diaphoretic tendency, which precludes any danger from these excesses.

He also made some comments on promiscuity:

This people exceeds in indulgences with women, and pays little regard to restraint or decency. The form of the houses already described secures no great secrecy to what is carried on within them, yet even the concealment which is thus offered, is not always sought. The shade of a tree, or long grass, is the sole temple required for the sacrifices to the primæval deity. In the course of licentious indulgence father and daughter, son and mother are sometimes mingled. The relations of brother and sister are exchanged for closer intercourse. … But however unbridled their appetites in other respects may be, paederasty, so common in Asia and the North of Africa, is in Soudan little known or practised.

'A company often sits from sun-rise to sun-set drinking and conversing, till a single man sometimes carries off near two gallons of that liquor.'

His most startling observations, however, relate to female genital mutilation, which he describes in great detail:

Thirteen or fourteen young females underwent *circumcision* in an house where I was. It was performed by a woman, and some of them complained much of the pain, both at and after it. They were prevented from locomotion, but permitted to eat meat. The parts were washed every twelve hours with warm water, which profuse suppuration rendered necessary. At the end of eight days the greater part were in a condition to walk, and liberated from their confinement. Three or four of them remained under restraint till the thirteenth day.

It often happens that another operation accompanies that of excision, which is not, like the latter, practised in Egypt, viz. producing an artificial impediment to the vagina, with a view to prevent coition. This happens most frequently in the cafe of slaves, whose value would be diminished by impregnation, or even by the necessary result of coition, though unaccompanied by conception. But it is also adopted towards girls who are free; the impulse being too strong to be counteracted by any less firm impediment. This operation, like the former, is performed at all ages from eight to sixteen, but commonly from eleven to twelve; nor are they who undergo it always virgins. In some the parts are more easily formed to cohere than in others. There are cafes in which the barrier becomes so firm, that the embrace cannot be received but by the previous application of a sharp instrument.

On his return from Africa, Browne, who admired many aspects of oriental life, subsequently travelled to Turkey, Armenia and Persia, where he was murdered near Tabriz by bandits in 1813. The location of his remains is not clear.

BIBLIOGRAPHIC REFERENCES AND FURTHER READING

Browne, W.G. 1799. *Travels in Africa, Egypt and Syria, from the Years 1792 to 1798.* London: Adell and Davies.
Garnett, R. 2004. Browne, William George (1768–1813). *Oxford Dictionary of National Biography online.*
Walpole, R. 1820. *Travels in Various Countries of the East; being a Continuation of Memoirs relating to European and Asiatic Turkey, &c.* London: Longman, Hurst, Rees, Orme, and Brown.

FRIEDRICH KONRAD HORNEMANN

FRIEDRICH HORNEMANN was born in Lower Saxony in Germany in 1772. In 1796 he offered his services to the African Association in London as an explorer. The association was seeking to resolve the mystery of the source of the Niger River, the direction of which had been a mystery since ancient times. One tactic was to approach from the west (as Scottish explorer Mungo Park, who discovered the central part of the river, had done) and the other was to approach it from the north by crossing the Sahara. This was the route chosen for Hornemann. The association sent him to the University of Göttingen to study Arabic, and in September 1797 he arrived in Cairo, where he continued his studies. A year later he joined a caravan returning to North Africa from Mecca, and was accompanied by Joseph Frendenburgh, a German convert to Islam. Their destination was Fezzan in southern Libya. They reached the town of Murzuk in November 1798, after two and a half months of travelling. Hornemann's companion died there from fever.

After setting out from Cairo (Figure 87) dressed as a Levantine trader, Hornemann was intrigued to discover the fossilised wood (Figure 88) for which Egypt's Western Desert is famous (*Travels from Cairo to Mourzouk*, 1802, p. 8):

> In this vast tract of sands, petrified wood is found, of various forms and size: sometimes are seen whole trunks of trees, of twelve feet circumference or more; sometimes only branches and twigs, scarcely

Figure 87. *Hornemann's route to Murzuk (Map drawn by Sebastian Ballard).*

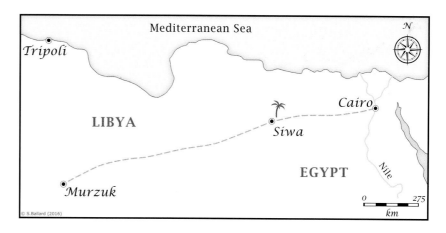

of a quarter of an inch diameter; and sometimes merely pieces of bark of various kinds, and in particular of the oak, are to be found. Many of the great stems yet retain their side branches, and in many the natural timber has undergone so little change, that the circular ranges of the wood are discernible, and especially in those trunks which apparently were of oak.

He then reached Siwa Oasis (p. 14):

Siwah is built upon, and round, a mass of rock; in which, according to tradition, the ancient people had only caves for their habitation. Indeed the style of building is such, that the actual houses might be taken for caves; they are raised so close to each other, that many of the streets, even at noon, are dark, and so intricate, that a stranger cannot find his way into or out of the town, small as it is, without a guide. Many of the houses built on the declivity of the rock, and especially those terminating the descent towards the plain, are of more than ordinary height, and their walls particularly thick and strong, so as to form a circumvallation of defence to the town within. The people of our caravan compared Siwah to a bee-hive, and the comparison is suitable, whether regarding the general appearance of the eminence thus covered with buildings, the swarm of its people crowded together, or the confused noise, or hum and buz from its narrow passages and streets, and which reach the ear to a considerable distance.

He described the people (p. 18):

The women of Siwah wear wide blue shifts, usually of cotton, which reach to the ankles, and a *melaye* (as above described), which they wrap round their head, from which it falls over the body in manner of a cloak,

They plait their hair into three tresses, one above the other; in; the lowermost tress they insert various ornaments of glass, or false coral, or silver, and twist in long stripes of black leather, hanging down the back, and to the ends of which they fasten little bells. On the crown of their heads, they fix a piece of silk or woollen cloth, which floats behind. As ear-rings they wear two, and some women three, large silver rings, inserted as links of a chain: their necklace is glass imitating coral; those of the higher class wear round their necks a solid ring of silver, somewhat thicker than the collar usually worn by criminals in some parts of Europe; from

Figure 88. *A petrified tree trunk from the Libyan Desert to the west of Cairo (author's image).*

this ring, by a chain of the same metal, hangs pendant a silver plate engraved with flowers and other ornaments, in the Arabian taste. They further decorate their arms and legs, (just above the ankle,) with rings of silver, of copper or of glass.

I can give no favourable account of the character of the people of Siwah, either from general repute, or from my own observation. I found them obtrusive and thievish. Our tents, and especially my own, were constantly surrounded and infested by this people; and our merchants were under the necessity of guarding their bales of goods, with more than ordinary attention, under apprehension not merely of pillage, but of general and hostile attack.

Hornemann was not the first European to visit Siwa. That prize had been claimed six years earlier by William George Browne (see p. 194).

Having reached Fezzan, Hornemann tried a local delicacy (p. 59):

We left the hospitable *Zuila* the ensuing morning, and having passed through a grove of date trees, came to an extensive and open plain over which we marched seven hours, and then arrived at *Hemara*; a small village, thin in people, and wretched in appearance, though the country round is most fertile. Here for the first time I was regaled with the great Fezzan dainty of locusts or grasshoppers, and a drink called *lugibi*. The latter is composed of the juice of date trees, and when fresh is sweet and agreeable enough to the taste, but is apt to produce flatulencies and diarrhoea. At first I did not relish the dried locusts, but when accustomed, grew fond of them: when eaten, the legs and wings are broken off and the inner part is scooped out, and what remains has a flavour similar to that of red herrings, but more delicious.

'At first I did not relish the dried locusts, but when accustomed, grew fond of them...'

In Murzuk he was not impressed by the local inhabitants (p. 70):

The mein, the walk, and every motion *and* gesture of the people of Fezzan, denote a want of energy, either of mind or body. The tyrannic government, the general poverty of the country, and their only food consisting of dates, or a kind of farinaceous pap, with no meat, and rarely with even a little rancid oil or fat, contribute at once to weakness of frame, and dejection of spirit. Even in those parts, where the race may be supposed to be ameliorated by a mixture with the Arabs, there is no energy of character, no industry.

He also commented on the question of alcohol (p. 72):

> The men of Fezzan are much addicted to drunkenness. Their beverage is the fresh juice of the date tree, called *lugibi*, or a drink called busa, which is prepared from the dates, and is very intoxicating. When friends assemble in the evening, the ordinary amusement is mere drinking; but sometimes a singing girl, or *kadanka*, is sent for: *kadanka* is a Soudan word, and answers to the term at Cairo.

Hornemann remained in Murzuk until June 1799, before going back to Tripoli, whence he dispatched his journals to London. He then returned to Murzuk with the intention of going south to Hausaland, a group of states in present-day northern Nigeria. After that he died, probably in February 1801, but precisely where and how is not known, although it may well have been on the banks of the Niger. The African Association published his journals as *Travels from Cairo to Mourzouk* (1802). Hornemann was the first European in modern times to have crossed the Sahara from north to south, and the first ever to do so from east to west.

BIBLIOGRAPHIC REFERENCES AND FURTHER READING

Hibbert, C. 1982. *Africa Explored. Europeans in the Dark Continent, 1769–1889*. London: Hamish Hamilton.
Hornemann, F. 1802. *Travels from Cairo to Mourzouk*. London: African Association.
Wellard, J. 1964. *The Great Sahara*. London: Hutchinson.

WILLIAM JOHN BANKES

I N THE COUNTY OF DORSET, in southern England, there is a verdant rural landscape dotted with small villages and large country houses. In one of these villages, Kingston Lacy, is just such an imposing house. One thing that makes this house different from others in the area is that in its exquisite gardens there is a huge granite obelisk which comes from Philae, a temple complex near Aswan in the desert of Nubia, in southern Egypt. The obelisk is there because of the labours of a member of one of the great Dorset families, William John Bankes (Figure 89). The family was noted for patience and solidity – William John did not share these characteristics.

He was born in 1786, educated at Westminster School and attended Trinity College, Cambridge, where he struck up an enduring friendship with Lord Byron. He was regarded as a handsome, boisterous, volatile, easy going, and magnetic personality with a great gift for conversation. During the Peninsular War he was briefly an aide-de-camp to the Duke of Wellington. It was here was while away during the war, in Spain and Portugal, that he started to purchase works of art to embellish his beloved Kingston Lacy.

Figure 89. *Bankes (A pencil sketch of Bankes by Maxim Gauci, c. 1820, in Victoria and Albert Collection in Usick, P. 2002. Adventures in Egypt and Nubia, figure 69).*

Figure 90. *Abu Simbel (author's image).*

Later, he became member of parliament, on and off, for a number of constituencies, including Truro, Cambridge, Marlborough and Dorset. Given his considerable wealth, Bankes could decide what, if anything, he wanted to do in life. He decided to travel and in so doing became a very significant Egyptologist.

During the period 1815–19, Bankes ventured to the Near East, where he visited Petra, Sinai, Egypt and Nubia. His most important expeditions were two voyages along the Nile, accompanied by Giovanni Finati, an Italian convert to Islam, who later wrote up their travels. He met many great figures on his journeys, including the architect Charles Barry and the Swiss explorer Johann Burckhardt, who, in 1813, had discovered Abu Simbel. Burckhardt advised Bankes to adopt a disguise and so he grew a beard and donned the turban. Burckhardt also inspired Bankes to explore and record Nubia in a serious fashion. Thus, in 1815, Bankes visited Abu Simbel (Figure 90). He and his colleagues produced 155 drawings of the temple and started to excavate one of the colossal figures that was covered in blown sand down to its feet. Of particular importance, however, is the amount of material that he gathered during his second Nubian expedition, which took him beyond the Second Cataract on the Nile, as far south as Amara.

Bankes, largely forgotten in comparison with other Egyptologists such as Giovanni Belzoni, a great discoverer and collector of antiquities whome Bankes also employed, Henry Salt, or Burkhardt with whom he worked, was important for his collections, drawings and transcriptions. His own deciphering of the name 'Cleopatra' on the Philae obelisk was to be instrumental in the race to decipher Egyptian hieroglyphics. His numerous site plans were meticulous and detailed (unlike many at that time), and are some of the earliest to be made of Nubia and Egypt. He carried out such work himself, but also employed other gifted artists such as Louis Linant de Bellefonds and Henry William Beechey. They give a record of objects and places that have since been lost, vandalized, destroyed or moved.

Although, as the obelisk from Philae at Kingston Lacy (Figure 91) demonstrates, Bankes was not completely averse to collecting Egyptian antiquities, he had a somewhat ambivalent attitude, and preferred to copy inscriptions. He certainly disapproved of damaging intact monuments by deliberately breaking them up and was scandalised by the way in which the Dendera zodiac was hacked out by 'French pilferers' and taken to France.

Bankes's fame would have been greater had he been less reluctant to put pen to paper. His later years were somewhat unfortunate and marred by scandal. In 1833 he was charged with meeting a guardsman, Thomas Flowers, for 'unnatural purposes', in a public convenience in Westminster. He was found not guilty, partly because of the character reference supplied by his friend the Duke of Wellington. However, in 1841 a similar charge was made against him. This time he was found with a guardsman in Green Park, London. He tried to bribe the police constable who had arrested him and also gave a false name. Sodomy carried the death sentence and so, given that the circumstances were damning, he was forced to flee speedily to Venice, where he died in 1855.

Many others were to visit Nubia after Burckhardt and Bankes. Particularly notable was the rather Bohemian amateur archaeologist Amelia Edwards (1831–1892), who, apart from writing about her trip up the Nile in a very charming fashion, was doubly instrumental in helping us to understand and conserve the great but threatened ruins, thanks to her support for British Egyptologist Sir Flinders Petrie and her role as co-founder of the Egypt Exploration Society.

Figure 91. *Kingston Lacy (author's image).*

BIBLIOGRAPHIC REFERENCES AND FURTHER READING

Baigent, E. 2004. Bankes, William John (1786–1855). *Oxford Dictionary of National Biography online.*
Sebba, A. 2004. *The Exiled Collector.* London: John Murray.
Usick, P. 2002. *Adventures in Egypt and Nubia. The Travels of William John Bankes (1786–1855).* London: The British Museum Press.

FRIEDRICH GERHARD ROHLFS

GERHARD ROHLFS explored both the western and eastern portions of the Sahara. Born near Bremen in Germany, in 1831, he travelled to Algeria and in 1855 enlisted in the Foreign Legion as a medic. Rohlfs took part in the French conquest of Algeria's Kabylia region, was decorated for bravery being appointed a Chevalier of the Legion of Honour, mastered Arabic, and became familiar with local customs. He was a scholarly looking man with a carefully waxed moustache and neatly brushed goatee, but on arriving in Morocco in 1862, he presented himself as a Muslim (Figure 92). With German thoroughness, he even had himself circumcised. Disguised as a Mohammedan physician, and calling himself Mustafa, Rohlfs travelled widely in Morocco, traversing the Wadi Draa and reaching the Saharan oases of Tafilet and Tuat (now in Algeria). This is all described in his book *Adventures in Morocco and Journey along the Oases of Draa and Tafilet* (1874), which, besides giving the narrative of his travels, is a remarkably full and informative account of the people, climate, politics, religions and diseases (syphilis appears to have been very prevalent).

In his *Adventures in Morocco* (p. 12) Rohlfs explained how he travelled:

> 'I had no weapons; a small note-book with a lead pencil was hidden in my pocket.'

I had reduced my baggage to the merest necessaries, namely a bundle of linen, which I carried on a stick hanging from my shoulder. My dress consisted of a *djelaba*, a long woollen shirt with a hood, yellow slippers on my bare feet, and a Spanish cap, within which I had stitched my whole stock of money, an English five-pound note; finally a black loose English overcoat served as my burnoose; I had no weapons; a small note-book with a lead pencil was hidden in my pocket.

He described the Berbers and the Arabs (p. 41):

> The physical type is both the same: slender, sinewy form, with good muscular development, brown skins, Caucasian form of countenance, aquiline noses, dark fiery eyes, smooth black hair, prominent cheek-bones, scanty beards.

Rohlfs also made some remarks about the women he encountered (p. 42):

> The Arab women appear to be somewhat shorter in stature than the women of the Berbers; but that is the only difference between them. Both pass prematurely from childhood to youth, have beautiful figures, and regularly-shaped features when they are young, but soon grown old and hideous hags, becoming dreadfully thin, on account of their meagre food, so that their skin hangs about them in folds.

While in the Draa oasis, Rohlfs was nearly murdered (p. 361):

> When I awoke I found the Schich of the oasis, my friendly host, standing over me, with the smoking mouth of his long gun still pointing at my breast. Luckily, he had not, as he intended struck my heart, but had only broken my left arm above the elbow. I was seizing my pistol, when he slashed my hand nearly off with his sabre. From that moment, what with pain and loss of blood, which was streaming from my arm, I became unconscious. … When I regained consciousness next morning, I found myself alone with nine wounds; for, after I had fainted, these ruffians had shot and slashed me, to make sure of me as they thought. They had robbed me of everything but the bloody clothes I had on.

Figure 92. *Rohlfs in Mohammedan attire (RGS).*

Luckily some locals came to his rescue and he survived.

Rohlfs also undertook a further series of journeys in Algeria and Tripolitania, in present-day Libya, and crossed the Sahara from Murzuk, in southern Libya, to Bornu in what is now north eastern Nigeria. In 1869 he travelled from Tripoli to Siwa and Alexandria in northern Egypt, but his greatest explorations took place in 1873–4, when the Khedive Ismail, known as Ismail the Magnificent, commissioned him to travel eastwards across the Libyan Desert. In 1878 he visited the oasis of Kufra, but the locals did not welcome him and he was forced to retreat to Benghazi. He died near Bonn, Germany, in 1896.

Rohlfs's expedition across the Libyan Desert, written up as *Drei Monate in der Libyschen Wüste* (1875), was notable for the impressive team of scientists that he recruited: Professor Ascherson, a botanist from the University of Berlin; Professor Zittel,of the University of Munich, a geologist and palaeontologist; Professor Wilhelm Jordan, a geodesist and astronomer from Karlsruhe, and Philipp Remelé, a photographer from Prussia. The expedition ascended the Nile to Asyut on the western bank, in the north of Upper Egypt, in a steamer provided by the Khedive. From here, with 140 camels, Rohlfs and his colleagues headed west and after 11 days reached the oasis of Farafra, located in the White Desert. They went on to Dakhla before crossing the 100-m high dunes of the Great Sand Sea and then on to Siwa, the oasis of the god Jupiter Ammon. This last phase took 15 days. They had no guide but the compass, sextant and theodolites they carried, and they encountered no source of water. They returned to Cairo via Dakhla, Kharga and the Nile. Such impressive scientific exploration of the Libyan Desert would not occur again until the late 1920s, when explorers such as Ralph Bagnold appeared on the scene in their Ford cars.

Sometimes regarded as the German version of Sir Richard Burton, Rohlf's work was appreciated by the Royal Geographical Society and in 1868 he received its Patron's Medal. His obituary by E.G. Ravenstein in the *Geographical Journal* (1896) summed up his career thus:

Dr Rohlfs, in the course of his extensive travels, made known to us wide regions in Africa, of which, up to his time, we only knew from the reports of earlier Arab explorers or from native information. He never made any astronomical observations, nor seems his knowledge of natural history to have been very

'He never made any astronomical observations, nor seems his knowledge of natural history to have been very profound; but he furnished excellent accounts of the countries he traversed...'

profound; but he furnished excellent accounts of the countries he traversed, and their inhabitants, laid down his routes from compass bearings, and kept a careful record of meteorological observations.

BIBLIOGRAPHIC REFERENCES AND FURTHER READING

Hibbert, C. 1982. *Africa Explored. Europeans in the Dark Continent, 1769–1889*. London: Hamish Hamilton.

Ravenstein, E.G. 1896. Gerhard Rohlfs. *Geographical Journal*, 8, 184–185.

Rohlfs, G. 1864–1865. Account of a journey across the Atlas Mountains and through the Oases Tuat and Tidikelt to Tripoli, by way of Ghadames, in the year 1864. *Proceedings of the Royal Geographical Society of London*, 9, 312–314.

Rohlfs, F.G. 1874. *Adventures in Morocco and Journey along the Oases of Draa and Tafilet*. London: Sampson Low.

Rohlfs, F.G. 1875. *Drei Monate in der Libyschen Wüste*. Cassel: Theodor Fischer.

GUSTAV NACHTIGAL

GUSTAV NACHTIGAL (Figure 93), one of the greatest of the German explorers of the deserts of northern Africa, was born in Saxony in 1834. He trained as a doctor and became a military surgeon. However, the climate of Germany was not good for his weak chest, so in 1862 he went to North Africa. After a short spell in Algeria, he practiced in Tunis as physician to the bey. His health improved greatly, but in 1869 his life was transformed still further when another great German explorer, Gerhard Rohlfs, acting on behalf of King William I of Prussia, charged him with conveying gifts to Shehu Umar, sultan of Bornu, in recognition of the sultan's protection and support for German explorers in the Lake Chad area. The gifts included a velvet chair of state, portraits of King William and his family, heavy guns and ammunition, Bibles in Arabic, a harmonium, a pendulum clock, and a silver tea service.

Nachtigal set out from Tripoli in 1869. He travelled with a compass in one hand and a watch in the other, measuring and counting paces, and thus reckoning the distances traversed. He also carried a thermometer, an aneroid barometer and a hypsometer so that he could make meteorological observations. He reached Murzuk, deep in southern Libya, in five weeks, and there met up with Alexandrine Tinné. Born in the Netherlands in 1835 and also known as Alexine, she was the first European woman to attempt to cross the Sahara. When her wealthy father, a Dutch merchant, died when Alexine was ten years old, she became the richest heiress in the country. She and her mother, Baroness Henriette van Capellen, travelled extensively in Norway, Italy and the Middle East, and between 1862 and 1864 journeyed up the Nile and through the uncharted Bahr al-Ghazal region of South Sudan. Her mother and her aunt, Addy, both perished from fever on this journey. In January 1869, like many other explorers, she left Tripoli with a caravan, intending to reach Lake Chad and thence head east by the regions of Wadai, Darfur and Kordofan to the upper Nile. However, west of Murzuk, on 1 August, Alexine was killed, probably by the Tuareg, who cut off her hand and left her to bleed to death. As there was no merchant caravan due to head south towards Bornu, Nachtigal decided to make a detour to Tibesti, the country of the Tubu. Luckily he left the gifts for Shehu Umar in Murzuk for safekeeping. His journey was tough, with little water available, and he found the Tubu to be unattractive, obstinate, vindictive and acquisitive. They imprisoned him in the town of Bardai for a while, but eventually he was able to escape and return to Murzuk.

Nachtigal gave a graphic account of the Tibesti landscape (*Sahara and Sudan*, 1, p. 235), which filled him:

> With an emotion of awe-struck horror, such as children might feel in a graveyard ay night. On the vertical walls of the ravines there frequently appeared in the depths grey, red, white, violet, brown or yellow limestone under the colossal covering of dark sandstone. Here were rounded hills covered with immense blocks of stone, there gigantic cubes strewn one above the other, forming either larger horizontal stone surfaces, or, if the ground around were broken or crumbling, real colossi of columns and pillars.

'... an emotion of awe-struck horror, such as children might feel in a graveyard ay night.'

He reckoned that the summit of the Tibesti Mountains lay at about 2,400–2,700 m above sea level, and recorded the presence of a crater at the summit.

Eventually Nachtigal was able to continue to Bornu, where he delivered his gifts and subsequently learnt the Bornu language. He then travelled extensively around Lake Chad in the Kanem region, and in Bodélé, the huge Saharan depression to the north of the lake. Chad and Bodélé were the prime focus of a paper he delivered to the Royal Geographical Society (*Journal of the Royal Geographical Society*, 1876). He noted the dense papyrus and reeds that often obscured the view of Lake Chad, its richness in fish and hippopotami, and the nature of the rivers such as the Logon and the Shari that flowed into it. He correctly identified that Chad had no outlet, but he suspected that there might have been one not that long ago and that Chad and Bodélé had at one time been united, containing a vast body of water. Subsequent investigations have proved this to be true.

Nachtigal also travelled to Wadai from Bornu in 1873, becoming the first European to visit the state and live to tell the tale. The people, he remarked (p. 409), 'even surpass the people of Bornu in

Figure 93. (opposite) *Gustav Nachtigal (RGS).*

their hatred of strangers, in their rudeness, and general lack of civilisation'. He then continued to Darfur, previously visited by only two Europeans, and Kordofan, and finally reached Cairo on 22 November 1874. Nachtigal returned to great acclaim in Europe, where he was fêted and lionised by kings, statesmen and scientific societies.

Nachtigal's journey had lasted five and a half years, covered nearly 10,000 km, and had taken him to places where no European had yet been, including the heart of Tibesti. His three-volume account of his travels makes colourful and riveting reading. His account is also highly informative; rather than being a mere travelogue or catalogue of dates and places, it contains a great deal of historical, political, topographical, meteorological, natural history and ethnographical data. In contrast to many of his contemporaries, and in spite of some of his experiences with the people of Tibesti and Wadai, Nachtigal did not seem to believe in the inferiority of Africans but hoped that European colonisation might stop slave hunting and slave keeping. Indeed, much of his success as a traveller was because of his ability to make friends and to establish a rapport with his African hosts. Nachtigal was awarded the RGS Founder's Medal in 1882. German chancellor Otto von Bismarck appointed him special commissioner for West Africa, and in this capacity he was involved with the acquisition of Togoland (Togo and part of present-day Ghana) and Kamerun (German Cameroon) as the first German colonial possessions. However, he died of fever on board a German gunboat, the *Möwe*, off the west coast of Africa, in 1885, aged 51.

BIBLIOGRAPHIC REFERENCES AND FURTHER READING

Anon. 1885. Dr Gustav Nachtigal. *Proceedings of the Royal Geographical Society of London and Monthly Record of Geography*, 7, 466.

Cardona, M. K. (2012). Alexine Tinné: Nineteenth-Century Explorer of Africa. *Terrae Incognitae*, 44(2), 124–138.

De Villers, M. and Hirtle, S. 2003. *Sahara. The Life of the Great Desert*. London: HarperCollins.

Gladstone, P. 1970. *Travels of Alexine. Alexine Tinne, 1835–1869*. London: John Murray.

Hibbert, C. 1982. *Africa Explored. Europeans in the Dark Continent, 1769–1889*. London: Hamish Hamilton.

Nachtigal, G. 1876. Journey to Lake Chad and neighbouring regions. *Journal of the Royal Geographical Society of London*, 46, 396–411.

Nachtigal, G. 1879–1881. *Sahara and Sudan*. 3 volumes. Berlin and Leipzig: F.A. Brockhaus.

JOHN BALL

Figure 94. *The Little Doctor – John Ball (RGS).*

EVEN IN THE 1950s, some desert explorers, notably Wilfred Thesiger, were still resistant to the idea of travelling by car. They preferred the camel. However, by contrast, Dr John Ball (1872–1941) (Figure 94) was one of the first enthusiasts for motor transport, as well as one of the most accomplished British scientific desert explorers of all.

Ball had a long career in the Libyan Desert, having joined the Egyptian Survey Department in 1897, which he served for 43 years. A highly qualified geologist, engineer and surveyor, who had trained at the Royal College of Science and the Royal School of Mines in London, as well as in Freiberg and the University of Zurich, he was described by Ralph Bagnold, to whom he gave great assistance, as 'the father of all modern investigations of the Libyan Desert' (*Libyan Sands*, p. 95). Barely 5 feet tall and almost totally deaf, at the turn of the century he surveyed the depressions of the Western Desert (Kharga, Bahariya and Kurkur). In the First World War, when attempting to combat the Senussi insurgence, he travelled by Model T Ford (Figure 95) with the newly formed Light Car Patrols. Ball prepared numerous maps for the British army's Egyptian Expeditionary Force and helped to develop sun compasses for navigation and condensers for the vehicles' boiling radiators. In 1917, while on patrol, he discovered 'Pottery Hill' (Abu Ballas,

Figure 95. *A Model T Ford Light Car Patrol in the First World War (Russell McGuirk).*

littered with piles of ancient pottery shards), skirted the southern edge of the Great Sand Sea that lies between Egypt and Libya (Figure 96), and reached the broken foothills of the great Gilf Kebir tableland without, however, recognising the true nature of the great sandstone plateau beyond. In a manuscript of 1917 he set out the ground rules for desert motoring, including the need for water condensors. In 1923, in the same year as Ahmed Hassenein's epic camel journey, Ball accompanied Prince Kemal el-Din Hussein on one of the first great motorised expeditions across the Libyan Desert. A new era of desert exploration had begun.

Ball found the motor car to be a boon for surveying in dune country, even though the dunes themselves posed one of the most formidable obstacles to movement. As he explained (*Geographical Journal*, 1927, p. 212):

Dunes are the most difficult of all desert features to map properly by ordinary reconnaissance methods with camel transport. Their smooth outlines provide no points on which intersections can be made, and no survey marks put on them will remain in place for more than a few hours, or at most a few days; they occur mostly in nearly level country, where it is impossible to find a station whence they can be overlooked; the absence of shadows on them renders it impossible to say whether one is looking at a single line of dunes, or at several lines, miles apart, one behind the other in echelon.

Ball found that the only sure way of mapping dunes was to follow their entire length, something that was impracticable with camels owing to the enormous distances which would have to be covered without water. However, using motor cars running at 40 km per hour instead of the camel's 4 km/h, they could soon be mapped and their distribution rapidly and easily ascertained.

Ball was a dedicated surveyor and achieved much in the face of indifference from the bureaucrats in Cairo. As Claude Scudamore Jarvis, his travelling companion with Prince Kemal el-Din, remarked (*Desert and Delta*, p. 86):

> Surveying a waterless desert under any conditions is not an easy task, but what makes the feat a definite accomplishment is the fact that the Egyptian Government themselves did not care whether the wastes were mapped or not. Ball and his small following succeeding in carrying out the work despite the Government indifference and not at its instigation or with its help. This was one of the queer anomalies of service in Egypt – one found oneself working desperately hard to accomplish some particular job of work and derived encouragement and enjoyment from the knowledge that, so far from giving satisfaction to one's employers, one was actually annoying them! Until one has tried it, it is impossible to realize what an inciting and impelling force this is.

Ball was 'game to the last ounce and fit for anything'. Jarvis recounted that it never mattered to Ball if the cars were hopelessly stuck in the sand and extraction seemed impossible, nor did he worry if water and food were running low and death from thirst seemed a possibility. Mundane matters like this were of no concern whatsoever to Ball. However, it was very different if anything happened to the car containing his instruments or if, when being driven, the driver changed direction so suddenly

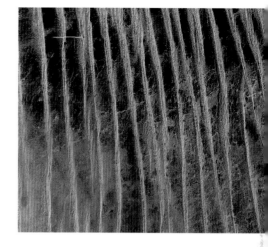

Figure 96. *Satellite image of linear dune chains of the Great Sand Sea. Scale bar 5 km (© Google Earth).*

that Ball was unable to get his speedometer reading and bearing. Jarvis believed (p. 87) that as a rule, surveyors are filled with the same sort of proselytising zeal that causes missionaries to end up in stew pans. On some occasions Ball's fanaticism caused friction. On the expedition with Prince Kemal el-Din, Jarvis recorded (p. 89) that he drove Ball in his car the whole time. It was fitted with a compass and a reliable speedometer, and as they went along Ball jotted down the various distances covered on every bearing. The trouble was that Ball frequently wanted to stop to take a few compass 'shots' on conspicuous hills, just when it was impossible for Jarvis to do so owing to the presence of soft sand. It was very difficult to reconcile the two ambitions: Jarvis's desire to keep travelling at speed, and Ball's desire to get out at the critical moment and take a shot at some particular hill. As a result, tempers sometimes got frayed and where it had been impossible to reconcile the two schools of thought, Ball and Jarvis frequently drove for hours without speaking. It was remarkable, however, how mellow they both became at the witching hour at 6 pm, when, with cars parked and the camp made, the whisky bottle was passed round after a tiring and nerve-racking day.

Ball received the Royal Geographical Society's Victoria Medal in 1926, retired in 1932, and died at Port Said in 1941. He was buried in the Protestant cemetery in Cairo and his tombstone inscription appropriately reads, 'I will even make a way in the wilderness'. Ball's obituary (Anon 1941) in *The Geographical Journal* paid tribute to his unbounded energy in the field, and remarked: 'A relentless critic of his own work and other people's work, he had an uncanny knack of laying a finger on the weak spot of an argument, method or instrument.' His most cherished maxim was 'never miss an opportunity of making a check'.

BIBLIOGRAPHIC REFERENCES AND FURTHER READING

Anon, 1941. Obituary: Dr John Ball. *Geographical Journal*, 98, 301–303.

Bagnold, R.A. 1935. *Libyan Sands*. London: Hodder and Stoughton.

Ball J., 1917. *Desert reconnaissance by motor-car. Primarily a handbook for patrol-officers in Western Egypt*. Western Frontier Force. 49 pp. MS in Royal Geographical Society.

Ball J., 1927. Problems of the Libyan Desert. *Geographical Journal*, 70, 21–38, 105–118, 209–224.

Jarvis C.S. 1938. *Desert and Delta* (p. 86). London: John Murray.

Goudie, A., 2008. *Wheels across the Desert. Exploration of the Libyan Desert by Motorcar 1916–1942*, London: Silphium Press.

ARTHUR EDWARD PEARSE BROME WEIGALL

Between the Nile and the Red Sea lies Egypt's Eastern Desert. It was here that British archaeologist and Egyptologist Arthur Weigall (Figure 97) made notable journeys of exploration. Born in 1880, Weigall never knew his father, an army officer who died the same year while on active service in Afghanistan. His mother was a revivalist missionary who worked to change the lives of destitute prostitutes. Weigall attended Wellington College, New College, Oxford and Leipzig University before finding work with Sir Flinders Petrie, a founder of scientific archaeology and a pioneer in meticulous excavation, first at University College London and then at the ancient city of Abydos in Upper Egypt. Subsequently, aged only 25, he was appointed to replace Howard Carter as chief inspector of antiquities for Upper Egypt at Luxor. He threw himself with enormous energy into trying to thwart the export of antiquities and to conserve what was left of Egypt's heritage. He was critical of Howard Carter's efforts in this area, but did a great deal to conserve, inter alia, some of the monuments that were threatened by the construction and heightening of the original Aswan Dam.

In 1909 Weigall published his account *Travels in the Upper Egyptian Deserts*, based on a series of expeditions that he conducted. He remarked that until then the Eastern Desert had been little studied. He was captivated by its clear atmosphere, the lack of evil odours, the purity of the wind, its richness of archaeological sites and ancient mines, the scatterings of prehistoric worked stones and the amazing night skies (p. 9):

The nights in the desert are as beautiful as the days, though in winter they are bitterly cold. With the assistance of a warm bed and plenty of blankets, however,

Figure 97. *Arthur Weigall and his wife, Hortense (Weigall, A. 1923.* The Glory of the Pharaohs. *London.*

one may sleep in the open in comfort: and only those who have known this vast bedroom will understand how beautiful night may be. If one turns to the east, one may stare at Mars flashing red somewhere over Arabia, and westwards there is Jupiter blazing above the Sahara. One looks up and up at the expanse of star-strewn blue, and one's mind journeys of itself into the place of dreams before sleep has come to conduct it thither.

Weigall travelled by camel, finding that for an expedition of 15 days' duration he needed about a dozen camels and one or two guides. He remarked (p. 25): 'With a steady steed and a good saddle there are few means of locomotion so enjoyable as camel-riding.' He reckoned that some 50 km a day could be covered with ease. However, even in 1909 he recognised that in the future travel might well be by motor car and that a journey from the Nile to the Red Sea might in due course be accomplished in a morning, with more and more travellers venturing out beyond 'the little garden of the Nile'.

Weigall, glad to get away from professional conflicts in Luxor, was a devotee of the wilderness (p. 150–1):

'The desert is the breathing-space of the world, and therein one truly breathes and lives.'

Here there are no cares, for there are no posts or newspapers; here there is no fretfulness, for one is taking almost continual exercise; here there is no irritation, for man, the arch-irritant, is absent; here there is no debility and fag, for one is drinking in renewed strength from the strong conditions around. … The desert is the breathing-space of the world, and therein one truly breathes and lives.

He delighted in the view of the blue waters of the Red Sea (p. 71):

There is always something which penetrates to the heart in one's first view of the sea after an interval of months; and now, the eyes having accustomed themselves to the barren desert, the old wonder came upon one with new weapons and attacked the sense with new vigour.

Weigall noted that hyenas were quite common in the desert and that they had been eaten by the ancient Egyptians. He reported that there were still trappers who made their living by snaring the beasts and that there was no part of the animal that did not have a marketable value (p. 132):

The skin has its obvious uses; the skull is sold as a charm and brings luck to any house under the threshold of which it is buried; the fat is roasted and eaten as a great delicacy; and the flesh is also used for eating, and for medical purposes, certain parts being stewed down and swallowed by women who desire to produce a family in spite of Nature's unwillingness.

Weigall remained in Luxor until 1911 and, following a breakdown largely brought about by professional rivalries, left Egypt in 1914. Thence he changed his career almost completely, transferring from the Eastern Desert to the West End of London, where he became a set designer, lyricist, novelist, film critic and journalist, before returning to Egypt in the 1920s to cover the opening of the Tomb of Tutankhamun for *The Daily Mail*. He died in 1934, aged only 53, after a quick and painful illness. Some suggested that he was the victim of the boy king's curse.

'The skin has its obvious uses; the skull is sold as a charm and brings luck to any house under the threshold of which it is buried...'

BIBLIOGRAPHIC REFERENCES AND FURTHER READING

Beuk, G. 2012. Arthur Weigall: a man out of time. *Egyptological* (http://www.egyptological.com/2012/02/arthur-weigall-a-man-out-of-time-part1-7525) and (http://www.egyptological.com/2012/02/arthur-weigall-a-man-out-of-time-part2-8394)

Hankey, J. 2001. *A Passion for Egypt*. London: I.B. Tauris.

Weigall, A., 1909. *Travels in the Upper Egyptian Deserts*. Edinburgh and London: William Blackwood and Sons.

AHMED HASSANEIN

Ahmed Hassanein (Figure 98), a member of the Turkish ruling class in Egypt, captained the Egyptian team at the Olympic Games in Brussels in 1920 (where he competed in the fencing) and, enjoyed the patronage of King Fuad I and his son, Farouk. Hassanein became an influential figure in palace affairs. Born in Cairo in 1889, where his father was a distinguished scholar at the thousand-year-old mosque of al-Azhar, he was educated at Balliol, an Oxford college at the time regarded by itself and by outsiders as an intellectual powerhouse. At Oxford he became a friend of Francis Rodd and they served together during the First World War on the British campaign against the Senussis which had so occupied Claud Williams and John Ball. It was at this time that they conceived the idea of travelling to the so-called secret oasis of Kufra, but in the event Rodd dropped out and was replaced by Rosita Forbes (Figure 99). Ms Forbes, who withstood the hardships of her journeys with great stamina and laudable fortitude, is often accused of writing up the expedition, magnifying her own role and downplaying that of her Egyptian colleague. This strikingly handsome divorcee, with dark hair and eyes, known in London for her huge Ascot hats, high heels and sophisticated make-up, dressed as a Muslim woman and posed as a relative of

Hassanein. She took the name of Khadija and invented a Circassian mother to account for her imperfect Arabic. Forbes is said to have attempted to seduce Hassanein but he resisted her advances. 'Sita', as she was also known, was born in England in 1890. Her journey with Hassanein in 1920–21 was her greatest feat of true exploration, but she later travelled very extensively, partly as the backdrop for a string of novels that she produced. Forbes visited Morocco, Abyssinia, Persia, Saudi Arabia, Yemen, Afghanistan and Central Asia. She died in 1967.

Hassanein next made his great camel trek from Sollum on the Egyptian northwest Mediterranean coast to El Obeid in Sudan in the first half of 1923 (Figure 100). He covered 3,500 km in over 7 months and 23 days. It was the climax of the pre-car desert explorations, and he was awarded the Founder's Medal by the Royal Geographical Society in 1924. The trip established the true location of some major landmarks of the Western Desert, including Kufra, Arkenu and Uweinat. As John Ball, head of the Egyptian government's Desert Survey Department, stated (*Geographical Journal* 64, p. 385):

> I may be permitted to remark that his expedition appears to me to be an almost unique achievement in the annals of geographical exploration. The journey of 3345 kms, from Sollum to El Obeid, most of it through inhospitable deserts sparsely inhabited by fanatical and predatory tribes, is one which, without a strong military escort, could have been undertaken only by a Moslem, and by one of remarkable grit, tact, and perseverance. But Hassenein Bey has not only accomplished this difficult journey and brought back interesting descriptions and photographs of the country through which he passed.

Ball, not an easy man to please when it came to mapping and surveying, was particularly impressed by the surveying skills Hassanein had learnt. Throughout his travels Hassenein made excellent use of the surveying knowledge he had acquired and managed somehow to carry out all his observations single-handed. He also succeeded in maintaining the continuity and accuracy of the measurements and records he took over the previously unmapped 2,000 km of his journey.

Figure 98. (opposite) *Hassanein Bey (RGS: from Hassanein Bey. 1925,* The Lost Oases, *82).*

Figure 99. (below) *Rosita Forbes (RGS: from Forbes, R. 1921.* The Secret of the Sahara, Kufara, *2).*

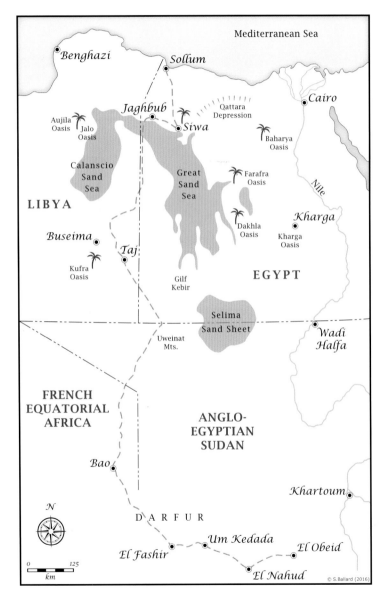

Hassanein found many rock pictures at Uweinat, prompting many later explorers to also visit the area. In an America gripped by the Rudolf Valentino film *The Sheik*, he became a celebrity. In Egypt his explorations were regarded as a patriotic achievement. He was feted at a ceremony in the Cairo Opera House, where King Fuad conferred on him the courtesy title of bey. In 1927 the British made him a Knight Commander of the Victorian Order. They also inadvertently killed him, for in February 1946 he died in a freak motor accident, when a British truck went into a skid and smashed into his car on a rain-swept Cairo bridge.

BIBLIOGRAPHIC REFERENCES AND FURTHER READING

Bald, M. 2010. *From the Sahara to Samarkand. Selected Travel Writings of Rosita Forbes, 1919–1937*. Mount Jackson, VA: Axios Press.

Ball, J. 1924. Note on the cartographical results of Hassanein Bey's journey. *Geographical Journal*, 64, 367–386.

Bey, H., 1925. *The Lost Oases*. London: Thomas Butterworth.

Forbes, R. 1921. *The Secret of the Sahara: Kufara*. London: Cassell.

Goudie, A. 2008. *Wheels across the Desert. Exploration of the Libyan Desert by Motorcar 1916–1942*, London: Silphium Press.

Hassanein Bey, A.M. 1924. Crossing the untraversed Libyan Desert. *National Geographic Magazine* 46(3), 49pp.

Figure 100. *Hassanein Bey's great journey of 1923 (map re-drawn by Sebastian Ballard, from Goudie, A. 2008).*

CLAUD WILLIAMS

CAPTAIN CLAUD WILLIAMS, MC, was born in Auckland, in February 1876. He was a pipe-smoking, violin-playing New Zealand sheep farmer, who enlisted in the British Army in 1915 and was stationed in the Western Desert with the Pembroke Yeomanry by April 1916. Williams is notable for pioneering the use of the Model T Ford (Figure 101) and the sun compass to navigate and negotiate the desert. He died in Gisborne, in New Zealand's North Island, in August 1970, aged 94, giving a foretaste of the longevity of many of the Libyan Desert's explorers – Ardito Desio, the greatest of the Italian explorers of the desert, lived to be 104.

The origins of motoring in the Libyan or Western Desert date back to the First World War with the formation of the Light Car Patrol. The patrols were established by the British to combat incursions by the Senussi, a Sufi brotherhood whose core area was among the Bedouin of Cyrenaica, in what is now eastern Libya. In 1895 the Senussi set up their centre at the secret oasis of Kufra. When the Italians invaded Libya in 1911, the Senussi leader, Ahmad al-Sharif – the Grand Sheikh – raised the call for a jihad and led a force against the invaders. In 1915, because the British were allies of the Italians and as a result of encouragement from the Turks and the Germans, the Senussi went on to attack the British in Egypt. In due course the Senussi had to be dislodged from the Mediterranean Egyptian coastal strip between Sollum and Mersa Matruh, and the interior oases of Dakhla, Farafra, Bahariya and Siwa (Massey, 1918). For more than a year they threatened the Nile Valley with invasion, tying up thousands of British and Empire troops who were badly needed in Palestine and elsewhere. Traditional horse-borne yeomanry were unable to operate effectively in the Western Desert, as they were too far from fodder and water. It was for this reason that the Light Car Patrols (LCPs) were established. The cars they used were 20-horsepower, 4-cylinder Model T Fords, fitted with what were then regarded as

Figure 101. *Claud Williams in A model T Ford of The Light Car Patrols (by kind permission of C.H. Williams's family).*

'oversized' three and a half inch (9cm) tyres. These were, by modern standards, horribly narrow for motoring in sand. Nonetheless, with these simple, cheap, but robust machines, with their high ground clearance and a relatively high power-to-weight ratio, the LCPs showed for the first time what cars could achieve in desert travel. With crews of three and rations for three days, the Fords could go practically anywhere that a camel could. They were sufficiently well armed to form a valuable adjunct to larger armed vehicles, while their mobility gave them a great advantage over enemy foot soldiers and camel-borne troops.

One of the LCPs was commanded by Williams, who was a great devotee of the Model T and noted that its ability to allow gear changes to be made easily and rapidly was a tremendous virtue in sandy country, where any loss of pace changing down could result in getting stuck. Other cars at the time often had less amenable gearboxes. He also remarked that 'It is difficult to put a Ford car out of action' (*Report on the Military Geography*, p. 123), though he did note that after a moist night or a sandstorm they could be tricky to start in the morning. He argued (p. 131): 'With complete equipment and proper preparation that there is hardly any limit to what Ford cars can accomplish in the desert.' Williams also remarked that 'The Ford has as many lives as a cat', and was impressed by the fact that they still ran even when the engine was held on by wire, leaky radiators plugged with chewing gum, wheels spliced with bits of petrol case, and holes plugged with corks. 'You can't', he remarked, 'kill a Ford Car.' (Williams, undated, pp. 84–5)

Williams (undated) gives a graphic account of their first operation from Wadi Natrun to Bahariya, during which they captured a group of Senussi travelling with an assortment of automatic pistols, dynamite and detonators. These men, intent on carrying out assassinations of Egyptian officials, were duly punished and two of them were shot. Williams was rather modest about the great triumph of removing the Senussi from Siwa Oasis, describing the actual battle as an 'opera bouffe' (p. 16), and 'a very safe and entertaining performance to have been mixed up in'. He called it 'the Siwa stunt'.

The Light Car Patrols were disbanded after the end of the Senussi campaign, but Williams produced a book in 1919 – for years classified by the military authorities because of its great potential strategic importance – entitled *Report on the Military Geography of the North-Western Desert of Egypt*. This small, khaki-covered volume gives details of routes, local caravan tracks (*masrabs*) and passes, particularly in the Siwa area. It also includes suggestions about the best oil and petrol containers, advice about the need to carry a canvas cover to put over the car and its passengers during the heat of the day, the recommendation that acetylene lights were better than electric as they did not suddenly dim when engine revs fell, the maximum safe load per car (around 550 kg), and ways of constructing condensers and sun compasses. He also produced an undated typescript, now held in the Royal Geographical Society archives, that describes some of the routes covered, to Bahariya, Siwa, Benghazi and beyond. Many of these routes followed old *masrabs*. Williams described them (in de Cosson, 1935, p. 159):

> They consist of wavy camel tracks a few feet apart, running parallel to one another, and varying in number from five or six to fifty or sixty, according to the importance of the route. …

'With complete equipment and proper preparation that there is hardly any limit to what Ford cars can accomplish in the desert.'

The course of a large masrab is generally marked at frequent intervals with camel bones and with human graves, which testify to the toll which the desert exacts from intruders into its solitudes. These, especially the tiny graves, present a rather pathetic appearance to the traveller by motor-car who traverses in an hour what would be a wearisome day's journey on camel back or on foot.

'We learnt to use compass and speedometer with skill and accuracy, and evolved a simple device for using the sun's shadow as a means of keeping a good direction.'

The journey he made to Benghazi and the Senussi centre of Zuetina was a round trip of just under 1200 miles (2000 km). Williams also undertook an aneroid survey, which gave an inkling of the depth of the great Qattara Depression.

The Light Car Patrols were undoubtedly innovative, as Williams explained (p. 5):

At first we were a bit shy about venturing very far afield. It seemed easy to get lost or to smash cars, or to run short of petrol or water; but we soon gained confidence in our ability to provide for all our needs. As a mere precaution we began to plot our course as we went. We learnt to use compass and speedometer with skill and accuracy, and evolved a simple device for using the sun's shadow as a means of keeping a good direction. Soon we found ourselves able to make a far more accurate dead reckoning than on a ship at sea; we began to chart our information and to build up gradually a fairly reliable map of the country'

The troops with the patrols had to be versatile (p. 77). They had to be 'soldier, chauffeur, mechanic, blood-hound, surveyor, signaller, astronomer and a few hundred other trades and callings'.

Williams appears to have had an ambivalent attitude to the desert. On the one hand he called it 'hateful, cruel, pitiless' and remarked that 'there is literally nothing to recommend this country'. He found the few scattered inhabitants of the more favoured parts to be 'squalid, miserable-looking specimens'. The scenery could be 'distinctly gruesome in its desolation'. He also noted: ' A remarkable feature of the desert is the absence of remarkable features … you may travel many a weary hundred miles for ever and ever amen.' On the other hand, he refers to the intense fascination that the desert exercises, the beauty of sun rise and sun set, the pure and vivid colouring of oasis lakes, and the attractive antics of that rampant rodent, the jerboa or desert rat (Parker, *Desert Rats*, p. 42–46).

BIBLIOGRAPHIC REFERENCES AND FURTHER READING

De Cosson, A. 1935. *Mareotis*. London: Country Life.

Parker J. 2004. *Desert Rats*. London: Headline.

Goudie, A. 2008. *Wheels across the Desert. Exploration of the Libyan Desert by Motorcar 1916–1942.* London: Silphium Press.

Harold, J. 2003. Deserts, cars, maps and names. Encountering traces of Claud H. Williams M.C., author of the one hundred and seventy-one page secret *Report on the Military Geography of the North-Western Desert of Egypt.* Paper presented at the ASTENE Conference, Worcester College, Oxford, July 2003.

Massey, W.T. 1918. *The Desert Campaigns*. London: Constable.

McGuirk, R. 2013. *Light Car Patrols, 1916–1919*. London: Silphium Press and Royal Geographical Society.

Williams, C.H. 1919. *Report on the Military Geography of the North-Western Desert of Egypt.* War Office Handbook.

Williams, C.H. undated. *Light Car Patrols in the Libyan Desert.* 85 pp. manuscript in the Royal Geographical Society.

LÁSZLÓ EDE ALMÁSY

Figure 102. *Almásy in his war-time uniform.*

ÁSZLÓ ALMÁSY (1895–1951) (Figure 102) was one of the most intriguing of the Libyan Desert explorers and the figure upon which the novel by Michael Ondaatje, *The English Patient* (and later film), was based. He has also often been seen as a promiscuous homosexual. Almásy was a great hunter, as well as an explorer, aviator (Figure 103) and motor enthusiast.

Almásy was born of an Austro-Hungarian aristocratic family in Borostyánkö (present-day Bernstein, Austria) in 1895. He developed an interest in motorised transport while at a 'crammer', a rather undistinguished private boarding school in southern England, where he gained his first pilot's license at the age of 17. He served in the Austro–Hungarian forces in the First World War and became a much-decorated pilot. After the war he claimed that he had been made a count by the exiled Karl IV, the last of the Hapsburg kings, but it seems that this may not have been true.

Almásy was always short of money and so tended to travel with the financial help of others. The first motive for his explorations was to test cars. He worked for the Steyr Company and in 1926, to demonstrate the capabilities of their vehicles, he drove a car along the Nile and into Sudan accompanied by a wealthy friend, Prince Antal Esterházy. In 1929 he drove with Prince Ferdinand von Liechtenstein from Wadi Halfa to Selima Oasis in Sudan, along the ancient desert track, the Darb el Arba'in (Forty Days' Road), and in 1930 conducted motor car trials for the Sudan government between Wadi Halfa and Uweinat. He also visited Kufra, where the Italians believed he was a British spy.

In 1932 he joined up with Sir Robert Clayton-East, a naval man and owner of *Rupert*, a second-hand Gypsy Moth biplane. They decided on an expedition to find the legendary but largely illusory lost oasis of Zerzura. From testing cars Almásy had gravitated to real exploration. On this innovative trip they combined the use of Ford Model A cars and *Rupert* to make a reconnaissance of the Gilf Kebir plateau. It was in the wadis that serrated the Gilf that the pair believed they had found Zerzura. It was also in one of these wadis that in 1933 on a further trip Almásy almost died of thirst. After a long walk he just made it back to his car, where he was revived by a bottle of Chianti.

Building on the successes of Ahmed Hassanein (see p. 220), Almásy and his colleagues became adept at finding cave paintings (Figure 104), including those in the Cave of Swimmers in the Wadi Sura. Almásy claimed that his art discoveries surpassed any previously known, anywhere in the world.

Shortly after the expedition exploring the western side of the Gilf Kebir, Sir Robert died suddenly and prematurely, in September 1932, having married only on 29 February of that year. Sir Robert's beautiful young widow, Dorothy, flew out to Egypt in 1933 to continue her late husband's work, but tragedy struck her as well. After her return to England, she was killed in a mysterious flying accident at Brooklands on 15 September 1933.

Other expeditions in 1935 took Almásy along the Darb el Arba'in to Wadi Howar in northern Sudan and across the Great Sand Sea from Ain Dalla to Siwa. On that journey, one of his colleagues was Hansjoachim von der Esch, one of the first Germans to study at Oxford University after the First World War. He wrote an accout of this and other explorations in *Weenat – die Karavane ruft* (1944). Von der Esch was no mean photographer, and he provided many of the plates in Almásy's book on his great journeys *Unbekannte Sahara* (1939). The 1935 journey was effectively the last that Almásy undertook before his exploits in the Second World War, and the British authorities, possibly sensing that he might be involved in espionage activities, seemed unwilling to give him the necessary travel

Figure 103. *László Almásy (left) with Nándor Zichy at Mátyásföld Airport, Budapest 1931.*

Figure 104. *Almasy (rear) and Richard Bermann (front) at Ain Doua, Uweinat, in 1933 (RGS).*

permits. However, he remained in Egypt, and set up a glider and aviation school in Cairo. In 1937 he was the first to fly a glider over the pyramids.

In 1939 Almásy returned to Hungary where he was recruited by the Abwehr, the German military intelligence service, and was assigned to the German Afrika Korps in 1941. In September 1941 Almásy developed a plan to drive 2,700 km via the Gialo Oasis in eastern Libya to the Gilf Kebir and thence to Kharga and Asyut. The purpose of the journey was to deliver German agents from Libya to the Nile Valley. Almásy used captured British vehicles for this endeavour, named 'Operation Salam' and meticulously described in a beautifully illustrated volume by Gross et al. (2013).

On 29 April 1942, Almásy and the agents set off from Tripoli, reaching Asyut on the Nile less than a month later. The two spies, Hans-Willi Eppler and Hans-Gerd Sandstede, of whom Almásy had a rather low opinion, were dropped off and duly made for Cairo, where they established themselves on a houseboat on the Nile, explored the nightspots, and made contact with various disaffected elements, including Anwar Sadat, a future president of Egypt. However, their presence was known to British counter-intelligence, and on the night of 24–25 July they were arrested. They spent the rest of the war as POWs. Almásy returned in his vehicles to Libya, reported back to Rommel and was promoted on the spot to major. He was later awarded the Iron Cross.

Almásy was plainly a complex individual. On the one hand he served Rommel in a most distinguished and daring way. On the other hand there is evidence that in Budapest in the winter of 1944–5 he offered sanctuary, shelter and food to Jews (*With Rommel's Army in Libya*). He also counted Jews among his friends, not least his travel companion Richard Bermann. Much of what drove Almásy was a profound love of the desert – this probably transcended political matters in his mind. As he wrote in his introduction to *The Unknown Sahara* (1934):

When I first set foot on the soil of Africa, I became acquainted with the desert, and this first impression was the deepest. Perhaps because driving at full speed into limitless distances is the most perfect expression of total freedom? … I love the endless plain flickering in the reflection of the mirage, the wild, broken rock peaks, the dune belts resembling frozen waves of the ocean. And I love the simple, tough life in the simple camp, both in the bitterly cold star filled nights and in the scorching sandstorms. In the infinity of the desert body, mind and soul are cleansed. Almost invisibly an unshakable belief in a mighty Power above us brings resignation to our humble human existence, even to the extent of offering our life to the desert without a grudge.

Rather surprisingly, after the war, Almásy was allowed to return to Egypt where in 1950 King Farouk I – possibly to cock a snook at Great Britain – appointed him director of the newly established Desert Institute in Cairo. But very shortly after this Almásy's health deteriorated and he was flown to Salzburg, where he died of dysentery and a severely diseased liver, in 1951 He was buried in Austria, where his epitaph includes the title *Abu Ramla*, father of the sand. His obituary notice in *The Geographical Journal* ended with the judgment that Almásy was 'a Nazi but a sportsman'. He was certainly a very great desert explorer and it is not entirely clear that he was a Nazi.

BIBLIOGRAPHIC REFERENCES AND FURTHER READING

Almásy, L. 1934. *The Unknown Sahara* (p. 6–7). Budapest: Franklin Tarsulat.

Almásy, L. 1939. *Unbekannte Sahara*. Leipzig: Brockhaus.

Almásy, L. 2001. *With Rommel's Army in Libya* (p. xii). Bloomington, Indiana: 1st Books Library.

Bierman, J. 2004. *The Secret Life of Laszlo Almasy*. London: Viking.

Esch, H. von der 1944. *Weenak – die Karavane ruft*. Leipzig: Brockhaus.

Goudie, A. 2008. *Wheels Across the Desert. Exploration of the Libyan Desert by Motorcar 1916–1942*, London: Silphium Press.

Gross, K., Rolke, M. and Zboray, A. 2013. *Operation Salam*. Munich: Belleville Verlag.

Kelly, S. 2002. *The Hunt for Zerzura. The Lost Oasis and the Desert War*. London: John Murray.

Murray, G.W. (1951). Obituary: Ladislas Almásy. *Geographical Journal*, 117(2), 253–254.

RALPH ALGER BAGNOLD

THE CENTRAL FIGURE in the exploration of the highly challenging Libyan Desert was Ralph Bagnold (1896–1990). He was born in Devonport, England. His father, Colonel Arthur Henry Bagnold (1854–1943) (Royal Engineers), participated in the expedition of 1884–85 to rescue General Gordon in Khartoum.

Bagnold was small and wiry, shy by nature, discerning and sociable with his friends. Extremely practical, he also had a knack for creating scientific instruments (Figure 105), and was a keen climber and snooker player. Remarkably for a soldier and explorer, he was made a fellow of the Royal Society. He was 'One of the founders of modern geomorphology despite having no formal academic affiliation, no cadre of students or postdocs under his command, no steady financial support, and no scientific training beyond a degree in engineering. What he did have, and used to great effect, were a deep curiosity about natural phenomena, a powerful physical intellect, a talent for clever experimentation, extensive opportunities to observe geomorphic processes at work in the field, and – perhaps most important of all – the time and freedom to focus his energies on significant scientific challenges.' (Kirchner, 2013)

In 1915 Bagnold enlisted in the British army's Royal Engineers and was sent to northern France. When the First World War ended he studied engineering at Cambridge University before returning to the army in 1921. In 1926 he was posted to Egypt and it was while on leave that he developed a passion for desert exploration by motor car, building upon the experience that Dr John Ball and others had gained in using Model T Fords for desert exploration during the Great War. After a couple of years in Egypt he was sent to India, but in 1931 was posted back to Catterick Garrison in the north of England. However, the army granted him permission to conduct an expedition in the Libyan Desert in 1932. Thereafter he served in the Far East but was taken ill with 'tropical sprue' (a digestive complaint) and was discharged from the army as 'a permanent invalid'.

After the army, Bagnold embarked with gusto on a new career in scientific investigation at Imperial College London with the aim of understanding the movement of sand and the development of dunes. To this end he conducted the first experiments by a geomorphologist with a wind tunnel and succeeded in devising a/published his formula for the movement of sand by wind in 1936.

In the winter of 1873–74, Gerhard Rohlfs had led a German expedition that attempted to cross the Great Sand Sea from Dakhla to Kufra. Since then, however, no expedition capable of making precise observations had penetrated this area of enormous dunes. It was generally thought that the terrain was just too difficult for motor vehicles, but Bagnold aimed to test this supposition. In November 1929, with five colleagues, he motored south-westwards from Cairo into dune country, before turning south-east towards Ain Dalla and thence back to Cairo. The oasis of Ain Dalla was a crucial location for those intending to travel into the Great Sand Sea, for it was a source of water. The expedition was equipped with two Ford trucks and a Model A car, the performance of which was such that by the end of the journey Bagnold was confident of getting across any dune country in these simple two-wheel drive vehicles. The car also had the advantage of having a relatively low petrol consumption while carrying a reasonable payload, and it gave promise of a self-contained range of driving of around 1,900 km. This was very evidently the way forward.

Indeed, the 1929 expedition had been so instructive, rewarding and revealing that Bagnold decided to attempt a still more ambitious journey in October and November 1930. This expedition left Cairo and made once more for Ain Dalla. From there, in four and a half days they travelled

Figure 105. *A bust of Bagnold which appears on the medal in his name, awarded by the European Geosciences Union (author's image).*

'We felt always in the presence of vast purposeful organisms, slowly creeping southwards through the ages...'

nearly 600 km over the dunes of the Great Sand Sea. Bagnold was plainly smitten (*The Times*, 3 January 1931):

We travelled in an unstable world of bare curving sand high above the rock. Strangest of all was the unnatural regularity of the dunes. They are identical in character and details of form, maintain their geometrical straightness throughout their great length, and are parallel to one another to within 2 deg. We felt always in the presence of vast purposeful organisms, slowly creeping southwards through the ages, engulfing all that might have been in their way.

During the second part of the journey they motored south to Uweinat, where water was available, and then across to Selima and Wadi Halfa before taking the Darb el Arba'in road back to Kharga, Asyut and Cairo. In 34 days they had travelled almost 5,000 km. The day's run, even in the most difficult dune country, never fell below around 100 km and the average was 220 km per day.

That such distances could be achieved quickly and safely was because of four devices that enabled cars to penetrate the deepest recesses of the desert: sand tracks for extricating vehicles when bogged down, a sun compass for navigating in featureless desert, a condenser to reduce water loss from boiling radiators, and broader tyres. The original model T Fords has tyres that were only about 3 inches (7.6 cm) wide, but after the introduction of the Model A Ford in 1927 (Figure 106), they used so-called 'airwheels' which were 9 inches (23 cm) wide and fitted specially for the trip. They were excellent in soft going. In addition, the cars were adapted so that weight was minimised and the risk of damage to stores due to vibration and bumping was reduced. Special box bodies were constructed into which everything had to fit tightly and yet could be be offloaded easily. As far as possible all stores – whether food, spares, tools, or petrol – were packed in wooden petrol cases, which were a convenient size and weight for handling. Bagnold, as Ball had before him, used shortwave radios to get the precise time signals that were so necessary for navigation and surveying.

In 1931 Bagnold returned to England from India and with fellow explorer Major Bill Shaw hatched the idea of embarking on an enormous journey to the north-west of Sudan and the unexplored frontier regions bordering the French province of Chad. It was decided to travel as a party of eight in four Model A Fords.

Figure 106. (opposite) *Model A Fords in the Libyan Desert (RGS).*

The first objective of the 1932 expedition was to reach the Uweinat mountains, the meeting point of the Egyptian and Libyan frontiers. This was to be the base where large stores of petrol and food could be dumped for a 1,900 km-journey westwards into the Sarra triangle (a tongue of the then Sudanese territory which juts out westwards towards the Tibesti Mountains and was ceded to Italy in 1934 and for a 2,200-km journey southwards to the Sudanese settlement of El Fasher, and then back to Cairo via Wadi Halfa. While at Uweinat the party scaled the summit and explored the volcanic craters between Uweinat and the Gilf Kebir.

All in all this was both a lengthy, inexpensive and successful trip. As Bagnold was to relate (*Geographical Journal* 82, p. 120):

The whole journey totalled over 6 000 miles, including the two runs from Kissu to Selima and back. Of this distance more that 5 000 miles was over country with no existing tracks. Much of it was very bad going for cars, being covered either with large stones and boulders, or, in the south, with hidden water runnels of hard mud. Apart from the cracking of one of the main engine-supporting brackets, which occurred within sight of the Tibesti Mountains and which was partly responsible for our decision not to go farther west, no serious fault occurred to any of the four cars, which at times were twisted and bumped about unmercifully.

In 1935 the Royal Geographical Society, which had supported the 1929, 1930 and 1932 expeditions, awarded Bagnold its Founder's Medal for all he had accomplished to date. However, more was to come. In 1938 Bagnold decided that he needed to validate the work he had been doing on sand movement in his pioneering wind tunnel experiments against real world conditions. Thus he returned to the Western Desert accompanied by archaeologists and surveyors. The journey took them to Uweinat, the Gilf Kebir and the Selima Sand Sheet in southern Egypt. For much of the time Bagnold's fieldwork involved waiting for a sandstorm to occur so that he could witness and measure sand grains in action, but he also wanted to do some real exploration. He wanted to drive to the top of the Gilf Kebir. Even though it was the size of Switzerland, this sandstone plateau had only been discovered in 1926, but its abrupt and steep cliffs had proved a deterrent in the past. However, Bagnold and his colleague, Ron Peel, managed to find a way up.

'Apart from the cracking of one of the main engine-supporting brackets ... no serious fault occurred to any of the four cars, which at times were twisted and bumped about unmercifully.'

One feature of Bagnold's expeditions was that besides exploring new regions and developing new techniques for desert travel, he also had time for science. Not only did he use the 1938 expedition to validate his own wind tunnel experiments. He also brought with him experts in a range of disciplines: geomorphology, archaeology, anthropology and geology. Expeditions can be self-indulgent stunts in which alpha males display their virility. Not so with Bagnold. His team made remarkable discoveries that included a profusion of archaeological sites and evidence of profound changes in past climatic conditions.

When the Second World War started, Bagnold returned to the army and used his unique experience to establish the Long Range Desert Group, to commit 'piracy on the high desert' and to harry the Axis powers in North Africa.

Bagnold wrote his classic book on dunes, *The Physics of Blown Sand and Desert Dunes*, in 1941, which is still much cited today. He attributed his fascination for dunes directly to the experience of motoring into the interior of an exceptionally dry desert. He died in 1990, aged 94, just after finishing his autobiography *Sand, Wind and War: Memoirs of a Desert Explorer*.

BIBLIOGRAPHIC REFERENCES AND FURTHER READING

Bagnold, R.A. (1933). A Further Journey Through the Libyan Desert. *The Geographical Journal*, 82(2), 103–126.

Bagnold, R.A. 1935. *Libyan Sands* (p. 95). London: Hodder and Stoughton.

Bagnold, R.A. 1941. *Physics of Blown Sand and Desert Dunes*. London: Methuen.

Bagnold, R.A. 1990. *Sand, Wind and War. Memoirs of a Desert Explorer.* Tucson: University of Arizona Press.

Gordon, J.W. 1987. *The Other Desert War. British Special Forces in North Africa, 1940–1943*, New York: Greenwood Press.

Goudie, A. 2008. *Wheels across the Desert. Exploration of the Libyan Desert by Motorcar 1916–1942*, London: Silphium Press.

Kelly, S. 2002. *The Hunt for Zerzura. The Lost Oasis and the Desert War.* London: John Murray.

Kirchner, J.W. 2013. The physics and chemistry of Earth's dynamic surface (Ralph Alger Bagnold Medal Lecture). In *EGU General Assembly Conference Abstracts* (Vol. 15, p. 14258).

Pittaway, J. 2008. *Long Range Desert Group, Rhodesia. The Men Speak.* Avondale, South Africa: Dandy Agencies.

CHAPTER 8
SOUTHERN AFRICA

Figure 107. (above) *The Kalahari and the Namib (Map drawn by Sebastian Ballard).*

Figure 108. (opposite) *The Namib Desert inland from Walvis Bay (author's image).*

SOUTHERN AFRICA has two main deserts, the Namib and the Kalahari (Figure 107). The former extends for 2,000 km along the South Atlantic coastline of southern Africa and occupies portions of South Africa, Namibia and Angola. It is, however, narrow (just 400–120 km wide), being bounded to the east by the Great Escarpment. It is hyper-arid (rainfall at the coast is often only 10–20 mm per annum), but is characterised by frequent wetting fogs. It has a distinctive fauna and flora, one component of which is the remarkable plant *Welwitschia mirabilis,* named after its discoverer, Friedrich Welwitsch.

Southern Africa's landscape demonstrates the importance of its tectonic setting and history. The Great Escarpment, the sloping plains of the Namib Desert itself, and the region's major inselbergs (large island hills), can be explained by the opening of the South Atlantic in the Early Cretaceous (around 120–130 million years ago), and the separation of southern Africa from South America. Igneous extrusive and intrusive activity occurred, leading to the formation of large spreads of lava (the Etendeka lavas) and the development of some inselbergs such as Erongo, Brandberg and Spitzkoppe.

The Namib is also an ancient desert, possibly one of the oldest in the world. The date of the onset of aridity is the subject of debate, but it could extend back to the Early Cretaceous.

The Namib today has a wide diversity of landforms that includes wind-fluted and blasted terrain (yardangs), especially in the southern Namib. There are also four major ergs or sand seas: from north to south, these are the Baia dos Tigres erg in Angola, the Cunene erg, the Skeleton Coast erg and the Namib Sand Sea (Figure 108). The wind has also created pans, wind streaks

and dust storms, produced particularly by high velocity '*berg* winds' blowing out from the interior plateau. They can make travel extremely unpleasant.

In the interior of southern Africa, much of it in Botswana, lies the Kalahari Desert. It provides a fine contrast to the Namib because of its relatively high rainfall and its basinal form. Most of it is not a true desert but an extensively wooded thirstland. Over enormous distances the relief is highly subdued and the landscape monotonous. In the extreme south-west, on the borders of Botswana, Namibia and South Africa, the rainfall (<200 mm per annum) is just sufficient to allow present-day dune activity, but to the north the Kalahari is largely a relict sand desert, or *sandveld*, which extends into Angola, Zambia, Zimbabwe and the Congo, and has a mean annual rainfall that exceeds 800 mm.

The Kalahari owes its gross form and subdued morphology to the fact that following the break-up of Gondwanaland it became an area of downwarping that was bounded on the west by the highlands of Namibia and Angola, and on the east by mountains such as the Drakensberg and Lubombo. It became a basin of sedimentation and this largely accounts for its flatness. The Kalahari Beds that fill this basin are, in parts of the Etosha region of northern Namibia, over 300 m thick.

Apart from its relict dunes, the Kalahari contains large numbers of pans and associated lunettes, together with two large closed depressions, the Etosha Pan and the Makgadikgadi Depression. Finally, in the north of the Kalahari lies the great inland delta of the Okavango River, which brings in flow from the Angolan Highlands to its north, and Lake Ngami to its south, the destination of explorers such as David Livingstone, Francis Galton, Thomas Baines, James Chapman, Charles Andersson and William Leonard Hunt.

FRIEDRICH MARTIN JOSEF WELWITSCH

IN A STRIP OF LAND in the hyper-arid Namib Desert, about 1,200 km long, lying along the south-western coast of Africa between the Saint Nicolau River in Angola and the Kuiseb River in Namibia, there grows a plant that is only found naturally in that location – *Welwitschia mirabilis*. It was discovered in southern Angola in 1859 and named after the discoverer, an Austrian doctor and botanist named Friedrich Welwitsch (Figure 109).

When Welwitsch saw it, 'he could do nothing but kneel down on the burning soil and gaze at it, half in fear lest a touch should prove it a figment of his imagination.' It caused a sensation at Kew, where Joseph Hooker, director of the Royal Botanic Gardens, wrote 'it is out of the question the most wonderful plant ever brought to this country, and the very ugliest.' It was Hooker who decreed that it should be named after its discoverer.

Charles Darwin described the *Welwitschia* (Figure 110) as the platypus of the plant kingdom. The plant is indeed remarkable. First of all, it can live to a great age, and some specimens are thought to be up to 2,000 years old. Secondly, it has only two permanent leaves. These are thick and leathery and can be over 8 m long. They are split into tatters by the desert winds as they get older and take on the appearance of 'a stranded octopus'. It is rare for desert plants to have large leaves. Thirdly, most desert succulents open their stomata at night and close them during the heat of the day in order to reduce water loss. Perversely, *Welwitschia mirabilis* opens its stomata during the day rather than at night. Moreover, although it lives in a fog desert, its leaves do not seem to be adapted to trap this source of moisture. Fourthly, it is the single species of a single family and is literally alone on the tree of life.

Figure 109. *Friedrich Welwitsch* (*http://en.wikipedia.org/wiki/File:Friedrich_Welwitsch.jpg*).

Figure 110. Welwitschia
mirabilis *(author's image)*.

Welwitsch was born in 1806 in Austria. He went to Lisbon in 1839, where he practised botany with considerable success. Between 1853 and 1861, he was employed by the Portuguese government to explore the fauna and flora of the Portuguese colony of Angola with a view to their possible exploitation. A truly meticulous and successful collector, he suffered from ulcerated legs, scurvy, dysentery and fever, and was wounded by local people who attacked the garrison in which he was staying at Lopollo. The financing from the Portuguese government was inadequate, so to raise money Welwitsch dispatched cases of plants, insects and seeds for sale in London. This was not popular with the Portuguese government, who were also disappointed with the seemingly slim commercial outcomes of his work. In 1863 the irascible and irritable Welwitsch left Lisbon with his great collections (around 5,000 species of plants and 3,000 species of insects and animals) and made for London, where he hoped the magnificent facilities of Kew and the British Museum would be at his disposal. For a while he received an allowance from the Portuguese government to sort out his material, but increasingly they were disappointed with the publication of his results and so they withdrew it. Welwitsch never returned to Lisbon, died in London in 1872 and was buried in Kensal Green Cemetery. After his death, his will caused protracted legal disputes between the government of Portugal and the British Museum as to who should have his collections.

As T.D.V. Swinscow wrote of Welwitsch on the centenary of his death (p. 287):

Dedicated from an early age to the study of natural history, he followed its call to the extent of parting from his father, his native land, and his adopted country. His passion for it sustained him through years of loneliness in Africa and destroyed his health with the hardships and diseases of the tropics.

'His passion for it sustained him through years of loneliness in Africa and destroyed his health with the hardships and diseases of the tropics.'

BIBLIOGRAPHIC REFERENCES AND FURTHER READING

Bustard, L. 1990. The ugliest plant in the world. The story of *Welwitschia mirabilis. Curtis's Botanical Magazine*, 7, 85–90.

Swinscow, T.D.V. 1972. Friedrich Welwitsch, 1806–72. A centennial memoir. *Biological Journal of the Linnean Society*, 4, 269–289.

Vicente, F.L. 2003. Travelling objects: The story of two natural history collections in the Nineteenth Century. *Portuguese Studies*, 19, 19–37.

SIR FRANCIS GALTON

Figure 111. *Francis Galton (RGS).*

FRANCIS GALTON (Figure 111) was born in 1822. He was the youngest child of a rich banker – Samuel Tertius Galton – and of Frances Darwin, a daughter of the great Erasmus Darwin, the English physician and natural philosopher. As a result Galton was never short of money and never *had* to work. He attended King Edward's School in Birmingham, and for a while became a medical student in Birmingham General Hospital and at King's College, London. However, he decided that a medical education and career were not for him and went to Trinity College, Cambridge, to read mathematics. Ill health forced him to leave Cambridge with a mere pass degree, whereupon he travelled in the Middle East, and up the Nile to Khartoum. Much of the second half of the 1840s, however, was spent in pursuit of sport. In 1850 Galton seems to have pulled himself together and decided that he would travel to south-western Africa. He joined the Geographical Society of London, as it then was, and started to arrange his one and only great expedition, an expedition which, in 1853, would gain him the society's Founder's Medal. When Galton received this medal, the president, Sir Roderick Impey Murchison, said:

So long as England possesses travellers with the resolution you have displayed, and so long as private gentlemen will devote themselves to accomplish what you have achieved, we shall always be able to boast that this country produces the best geographers of the day.

Galton's prime motive was the love of adventure, followed by the shooting of game, though he also hoped to obtain useful and interesting information about immense regions that were then utterly unknown. He hoped that he might reach Lake Ngami, which had just been discovered by David Livingstone. Galton's route (Figure 112) took him up the Kuiseb Valley inland from Walvis Bay, across the gravel plains of the Namib, into the Swakop Valley, through Damaraland (Figure 113) to Etosha Pan and Ovamboland in present-day northern Namibia. He was accompanied by Charles John Andersson, 'a Swedish gentleman and a naturalist', who was born in Sweden in 1827 and was the illegitimate son of an English bear hunter and his Swedish servant. Galton and Andersson travelled some of the way by ox and ox-cart. The expedition lasted almost exactly two years. When Galton returned to England, Andersson stayed on and managed to reach Lake Ngami in 1853. Andersson also visited the valleys of the Cunene and the Okavango. Rendered a cripple after being shot in the leg by the Namaquas when he was fighting them on behalf of the Damaras, he later developed various disorders and died in pain, aged 40, in 1867. IHe was buried in the region that is now on the border between southern Angola and northern Namibia.

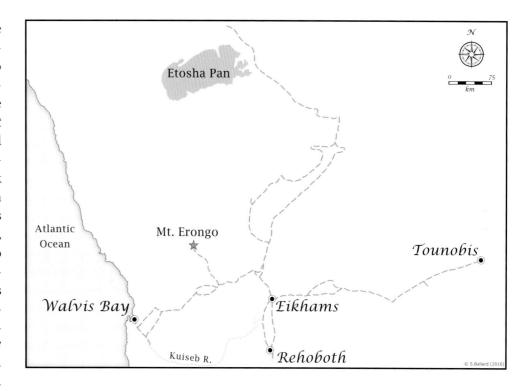

Figure 112. *Galton's route (Map drawn by Sebastian Ballard).*

Galton's descriptions of the indigenous people he encountered on his journey are, even by Victorian standards, ethnocentric and racist. He never showed the genuine sympathy for Africans which marked such contemporaries as David Livingstone and John Hanning Speke. He was exceptionally rude and dismissive of the Damara people (*Journal of the Royal Geographical Society,* 1852,

p. 159). After admitting that the men were very handsome, with fine, manly, open countenances, and often beautifully chiselled features, he went on:

> Morally they are the most worthless, thieving, and murderous of vagabonds, and at the least irritation their usually placid countenance changes into one of the most diabolical expression. Much as I was struck with them at first, I came ultimately to the conclusion that, except their general good humour, there was not a single good point in their character.

He even averred that their personal strength was 'wonderfully small considering their immense muscular development' and that none of them was a match for the average of his own men. In his book *Narrative of an Explorer in Tropical South Africa being an Account of a Visit to Damaraland in 1851*, he expressed distaste at the way these 'dirtiest and most vermin-covered of savages' (p. 60)

Figure 113. *The Etendeka mountains of central Namibia (author's image).*

Figure 114. *Lake Otjikoto, Namibia (author's image).*

clustered around them, suggested that his spaniel was better at counting than they were (p. 82), and noted that when they slept they 'lie huddled up together like pigs' (p. 116).

By contrast he found the Ovampo to be 'orderly, centralised, hard-working, neat, and scrupulously honest', something which Andersson doubted. Galton was also interested in the physical characteristics of the Hottentot women, with their large buttocks and breasts. He encountered a 'Venus among Hottentots' and was 'perfectly aghast at her development'. Using a sextant and a measuring tape he calculated her dimensions at a distance, using trigonometry and log tables. Overall, however, he remarked (p. 75):

> The greater part of the Hottentots about me had that peculiar set of features which is so characteristic of bad characters in England, and so generally among prisoners that it is usually, I believe, known by the name of the "felon face".

On one occasion (p. 55) he had 'the grand idea' of using an old 'Bushwoman' (more correctly, San woman) as bait for a marauding hyena. The woman survived but the hyena did not. It received its quietus from Galton and a colleague.

He returned from Africa with a strong impression of the diversity of the indigenous people and the conviction that they were, to varying degrees, inferior to Europeans. This was an important stimulus to his later work on inheritance and genetics.

Galton did not just make ethnographic observations or merely discuss his encounters with big game, he also provided valuable geographical information on, for example, the occasional floods that came down the Swakop and Kuiseb rivers, and the limestone country near Etosha, with its solutionally serrated rocks, cavities and deep lakes, including Otjikoto (Figure 114).

Even after his days of exploration were over, Galton exerted great influence through his position in the Royal Geographical Society and the publication of his book *The Art of Travel or Shifts and Contrivances Available in Wild Countries* (1872). This provided a vade mecum on how to conduct expeditions, giving details inter alia of equipment, food, medicine, surveying and the 'Management of Savages'. Galton was knighted in 1909 and died in 1911, aged 88, in Haselmere, England.

'Much as I was struck with them at first, I came ultimately to the conclusion that, except their general good humour, there was not a single good point in their character.'

BIBLIOGRAPHIC REFERENCES AND FURTHER READING

Cowan, R.S. 2005. Galton, Sir Francis (1822–1911). *Oxford Dictionary of National Biography online.*

Fancher, R.E. 1982. Galton in Africa. *American Psychologist*, 37, 713–714.

Freshfield, D.W. 1911. Obituary: Sir Francis Galton, F.R.S. etc. *Geographical Journal*, 37, 323–325.

Galton, F. 1852. Recent expedition to the interior of South-Western Africa. *Journal of the Royal Geographical Society*, 22, 140–163.

Galton, F. 1853. *Narrative of an Explorer in Tropical South Africa being an Account of a Visit to Damaraland in 1851.* London: John Murray.

Galton, F. 1872. *The Art of Travel, or, Shifts and Contrivances Available in Wild Countries.* London: John Murray.

Gillham, N.W. 2001. *A Life of Sir Francis Galton.* Oxford: Oxford University Press.

WILLIAM LEONARD HUNT

Figure 115. *Farini (RGS).*

WILLIAM LEONARD HUNT, besides being an acrobat and showman, also made one of the first trans-Kalahari expeditions on foot. He was born in Lockport, New York, in 1838, but his family later moved to Canada. Of a rebellious nature, while living at Bowmanville, Ontario, Hunt sneaked out to see a visiting circus, and immediately decided that he wanted to enter showbusiness. Adopting the stage name of Signor Guillermo Antonio Farini (later 'The Great Farini') (Figure 115), he became a professional high wire performer, and in 1860 made his debut performance over the Niagara Falls (Figure 116). Subsequently, he developed a human cannon ball act and for a while worked with the famous showman P.T. Barnum. One of his co-performers was Samuel Wasgatt, who, as a child acrobat was known as El Niño and billed, when he was adopted by Hunt, as Farini's son. Once he became an adult, Wasgatt adopted the persona Lulu, and performed in female dress. As Shane Peacock remarked of Farini, (p. vii), 'He created some of the most thrilling entertainment the world has ever seen, putting staid Victorians momentarily in touch with dangerous, almost-erotic sensations that sometimes alarmed them.'

One area in which Hunt as Farini used his showman's abilities was in displaying freaks, including Zulus and San Bushmen.

Thus it was that in 1885 Hunt decided to visit the Kalahari Desert, covering large tracts of what are now South Africa and Botswana but which were then the Cape Colony and the Bechuanaland Protectorate. The reasons for the journey included his familiarity with Africans through his displays of them in his shows, the possibility of hunting, the desire to find diamonds, and a concern about his health and fitness. He

travelled with Lulu, who was a gifted photographer, and 'Kert' (Gert Louw), 'an old half-breed hunter'. Using Hunt's stage name, an account of their journey was presented *in absentia* at the Royal Geographical Society the following year (*Proceedings of the Royal Geographical Society*, 1886). They travelled on foot and horseback, using oxen to carry their baggage.

The expedition's route started in the diamond town of Kimberley, passed through the Langeberg range and Griqualand West to Upington on the Orange River, and then headed northwards via the villages of Kuis and Kang to Ghanzi and Lake Ngami. The return journey followed a route further to the west and crossed the Auob and Nossob rivers before reaching the Orange River at the Augrabies Falls.

At the Langeberg, Hunt came across his first San people, who were taller than he expected. He evidently liked them (p. 439):

I admired their calm demeanour, and was astonished at their neither asking questions nor soliciting alms, which contrasted so strongly with the impertinent curiosity and mendacity of the half breeds.

Figure 116. Farini on a tightrope, Niagra Falls, 1860 (Niagra Falls Heritage Foundation Collection).

He supplied them with *dokka* (dagga or cannabis), listened with disapproval to the 'wild and weird' music this generated, and sketched some of their cave drawings. Further on he met some other nomadic people (p. 443):

The young girls were perfectly formed, the little black-eyed children really pretty, but the old and middle-aged women, some of whom judging from appearances, might have seen a hundred years, were the veriest hags.

Hunt was impressed by the amount of vegetation in the area, the huge quantities of game (some of which he shot), and the possibilities that existed for cattle ranching. He noted, however, that Lake

Ngami appeared to be shrinking, not, he thought, for a want of rain, but because the country was gradually rising. He made some substantial collections of plants, insects, birds and geological specimens.

During one of his hunting expeditions, he came across a collection of large rocks and boulders which he thought were the remains of a lost city. He described finding masonry of cyclopean character, walled enclosures, pavements and a broken column. Subsequent researchers believed that these features were natural and the result of the weathering of a dolerite dyke. No lost city ever seems to have existed and Hunt's directions and descriptions are vague.

Towards the end of the expedition, Hunt visited and photographed the great falls cut into granite on the Orange River, which in flood he believed would rival the great Niagara. He spoke of their 'picturesque grandeur' and 'fantastic beauty', and gave the different sections of the falls names, including Lulu Falls and Farini Falls.

As the conclusion to his paper, Hunt spoke up for the indigenous peoples (p. 450):

> I will conclude with the hope that now this great district has become part of the British Empire, these interesting native races will be preserved, and that the English public, in opening up this district for civilisation and trade, will also give lasting protection to the natives.

His book of the journey was successful and editions were published in England, America, France and Germany. Active and inventive to the end, Hunt, impeccably dressed, with bright blue eyes, snow-white hair and a perfectly coiffed beard, died of influenza in 1929 at the age of 91 in Canada, but the veracity of all his accounts is doubted by some and also that he covered all the ground he claimed in the time available.

BIBLIOGRAPHIC REFERENCES AND FURTHER READING

Farini, G.A. 1886. A recent journey in the Kalahari. *Proceedings of the Royal Geographical Society*, 8, 437–453.

Farini, G.A. 1886. *Through the Kalahari Desert. A Narrative of a Journey with Gun, Camera and Notebook to Lake N'Gami and Back* (1886). New York: Scribner and Welford.

Main, M. 1987. *Kalahari. Life's Variety in Dune and Delta*. Johannesburg: Southern Book Publishers.

Peacock, S. 1995. *The Great Farini. The High-wire Life of William Hunt*. Harmondsworth: Penguin Books.

SIR BEDE EDMUND HUGH CLIFFORD

Figure 117. (opposite)
Clifford in the cab (From Makin, W.J. 1929. Across, the Kalahari Desert, 92. London: Arrowsmith).

BEDE CLIFFORD (Figure 117), born on a sheep farm on the South Island of New Zealand in 1890, was educated in Melbourne, Australia, and then made his way by tramp steamer to England. When war broke out in 1914 he enlisted in the Royal Fusiliers, but was gassed and invalided out of the army in 1917. In 1924 he became imperial secretary to the South African High Commission, and the three British protectorates – Swaziland, Basutoland (now Lesotho) and Bechuanaland (now Botswana) were under his jurisdiction. It was in this capacity that he became, in 1928, one of the first white men to traverse the Kalahari Desert and to use motor lorries to do so. He subsequently carried out a small series of surveys of the Great Makarikari (now Makgadikgadi) salt lake.

The Kalahari, for the most part a rather featureless plain, lies in a great basin in the centre of southern Africa. Although it is often called a desert, it is semi-arid rather than arid, and has large areas of savanna woodland. In the Ice Age, however, it was drier than now, so large areas are underlain by ancient sand dunes, and it is these than can make the going tough for wheeled transport. Also, during the long winter dry season, there are few or no sources of water between the Orange and Okavango rivers, so it is often termed a 'thirstland'. In the 1920s the Kalahari was still very little known to Europeans, but Clifford sought to change this situation.

Clifford's great expedition left Mahalapye in eastern Bechuanaland for Ghanzi in the north-west in June 1928. He employed two six-wheeled Morris trucks. The party consisted not only of the Captain the Honourable Bede Clifford, but also Lieutenant Harry Beeching (Bechuanaland Protectorate Police), Bill Grantham (protectorate desert officer), a Morris mechanic, William J. Makin (special correspondent of *The Daily Mail*), two chauffeurs, three local constables, with a local corporal and cook. The trucks carried a heavy load, which included 680 litres of water, for they were travelling in the winter dry season when the Kalahari is very parched. The trucks were also thirsty in terms of petrol consumption so they had to carry 1,455 litres of fuel, allowing for a minimum consumption of 4.5 litres per 6.5 km (4 miles to the gallon), though in the event this proved optimistic. Besides the petrol and water there were spare tyres, bedding, food, tents, tools and caterpillar tracks, which were to be used where the Kalahari sand proved too soft and deep for wheels.

Harry Beeching (Figure 118) was plainly a very important member of the expedition, for he had spent many years patrolling the Kalahari by camel. As W.J. Makin described him in his account of the journey (*Across the Kalahari Desert*, p. 39):

> With blue eyes, fan-wrinkled at the edges through gazing at far horizons, a tousled head of hair and a pipe eternally stuck in his mouth, he was a real desert man. … He was in love with the desert and his dog. Nothing else seemed to matter. … Each year he managed to get over some seven thousand miles of desert travel. He travels with two or three native boys, and has to find his way into areas where the white man is unknown.

The expedition soon found that if they travelled during the heat of the day through the heavy sand that mantles much of the desert, using a low gear, the trucks consumed prodigious amounts of water. So they often travelled at night instead, which they found bitterly cold, to the extent that their water bottles froze. Another

problem they encountered – often as frequently as one an hour – were punctures, caused by thorns and sharp shrubs, which had to be repaired with half-frozen fingers by the light of the headlamps. In spite of such travails, three weeks after they set out, they reached Victoria Falls via Ghanzi, Ngamiland, Maun and the Mababe Depression.

On the journey they met occasional San people, one of whom was described in less than glowing terms (*Geographical Journal*, 1929, p. 349):

He was carrying a number of desert melons in his arms, which in the absence of water no doubt accounted for the giraffe and big game spoor we had recently seen. … He was a dirty-looking specimen, naked but for a grimy skin pulled over his shoulders, and an even grimier skin round his loins. His scalp was shaved except for a narrow ring of short black curls, clotted together with dirt, which encircled his head and gave him the appearance of a diminutive monk who had deserted the cloister and reverted to primitive type. His nose was almost flat on his face, and his features repulsive.

Clifford was fairly gloomy about the prospects for using motor transport to haul heavy goods across the Kalahari, largely because the trucks were so slow and because the life

Figure 118. *Harry Beeching (From Makin, W.J. 1929. Across the Kalahari Desert, 41. London: Arrowsmith).*

of the expensive tyres was so short. Thus it was in the following year he visited the Makarikari in northern Bechuanaland to see whether it might be feasible to construct a railway from Bulawayo in Southern Rhodesia (now Zimbabwe) to the port of Walvis Bay in South West Africa (now Namibia). The Makarikari was a shrunken remnant of a great lake, which in the late Ice Age had once covered an area of over 120,000 km^2 – much greater than present day Lake Victoria. What was the shape of the depression and would it prove an obstacle to railway construction and operation? They carried out a complete anticlockwise circumnavigation of the lake by truck, concluding that there would be no great obstacles to railway construction and that the costs would be low. Clifford's third expedition in 1931 again used six-wheeled trucks and once more took him back to the Great Makarikari salt lake, where he undertook detailed surveying. In later years he became governor of the Bahamas, Mauritius and Trinidad. He died in Surrey, England, in 1969.

BIBLIOGRAPHIC REFERENCES AND FURTHER READING

Clifford, B.E.H. 1929. A journey by motor lorry from Mahalapye through the Kalahari Desert. *Geographical Journal*, 73, 342–358.

Clifford, B.E.H. 1930. A reconnaissance of the Great Makarikari Lake. *Geographical Journal*, 75, 16–26.

Clifford, B.E.H. 1938. Across the Great Makarikari Salt Lake. *Geographical Journal*, 91, 233–241.

Makin, W.J. 1929. *Across the Kalahari Desert*. London: Arrowsmith.

Smith, H.A. 2004. Clifford, Sir Bede Edmund Hugh (1890–1969). *Oxford Dictionary of National Biography online*.

CHAPTER 9
NORTH AMERICA

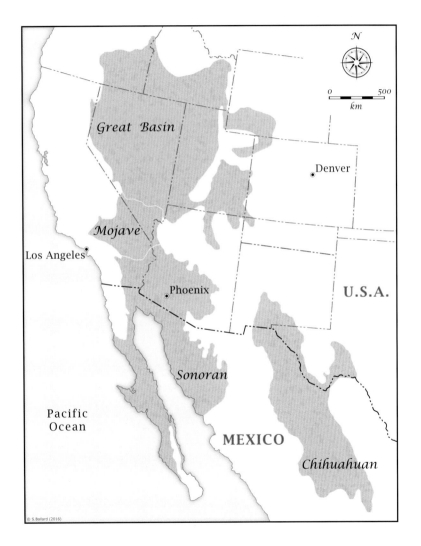

TWO MAIN PHYSIOGRAPHICAL provinces – The Basin and Range and The Colorado Plateau – contain the most important of the North American deserts, but there are marked differences between them. Within the Basin and Range Province lie the Sonoran, Chihuahuan, Mojave and Great Basin deserts, the last of which was explored by John C. Frémont. They are characterised by more or less north-to-south trending mountain ranges and basins. The juxtaposition of topographic highs and lows – of which Death Valley is the supreme example – provides a situation where there are many alluvial fans, extensive pediments and active runoff. The many closed basins that existed in pluvial times of the Pleistocene epoch contained large lakes. Notable among these were lakes Bonneville and Lahontan, and, in the Death Valley region, Lake Manly, named after William Lewis Manly, one of the greatest explorers of North America.

The Colorado Plateau is very different. It exhibits sedimentary strata, which on account of their very limited dips give rise to extensive mesa and scarp landscapes, sandstone canyons and intricately dissected fluvial landscapes. Rapid denudation has created the great cliffs of the plateau, with their magnificent escarpments, mesas, natural arches, box canyons and ground water-sapped alcoves (Figure 120).

Although these two provinces contain some dune fields (Algodones, White Sands, etc.) and generate dust from desiccated lakes, they are not areas where aeolian processes and phenomena are generally dominant. They do not possess the great sand seas that characterise Arabia and the Sahara. Fluvial and slope processes, driven by water and gravity, give these North American deserts their distinctiveness, as demonstrated so dramatically by the Grand Canyon (Figure 121). This vast chasm was first encountered by Europeans in 1540, when a great expedition led by Francisco Vázquez de Coronado reached it. Another pioneering Spanish explorer was Francisco Hermenegildo Tomás Garcés (1738–1781), a Franciscan friar, who served as a missionary and explorer

Figure 119. (opposite) *The North American Deserts (Map by Sebastian Ballard).*

Figure 120. (left) *Sandstone Cliffs in the Capitol Reef Natonal Park, Utah (author's image).*

in the colonial Viceroyalty of New Spain. He explored much of the southwestern region of North America, including present day Sonora and Baja California in Mexico, and the U.S. states of Arizona and Southern California. Among other places he visited were Soda Lake and the Mojave River and it was Garcés who gave the Colorado River its name. He died in the Yuma uprising in July 1781, aged 43.

In the nineteenth century there was a phase of westward expansion, a desire to find routes through the mountains and deserts of the west, and a wish to establish the resources (gold, for example) that might be available for exploitation. There was also a desire to explore the Colorado River, such as the expedition commanded by Joseph Ives between 1857 and 1858 to explore the river upstream from its mouth. At Robinson's Landing, Ives assembled and the used the 54-foot (16.5-m) paddlewheel steamboat *Explorer* to survey and map the river. His party included John Strong Newberry as medic, geologist and botanist. He led them up the Colorado to the lower end of the Grand Canyon, then struck out across the desert to Fort Defiance in Colorado. Ives gave an account of his findings in his *Report upon the Colorado River of the West* (1861). The Ives expedition produced one of the important early maps of the Grand Canyon drawn by Frederick W. von Egloffstein, the expedition's topographer.

In 1857 and 1858 Lieutenant Ned Beale surveyed an east-to-west route just to the south of the Grand Canyon. He was notable for employing imported camels. Later in the nineteenth century, John Wesley Powell (see p. 279) led an expedition that also surveyed the Colorado, but on that journey the party travelled downstream.

Figure 121. (opposite) *The Grand Canyon from the south rim, with the Colorado River at its base (author's image).*

JEDEDIAH STRONG SMITH

JEDEDIAH SMITH (Figure 122), hunter, trapper, fur trader and explorer, was born in New York State in 1799. As a young man he worked for General Ashley's Rocky Mountain Fur Company and travelled up the Missouri River, trapping beaver and hunting buffalo. In 1822 he was involved in a battle with the Arikara Native Americans in which 13 of Ashley's men were killed. Smith conducted himself well in this battle and was promoted by Ashley and led various expeditions to the Rocky Mountains. In 1824 he reached the Snake River from the Green River by way of South Pass on the Continental Divide in the Rocky Mountains, and by doing so he effectively opened up the Oregon Trail, which later was to carry thousands of settlers from St Louis and Independence, Missouri, to the Pacific coast. In that same year, while along the Cheyenne River, he was badly mauled by a grizzly bear. In 1826–7 (Figure 123), and now running his own company, Smith once more left camp on the Green River and followed the Colorado River deep into the west, before travelling through the Mojave Desert into California, which was then part of Mexico.

From Soda Lake (Figure 124) they followed the ephemeral Mojave River into the San Bernadino Mountains. They arrived at San Gabriel Mission near Los Angeles. Smith and his party had become the first Americans to cross overland to California, entering from the east. On the way back they crossed the Sierra Nevada and into what is now known as the Great Basin named by John C. Frémont, and eventually reached the Great Salt Lake. Smith was thus also the first American to make the journey back from California by an overland route and to traverse the Great Basin, which covers most of Nevada and parts of several other states.

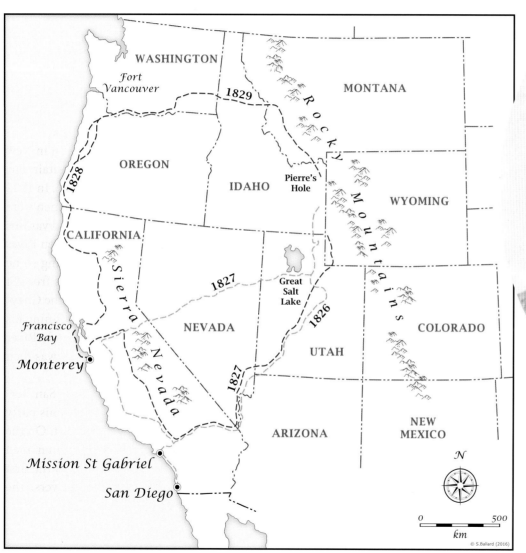

Figure 122. (above) *Jed Smith (from Frontispiece, Morgan, D.L. 1953. Jedediah Smith and the Opening of the West. Lincoln: University of Nebraska Press).*

Figure 123. (left) *Smith's routes (Map drawn by Sebastian Ballard).*

In his diary of the journey, Smith made some observations on the Mojave people:

The women are generally very fleshy with tolerable features. The men when dressed at all have a Spanish Blanket thrown over the left shoulder and passing under the right arm it is pinned on the breast with a wooden pin. They wear no head dress, moccasins or leggings. The dress of the women is a petticoat made of a material like flax just broken, which is banded with a plait on the upper edge like corn husks. It is fastened around the waist extending down to the knee and constitutes with whole of their clothing. They are in general much more cleanly than the Pautch. They make a kind of earthenware and in large crocks of this they boil their beans corn pumpkins &c.

The men appear to work as much in the field as the women which is quite an unusual sight among Indians. But few of them have bows and arrows. The bows are 5 feet long and the arrows very long and made of cane grass with a wooden splice 6 inches long for a head. It is fashion with these indians to fill the hair full of mud and wind it around the head until the top resembles in shape of a tin pan.

'It is fashion with these indians to fill the hair full of mud and wind it around the head until the top resembles in shape of a tin pan.'

From time to time Smith and his men suffered grievously from thirst and hunger. As he recorded in his diary:

I cut the horse meat and spread it out to dry, and determined to remain for the rest of the day that we might repose our wearied and emaciated bodies. I have at different times suffered the extremes of hunger and thirst. Hard as it is to bear for successive days the knawings of hunger, yet it is light in comparison to the agony of burning thirst and, on the other hand, I have observed that a man reduced by hunger is some days in recovering his strength. A man equally reduced by thirst seems renovated almost instantaneously. Hunger can be endured more than twice as long as thirst. To some it may appear surprising that a man who has been for several days without eating has a most incessant desire to drink, and although he can drink but little at a time, yet he wants it much oftener than in ordinary circumstances.

In 1827–28 Smith made a second trip to California, again following the Colorado River and into the Mojave Desert, where the Mojave Native Americans killed ten of his men. In 1831, aged 32,

Figure 124. (opposite) *Soda Lake, Mojave Desert (author's image).*

Smith himself was shot, stabbed to death and then scalped by a group of Comanches while en route to Santa Fe. His body was never found.

Trappers and hunters in North America, such as Smith, largely unaided by the government of their country, pushed boldly out into terra incognita. As J.M. Guinn wrote in an article on Smith in the *Annual Publication of the Historical Society of Southern California* (1896), they crossed alkaline deserts, penetrated dark and dangerous defiles, launched frail canoes on nameless rivers, and were forever in danger from savage foes, whether man or beast.

The child of Methodist parents, Smith appears to have been a tall, spare, generally humourless, devout and religious man. He never smoked, got drunk, consorted with Native American women, or used profanity. On his travels his rifle and his Bible were his inseparable companions. It was said that he made the lone wilderness his place of meditation and the mountaintop his altar.

BIBLIOGRAPHIC REFERENCES AND FURTHER READING

Guinn, J.M. 1896. Captain Jedediah S. Smith: the pathfinder of the Sierras. *Annual Publication of the Historical Society of Southern California*, Los Angeles, 3, 45–63.

Morgan, D.L. 1953. *Jedediah Smith and the Opening of the West*. Lincoln: University of Nebraska Press.

Smith, J. Diary, http://mtmen.org/mtman/html/jsmith/jedexped1.html, accessed online 15 November 2015.

JOHN CHARLES FRÉMONT

JOHN C. FRÉMONT, 'the Great Pathfinder', was born, illegitimate, in Savannah, Georgia, in 1813. As a young man he demonstrated his mathematical ability and became a topographical surveyor in the U.S. Army's Corps of Topographical Engineers. Reputed in his early years to be lean, wiry, as handsome as Lord Byron and as mysterious as Sir Richard Burton, he had the carriage of a soldier and the face of a poet (Figure 125). Initially, Frémont worked in the eastern part of the United States, but in due course, in Washington DC, he met Senator Thomas Hart Benton, one of the leading advocates of western expansion. Frémont eloped with Benton's daughter, Jessie in 1841, but in the following year her father arranged for his son-in-law to carry out an expedition to map and survey the emerging Oregon Trail through South Pass on the Continental Divide (Figure 126). In this and subsequent endeavours he was assisted by the hunter Kit Carson, whom Frémont through his writings turned into a legend. In 1843 he took on a second government-sponsored expedition that took him across what became known as the Great Basin and then across the Sierra Nevada into California. It was on this expedition that his principal encounters with desert areas occurred. Frémont's third expedition took him through California to the Pacific coast, but his involvement with political controversies in California during the Mexican–American War caused him to be subjected to a court-martial, and not for the last time, for he was also accused of insubordination in the Civil War by Abraham Lincoln. Found guilty of

Figure 125. *Frémont: the carriage of a soldier and the face of a poet (RGS).*

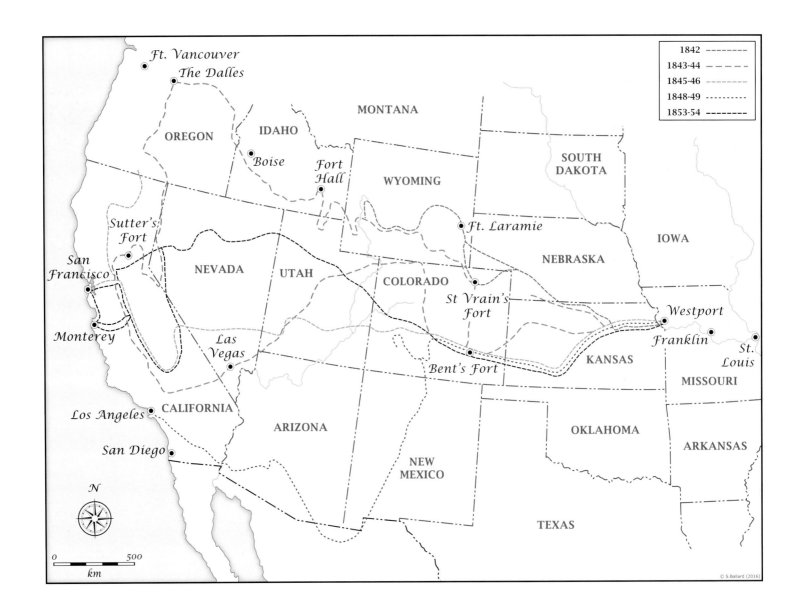

Ft. Vancouver
The Dalles

MONTANA

OREGON

IDAHO

Boise

Fort
Hall

WYOMING

SOUTH
DAKOTA

Sutter's
Fort

Ft. Laramie

IOWA

San
Francisco

NEVADA

UTAH

COLORADO

NEBRASKA

St Vrain's
Fort

Westport

Monterey

Las
Vegas

Bent's Fort

KANSAS

Franklin

St.
Louis

MISSOURI

Los Angeles

CALIFORNIA

ARIZONA

OKLAHOMA

ARKANSAS

San Diego

NEW
MEXICO

TEXAS

N

0   500
km

© S.Ballard (2016)

mutiny, disobeying orders and undisciplined conduct, he was dismissed from the army. Frémont subsequently made two further expeditions to seek routes through the Rockies, but both were disastrous and unsuccessful. On one of them, ten of his party perished in the snow.

Frémont later became increasingly involved in politics. During the Mexican American War, Frémont, a major in the U.S. Army, took control of California from the Bear Flag Republic in 1846. He proclaimed himself military governor of California. He served as major general in the American Civil War, was governor of Arizona Territory, and even became a Republican candidate for the presidency of the United States. He died, destitute and largely forgotten, in New York City in 1890. Frémont disliked routine and discipline, often displayed a career-crippling disdain for authority, was probably narcissistic, proved to be financially incompetent, and was dangerously impetuous and unpredictable. On the other hand be brought courage, great enthusiasm, mapping skills and scientific knowledge to his explorations. Clad in buckskin, he covered more ground than any other government explorer, including Lewis and Clark, but above all he was a serious scientist. As Rolle's book (p. 46) recounts:

> Each evening he ordered the expedition to pitch tens early so that he could gather botanical and geological specimens before nightfall set in. His science was never suspect, for he was the personification of mapmaking no longer based upon rumors, guesses, and estimates that could be inaccurate by hundreds of miles. Nightly star sightings, frequent sketches, and detailed study of the landscape often produced accuracy to within a few hundred feet.

Frémont's *Report of the Exploring Expedition to the Rocky Mountains in the Year 1842, and to California in the year 1843-'44* was a U.S. government publication that was at once an heroic adventure story, a travel book and an emigrants' guide to settlement of the American West. Much of it may have been crafted by his talented wife, who turned it into a literary classic. It provided the American government and the American people with their first connected view of the Great Plains, the Great Basin, the Rocky Mountains, and Oregon and California. It stimulated a national urge for westward expansion. He was the first American explorer to accurately record the wilderness beyond the Rockies and to address the geographical problems that might await the prospective settler. His report also presented drawings of new plants and fossils as well as describing the essentials of the geography of the West. It contained detailed maps based on countless readings of

Figure 126. (opposite) *Frémont's routes (Map drawn by Sebastian Ballard).*

Figure 127. *Frémont's view of Pyramid Lake (RGS: From Frémont, J.C. 1845.* Report of the Exploring Expedition to the Rocky Mountains in the Year 1842, and to California in the year 1843-'44. *Washington, D.C.: Senate of the United States).*

latitude and longitude. This filled in what he described as 'a vast geographical chasm' between the Missouri River and the Pacific Coast region.

Frémont's greatest contribution to understanding the geography of the American West was his circuit of what he named the Great Basin, an area of land that stretches between the Columbia River drainage in the north and the Colorado River drainage in the south, and between the Sierra Nevada in the west and the Rocky Mountains in the east. He was the first to recognise that it was an area of interior drainage, though he generously recorded that he had obtained much geographical intelligence from traders and hunters like Joseph Walker. He described the Great Basin thus (*Geographical Memoir*, cited in Gilbert, p. 188):

> Partly arid, and sparsely inhabited, the general character of the GREAT BASIN is that of desert, but with great exceptions, there being many parts of it very fit for the residence of a civilized people. … Mountain is the predominating structure of the interior of the Basin, with plains

between – the mountains wooded and watered, the plains arid and sterile. … Such is the general structure of the interior of the Great Basin, more Asiatic than American in its character, and much resembling the elevated region between the Caspian sea and northern Persia.

By demonstrating the centripetal nature of drainage in the Great Basin and its many salt lakes (Figure 127), Frémont had effectively scuppered the myth of a fabled Buenaventura river flowing from the Rocky Mountains to the Pacific at San Francisco Bay. He proved that the two great rivers flowing into the bay, the Sacramento and San Joaquin, did not arise at the western base of the Rocky Mountains. He showed that there was no possible trans-western river trade route, and that the Sierra Nevada formed an unbroken barricade that trapped interior rivers in the Great Basin. Maps by such figures as Albert Finley and John Melish, which purported to portray the course of the Buenaventura, were shown to be figments of the imagination.

Frémont visited the Great Salt Lake in Utah, and his favourable description of that location was one of the factors that led Brigham Young, the Mormon leader, to settle his people in what is now Salt Lake City. As Frémont's wife Jessie wrote, 'From the ashes of his campfires have sprung cities.' Frémont also visited Lake Abert in Oregon of which he said 'the white efflorescences which lined the shore like a bank of snow, and the disagreeable odour which filled the air, informed us too plainly that the water belonged to one of those fetid salt lakes which are common in this region.'

Frémont never showed any fondness for deserts. For them he had an arsenal of adjectival abuse. He preferred mountains and plains – the former for their scenery and the latter for their animation supplied by buffalo and the indigenous people. He disliked deserts because they formed a barrier to travel. The Mohave valley, for example, passed through a desert which in his view was 'most sterile and repulsive'.

In 1850, the same year in which the Geographical Society presented a chronometer to David Livingstone for his explorations in central Africa, the society awarded Frémont its Patron's Medal. This was richly deserved, for as Tom Chaffin has remarked (2002, p. xxi):

A born geographer, the Pathfinder possessed a jeweler's eye for assaying landscapes and ascertaining how mountains, river drainages, valleys, and lakes link up into a continental whole. … During his expeditions, Frémont and the men of his exploring parties walked thousands of miles, surviving on paltry rations and whatever game they could find. They endured extremes

of cold, heat, wind and rain, as well as dangers incomprehensible to modern sensibilities. …
And in an era before specialists came to dominate scientific exploration, he functioned as
a one-man-band scientist – expedition geologist, meteorologist, astronomer, and botanist.

BIBLIOGRAPHIC REFERENCES AND FURTHER READING

Chaffin, T. 2002. *Pathfinder. John Charles Frémont and the Course of American Empire.* Norman: University of Oklahoma Press.

Egan, F. 1977. *Fremont, Explorer for a Restless Nation.* Reno: University of Nevada Press.

Frémont, J.C. 1845. *Report of the Exploring Expedition to the Rocky Mountains in the Year 1842, and to California in the year 1843–'44.* Washington, D.C.: Senate of the United States.

Gilbert, E.W. 1933. *The Exploration of Western America.* Cambridge: Cambridge University Press.

Grayson, D.K. 1993. *The Desert's Past. A Natural History of the Great Basin.* Washington: Smithsonian Institution Press.

Gregory, H.E. 1945. Scientific explorations in southern Utah. *American Journal of Science*, 243(10), 527–549.

Herr, P. 2000. Frémont, John Charles. *American National Biography online.*

Limerick, P.N. 1985. *Desert Passages. Encounters with the American Deserts.* Albuquerque: University of New Mexico Press.

Roberts, D. (2002). *A Newer World: Kit Carson, John C. Frémont and the Claiming of the American West.* New York: Simon and Schuster.

Rolle, A. 1982, Exploring an explorer: psychohistory and John Charles Frémont. *Pacific Historical Review*, 51, 135–163.

Weiss, S.C. 1999. John C. Frémont 1842, 1843–'44 *Report* and Map. *Journal of Government Information*, 26, 297–313.

WILLIAM LEWIS MANLY

WILLIAM LEWIS MANLY, born in 1820, was a Vermonter who at the age of 20 moved to Wisconsin and became a fur hunter, trapper and lead miner. However, in 1848, on hearing of the California Gold Rush, he set out to make his fortune. At the city of Council Bluffs, Iowa, he met John Haney Rogers, and together they served as ox drivers on a wagon train that was headed for California. Initially, they took an abandoned ferryboat down the Green River in the hope of eventually reaching the Pacific Ocean. However, when this proved impossible, they headed into Utah where they met up with some other gold seekers. Manly and Rogers led or two families with children (the Bennett-Arcane party) on a purported shortcut to California that crossed south-central Nevada. Unfortunately this proved to be an unwise move and the information upon which they based their decision was faulty.

The route took them through barren sagebrush desert, with hardly any water or forage for their oxen and horses, and with little or no game to shoot. The party had to cross the Amargosa Range in eastern California and then descend a dry arroyo (gully) now known as Furnace Creek Wash. This brought them to the base of what Manly called 'Death Valley'. Here they found their westward progress blocked by the mountains of the Panamint Range. They were probably the first European Americans to see Death Valley, the lowest and one of the driest and hottest places in North America (Figure 128). They became lost and were on the brink of starvation. The only possibility for survival was for a small party to try and scout out a route to seek help. Manly and Rogers volunteered to do this, and with little more than a few pounds of dry meat and makeshift cans of water, they trekked nearly 400 km through the Mojave Desert before reaching Rancho San Francisco, a settlement not far from Los Angeles. Here they obtained supplies, and a month after leaving Death Valley, were able to return to the desperate families, who, with one exception – a Captain Culverwell – had survived.

In 1894 Manly published his account of the travails and heroics of his experiences in *Death Valley in '49*.

He recounted the gradual decline of the oxen that were so essential for pulling the wagons (p. 66):

Our oxen began to look bad, for they had poor food. Grass had been very scarce, and now when we unyoked them and turned them out they did not care to look around much for something to eat. They moved slowly and cropped disdainfully the dry scattering shrubs and bunches of grass. … Spending many nights and days on such dry food and without water they suffered fearfully, and though fat and sleek when we started from salt Lake, they now looked gaunt and poor, and dragged themselves along, poor faithful servants of mankind. No one knew how long before we might have to kill some of them to get food to save our own lives.

Manly became depressed (p. 72):

I thought of the bounteous stock of bread and beans upon my father's table … and here was I, the oldest son, away out in the center of the Great American Desert, with an empty stomach and a dry and parched throat, and clothes fast wearing out with constant wear. And perhaps I had not yet seen the worst of it. I might be forced to see men, and the women and children of our party, choke and die, powerless to help them. It was a darker, gloomier day than I had ever known could be, and alone I wept aloud, for I believed I could see the future, and the results were bitter to contemplate.

Manly and Rogers now prepared to set off to seek rescue (p. 83):

Mr Arcane killed the ox which had so nearly failed, and all the men went to drying and preparing meat. Others made us some new mocassins out of rawhide, and the women made us each a knapsack. Our meat was closely packed, and one can form an idea how poor are cattle were from the fact that John and I actually packed seven-eighths of all the flesh of an ox into our knapsacks and carried it away. They put in a couple of spoonfuls of rice and about as much tea … I wore no coat or vest, but took half of a light blanket, while Rogers wore a thin summer coat and took no blanket.

Figure 128. *Death Valley. Below: As it is today (author's image). Right: As depicted by Manley.*

Eventually, after many privations, and a month of travel, they reached the summit of a hill and looked down upon a joyous scene, full of grass meadows and grazing cattle (p. 95):

> such a scene of abundance and rich plenty and comfort bursting thus upon our eyes which for months had seen only the desolation and sadness of the desert, was like getting a glimpse of Paradise, and tears of joy ran down our faces.

The Catholic mission of San Francisco gave them food, horses, and a particularly useful and intelligent mule. They retraced their steps, rescued their party, and got them to Los Angeles. Manly was pleased to see the back of Death Valley (p. 141):

> We were out of the dreadful sands and shadows of Death Valley, its exhausting phantoms, its salty columns bitter lakes and wild, dreary sunken desolation. If the waves of the sea could flow in and cover its barren nakedness, as we now know they might if a few sandy barriers were swept away, it would be indeed, a blessing, for in it there is naught of good, comfort, or satisfaction, but ever in the minds of those who braved its heat and sands, a thought of a horrid Charnel house, a corner of the earth so dreary that it requires an exercise of the strongest faith to believe that the great Creator ever smiled upon it as a portion of his work and pronounced it "Very good".

Manly eventually settled in California and died there in 1903 at the age of 83. Rogers also settled in California, and died in 1906, having suffered from the effects of the mercury he had used to extract gold from low-grade ore. Parts of his feet had had to be amputated because of mercury-induced gangrene.

BIBLIOGRAPHIC REFERENCES AND FURTHER READING

Kowalewski, M. 2000. Manly, William Lewis. *American National Biography online*.
Limerick, P.N. 1985. *Desert Passages. Encounters with the American Deserts*. Albuquerque: University of New Mexico Press.
Manly, W.L. 1894. *Death Valley in '49*. San Jose, CA: Pacific Tree and Vine Company.

JOHN WESLEY POWELL

JOHN WESLEY POWELL, a great geologist, anthropologist and explorer, was born in 1834 in Mount Morris, New York. He was the son of an impoverished wandering preacher or 'exhorter'. After a spell of teaching, museum work and fighting on the side of the Union in the American Civil War, where he lost part of one arm at the Battle of Shiloh, he became a professor of geology at Illinois Wesleyan University in Bloomington (Figure 129). In May 1869, having obtained funds and equipment from various sources, he set out on his first journey – the Rocky Mountain Scientific Exploring Expedition – to navigate the largely unknown Green and Colorado rivers. Manly, some decades earlier had attempted to float down the Green River, and parts of the Colorado had also been navigated before, notably by Joseph C. Ives and John Strong Newberry in 1857, but Major Powell's party went much further and when he emerged from the Grand Canyon he was treated as a hero. He made a second river trip in 1871–72, in which he retraced part of the 1869 route, travelling the Colorado River from Green River, Wyoming to Kanab Creek in the Grand Canyon.

While Ives and Newberry had tried to navigate *up* the Colorado from the Gulf of California using heavy steamboats, Wes Powell's pioneering trip *down* the Colorado and its tributaries was undertaken in four small wooden boats that were transported on the new transcontinental railroad to the point where it crossed the Green

Figure 129. *The Major's bust at his memorial on the south rim of the Grand Canyon (author's image).*

River. Powell's party went with the current, but from time to time the boats had to be carried around obstacles such as rapids and rock falls. Such portages could be exhausting. On one scary occasion at Lodore (Figure 130) on the Green River, in a stretch of rapids and whirlpools, one of the vessels capsized and much equipment were lost, including their all-important surveying barometers. The trip was to be long, bruising, cold, dangerous, and – when hemmed in by cliffs – claustrophobic.

As the Big Canyon was approached,, the tension grew. As Powell recounted (*The Exploration of the Colorado River and its Canyons*, p. 247):

We are now ready to start on our way down the Great Unknown. Our boats, tied to a common stake, are chafing each other, as they are tossed by the fretful river. … We have but a month's rations remaining. The flour has been resifted through the mosquito-net sieve, the spoiled bacon has been dried, and the worst of it boiled; the few pounds of dried apples have been spread in the sun, and reshrunken to their normal bulk; the sugar has all melted, and gone on its way down the river; but we have a large sack of coffee.

Powell wrote thus of the impact upon his senses of the Grand Canyon (p. 390):

Figure 130. *The Heart of Lodore, Green River: Frederick S. Dellenbaugh seated on the bank, 1871. Taken on John Wesley Powell's second expedition down the Colorado River, 1871–72 (RGS).*

The Grand Canyon of the Colorado is a canyon composed of many canyons. It is a composite of thousands of gorges. In like manner, each wall of the canyon is a composite structure, a wall composed of many walls, but never a repetition. Every one of these almost innumerable gorges is a world of beauty in itself. In the Grand Canyon there are thousands of gorges like that below Niagara Falls, and there are a thousand Yosemites. Yet all the canyons unite to form one Grand Canyon, the most sublime spectacle on the earth.

The rapids were horrendously dangerous and physically challenging (Figure 131). Moreover, notwithstanding only having one arm, which gave rise to his Ute name Kapurats, Powell climbed the sides of the canyons on numerous occasions to record the geology and to spy out the land. On one occasion he found himself stranded on a high ledge, unable to go on up or to go back. He only survived because his companion, who was higher up, took off his trousers, and dangled them down so that Powell could grasp them with his one arm (Figure 132).

Powell's experiences in the Colorado Plateau and the Uinta Basin were crucial for the development of ideas in geomorphology. He appreciated the sheer power of river erosion, and could see from the unconformities present in the area's starkly exposed stratigraphic columns that rivers could cut down to a 'base-level of erosion', and continue to cut down through deep layers of slowly uplifting strata.

In 1870 Congress granted Powell funds for what came to be designated the 'Geographical and Geological Survey of the Rocky Mountain Region, J.W. Powell in charge'. In the event the Rockies hardly figured at all in his programme, and Donald Worster in *A River Running West*, 2001 has suggested that a better name might have been 'The survey of the high plateau country of Utah and Arizona through which the Colorado River flows'. Within six years of the first river expedition and three years of the second, the work of Powell's surveyors and geologists in the Colorado Plateau had become hugely appreciated for their results and their professionalism. In this role he employed and encouraged some other great investigators of the arid west, including Grove Karl Gilbert and Clarence Dutton (Figure 133). So it was that Powell became director of the U.S. Geological Survey from 1881 to 1894. He also became a great

Figure 131. *Powell's little boats in big rapids (RGS: Powell, J.W. 1961.* The Exploration of the Colorado River and its Canyons, *250. New York, NY: Dover Publications).*

authority on Native Americans and for a while was director of the Bureau of Ethnology. His report on *The Lands of the Arid Region of the United States* (1878) recognised the particular problems for land development caused by aridity. Powell died in Maine in 1902, aged 69, and was buried in Arlington Cemetery.

BIBLIOGRAPHIC REFERENCES AND FURTHER READING

Fowler, D.D. 2000. Powell, John Wesley. *American National Biography online.*

Freeman, L.R. 1923. *The Colorado River, Yesterday, To-day and To-morrow*. London: William Heinemann.

Gregory, H.E. 1945. Scientific explorations in southern Utah. *American Journal of Science*, 243(10), 527–549.

Powell, J.W. 1878. *The Lands of the Arid Region of the United States*. Washington, D.C.: Government Printing Office.

Powell, J.W. 1961. *The Exploration of the Colorado River and its Canyons*. New York, NY: Dover Publications.

Pyne, S.J. 1998. *How the Canyon Became Grand*. Harmondsworth: Penguin Books.

Stenger, W. 1954. *Beyond the Hundredth Meridian*. New York: Houghton Mifflin Company.

Worster, D. 2001. *A River Running West. The Life of John Wesley Powell*. New York: Oxford University Press.

Figure 132. (left) *Powell dangling from trousers RGS: Powell, J.W. 1961.* The Exploration of the Colorado River and its Canyons, *169. New York, NY: Dover Publications).*

Figure 133. (opposite) *Point Sublime, Grand Canyon, from Clarence Dutton (this panoramic image of Point Sublime by William Henry Holmes was one of several included in Clarence E. Dutton's 1882 publication* Tertiary History of the Grand Canon District).

CHAPTER 10

NORTH AFRICA

Figure 134. (opposite)
*Explorers' routes in the Sahara
and West Africa (Map drawn by
Sebastian Ballard).*

THE SAHARA, the world's largest desert, covers an area which is similar in extent to that of the United States (including Alaska). Occupying approximately one third of the African continent, it stretches from the Atlantic to the Red Sea and from the Mediterranean to the Sahel zone of West Africa. Its heart is dry, with mean annual rainfall dropping to less than 10 mm. Vegetation is largely absent. Sometimes the Sahara is subdivided into two or more parts, with the eastern portion being called the Libyan Desert (or, in Egypt, the Western Desert) and the western part being regarded as the Sahara proper. This same division is followed in this book.

The most distinctive characteristic of the Sahara – save only the relief provided by the Hoggar, Tibesti and other massifs – is its flatness. This is associated with great sandstone plateaux, a series of broad, closed basins, and a series of wind-moulded landscapes and areas of sand deposition (ergs).

The uplift of the central uplands – including Jebel Marra, Tibesti, Hoggar and the Aïr – was accompanied by massive outpouring of lava and the creation of striking volcanic craters and pinnacles. These uplands form a very important component of the Sahara. They rise to considerable altitudes: Tibesti to over 3,400 m, Jebel Marra to over 3,000 m, Hoggar to over 2,900 m and Aïr to over 2,000 m.

The Sahara displays many features that result, at least in part, from wind action, including some enormous ridge and swale systems produced by wind erosion of bedrock. The Sahara contains a significant proportion of the global inventory of wind-blown sand as well as some of the world's largest sand seas, and dunes cover just over a quarter of the total area. On the north side of the Sahara, in a belt that runs through the centre of Tunisia westwards towards the high plateaux of Algeria, is a line of depressions called *chotts*. Another great topographic depression on the south side of the Sahara is the Chad Basin. Covering a total area of 2.5 million km ^{2}, it stretches for over 1,500 km from the low watershed of the Congo into the heart of the Sahara, where it receives run-off from the Tibesti and Hoggar massifs. The lowest point of the basin is the dusty Bodelé Depression, the altitude of which is only 150 m above sea level.

Among the inhabitants of the Sahara are the Tuareg. Their most striking attribute is the indigo veil, worn by the men but not the women, giving rise to the popular name the 'Blue Men of the

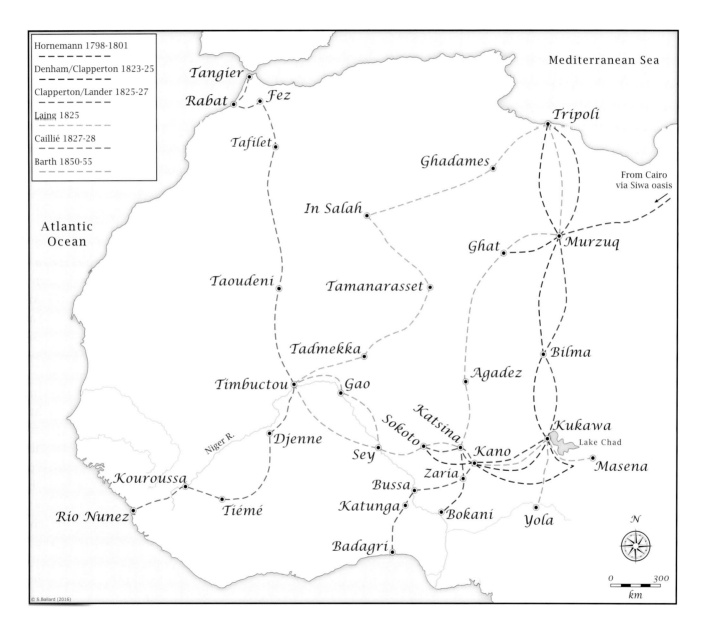

Hornemann 1798-1801

Denham/Clapperton 1823-25

Clapperton/Lander 1825-27

Laing 1825

Caillié 1827-28

Barth 1850-55

Mediterranean Sea

Tangier

Rabat · Fez

Tripoli

Tafilet

Ghadames

From Cairo
via Siwa oasis

Atlantic
Ocean

In Salah

Ghat · Murzuq

Taoudeni

Tamanarasset

Bilma

Tadmekka

Agadez

Timbuctou · Gao

Katsina

Kukawa

Niger R. · Djenne

Sokoto

Lake Chad

Sey

Kano

Kouroussa

Zaria

Masena

Bussa

Rio Nunez

Tiémé

Katunga

Bokani

Badagri

Yola

N

0   300

km

© S.Ballard (2016)

Sahara', or 'Men of the Veil'. They are a Berber people with a traditionally nomadic pastoralist life-style. Most Tuareg live in the Saharan parts of Niger, Mali and Algeria. In the late nineteenth century, they resisted both the early explorers – some of whom they killed, notably Scottish explorer Alexander Gordon Laing – and the later French colonial invasion of their central Saharan homelands. Deeply shocking to France in 1881 was the almost total extermination by the Tuareg of the large expedition that had been led by Colonel Paul Flatters in search of a suitable route for a railway across the desert. The exploration of the Sahara was, from the late eighteenth century, very much concerned with the search for Timbuktu (also spelled Tombouctou, Timbuctoo and Timbuktoo) (Figure 134), a city in Mali situated 20 km north of the River Niger. In 1788 a group of titled Englishmen formed the African Association with the goal of finding the city and charting the course of the Niger River, while in 1824 the Paris-based Société de Géographie offered a 10,000 franc prize to the first non-Muslim to reach the town and return with information about it. This ultimately rather unprepossessing city lured a large number of European travellers towards it, but also, to their deaths. Disease, privation and the Tuareg took their toll. Many of the explorations, including the ill-fated journey to Murzuk by George Lyon and Joseph Ritchie, started from Tripoli in Libya, and followed old trading routes.

In the nineteenth century, as France started to exert its colonial muscle, its missionaries, scientists, soldiers and administrators began to make their contribution, as described in Douglas Porch's *The Conquest of the Sahara* (1984). Finally, in the twentieth century, tracked motor vehicles permitted rapid trans-Saharan journeys. There was also serious scientific exploration by French geographers such as René Chudeau, Émile-Félix Gautier, Robert Capot-Rey and Théodore Monod. Capot-Rey (1897–1977) was seriously wounded in the First World War and had his right leg amputated in March 1917. Notwithstanding this severe disability, he undertook many camel journeys in the Sahara and became secretary and then director of the Institut de Recherches Sahariennes in Algiers (founded in 1937).

Each Saharan expedition faced many of the same problems: the sheer size of the desert, its severely parched nature, the shortage of water, the scourge of dust and sandstorms, and the drudgery of trudging across enormous chains of dunes. It could also be a dangerous or even fatal affair. The promiscuous and drug-using Isabelle Eberhardt, drowned in the desert during a flash flood on 21 October 1904. She was only 27 years old.

BAIN HUGH CLAPPERTON

HUGH CLAPPERTON (Figure 135) was a Scottish naval officer, who was born in Dumfriesshire, Scotland, in 1788. He took part in an early journey across the Sahara from Tripoli to Murzuk in present-day southern Libya, and on to Lake Chad at the southern edge of the Sahara. The second member of the expedition was English soldier Dixon Denham (1786–1828), who has been described as odious, pushy, self-important and malicious. He spread unsubstantiated gossip that Clapperton had had sexual relations with an Arab assistant and dismissed Clapperton unjustly as 'vulgar, conceited and quarrelsome'. The other member of the team was Walter Oudney (1790–1824), a pale, grave, slightly built Scottish naval doctor. He was a neighbour of Clapperton in Edinburgh and had aroused Clapperton's interest in African travel, having himself been intrigued by the life of fellow Scotsman Mungo Park and his exploration of the Niger. The trio were the first Europeans to see Lake Chad. A record of their journey is given in *Narrative of Travels and Discoveries in northern and central Africa in the Years 1822, 1823 and 1824*. London: John Murray, 3rd edition (1828). Clapperton's journal, 'a spontaneous, modest and uncomplicated record', has recently been published as *Difficult and Dangerous Roads* edited by James Bruce-Lockhart and John Wright (2000).

In the early nineteenth century, Tripoli was the scene of great interest to Britain, partly because of its proximity to Malta (which had been occupied by Britain since 1800) and partly because it was thought to be a good base for African exploration and in particular to establish the course of the Niger.

Figure 135. *Hugh Clapperton (RGS).*

The British consul general in Tripoli, Colonel Hanmer Warrington, was a firm supporter of exploration during his long tenure of the post (1814–1846). Also, Yusuf Pasha Karamanli, who had usurped the throne of Tripoli in 1795, was keen to project the city's power. So it was that the expedition – the Borno Mission – left Tripoli in early 1822 and reached Lake Chad after 11 months. In the introduction to the *Narrative of Travels and Discoveries*, Denham explained the good and bad aspects of the outward desert crossing:

> It will, perhaps, be thought by some, that I have been more minute than necessary in the account of our journey across that tremendous desert which lies between Mourzuk and Bornou, and which, generally speaking, is made up of dark frowning hills of naked rock, or interminable plains, strewed in some places with fragments of stone and pebbles, in others of one vast level surface of sand, and, in others again, the same material rising into immense mounds, altering their form and position according to the strength and direction of the winds. But, even in the midst of this dreary waste, towns, villages, wandering tribes, and kafilas, or caravans, sometimes occur to break the solitude of this dismal belt, which seems to stretch across Northern Africa, and, on many parts of which, not a living creature, even an insect, enlivens the scene. Still, however, the halting places at the wells, and the wadeys or valleys, afford an endless source of amusement to the traveller, in witnessing the manners, and listening to the conversation, of the various tribes of natives, who, by their singing and dancing, their storytelling, their quarrelling and fighting, make him forget, for a time, the ennui and fatigue of the day's journey.

The authors also had good things to say about the Arabs they encountered (p. 58):

> Arabs are generally thin meagre figures, though possessing expressive and sometimes handsome features, great violence of gesture and muscular action. Irritable and fiery, they are unlike the dwellers in towns and cities: noisy and loud, their common conversational intercourse appears to be a continual strife and quarrel; they are, however, brave, eloquent, and deeply sensible of shame. … I should, however, without hesitation, pronounce them to be much more cleanly than the lower order of people in any European country. Circumcision, and the shaving the hair from the head, and every other part of the body; the frequent ablutions which their religion compels them to perform; all tend to enforce practices of cleanliness. Vermin, from the climate of their country,

they, as well as every other person, must be annoyed with; and although the lower ranks have not the means of frequently changing their covering (for it scarcely can be called apparel), yet they endeavour to free themselves as much as possible from the persecuting vermin.

They gave details of their positive virtues (p. 62):

Arabs have always been commended by the ancients for the fidelity of their attachments, and they are still scrupulously exact to their words, and respectful to their kindred; they have been universally celebrated for their quickness of apprehension and penetration, and the vivacity of their wit. Their language is certainly one of the most ancient in the world; but it has many dialects. The Arabs, however, have their vices and their defects; they are naturally addicted to war, bloodshed, and cruelty; and so malicious as scarcely ever to forget an injury.

Their frequent robberies committed on traders and travellers have rendered the name of an Arab almost infamous in Europe. Amongst themselves, however, they are most honest, and true to the rites of hospitality; and towards those whom they receive as friends into their camp, every thing is open, and nothing ever known to be stolen: enter but once into the tent of an Arab, and by the pressure of his hand he ensures you protection, at the hazard of his life. An Arab is ever true to his bread and salt; once eat with him, and a knot of friendship is tied which cannot easily be loosened.

'Their frequent robberies committed on traders and travellers have rendered the name of an Arab almost infamous in Europe.'

Near Bilma oasis, in south-central Sahara, they encountered a group of local people whose appearance they appreciated (p. 149):

The men had most of them bows and arrows, and all carried spears: they approached Boo-Khaloom, shaking them in the air over their heads; and after this salutation we all moved on towards the town, the females dancing, and throwing themselves about with screams and songs in a manner to us quite original. They were of a superior class to those of the minor towns; some having extremely pleasing features, while the pearly white of their regular teeth was beautifully contrasted with the glossy black of their skin, and the triangular flaps of plaited hair, which hung down on each side of their faces, streaming with oil, with the addition of the coral in the nose, and large amber necklaces, gave them a very seducing appearance.

Denham remarked on the horrors of sandstorms and the pleasurable solution to the discomfort caused (p. 167):

Jan. 30.—The wind and drifting sand were so violent, that we were obliged to keep our tents the whole day; besides this, I was more disordered than I had been since leaving Mourzuk. I found a loose shirt only the most convenient covering, as the sand could be shaken off as soon as it made a lodgment, which, with other articles of dress, could not be done, and the irritation it caused produced a soreness almost intolerable: a little oil or fat from the hand of a negress (all of whom are early taught the art of shampooing to perfection), rubbed well round the neck, loins, and back, is the best cure, and the greatest comfort, in cases of this kind.

Eventually they reached Lake Chad (Figure 136) and remarked upon its beauty (p. 182):

The great lake Tchad, glowing with the golden rays of the sun in its strength, appeared to be within a mile of the spot on which we stood. My heart bounded within me at the prospect, for I believed this lake to be the key to the great object of our search, and I could not refrain from silently imploring Heaven's continued protection, which had enabled us to proceed so far in health and strength even to the accomplishment of our task. … Flocks of geese and wild ducks, of a most beautiful plumage, were quietly feeding at within half pistol shot of where I stood. … Pelicans, cranes, four and five feet in height, grey, variegated, and white, were scarcely so many yards from my side, and a bird, between a snipe and a woodcock, resembling both, and larger than either; immense spoonbills of a snowy whiteness, widgeon, teal, yellow-legged plover, and a hundred species of (to me at least) unknown water fowl, were sporting before me; and it was long before I could disturb the tranquillity of the dwellers on these waters by firing a gun. … The water is sweet and pleasant, and abounds with fish; which the natives have a curious way of catching. Some thirty or forty women go into the lake, with their wrappers brought up between their legs, and tied round their middles, as I should say, by single files, and forming a line at some distance in the water, fronting the land, for it is very shallow near the edges, and absolutely charge the fish before them so close, that they are caught by the hand, or leap upon the shore. We purchased some, and the best flavoured was a sort of bream.

'My heart bounded within me at the prospect, for I believed this lake to be the key to the great object of our search...'

Having found and explored the lake, the party split up. Denham set off to follow the River Shari, while Clapperton and Oudney travelled westwards towards Kano in present-day northern Nigeria. Oudney, however, fell ill and died before they reached their destination. Clapperton then went on to the region of Sokoto, before meeting up with Denham back at Kukawa. Together they made a return journey across the Sahara and back to Tripoli, arriving in January 1825. Clapperton returned to West Africa later in the year, but died near Sokoto on 13 April 1827, as a result of fever and dysentery. Denham died of fever in Sierra Leone, aged 42, in the following year. The Borno Mission of 1822–25 was, in the words of John Wright, 'the most dramatically successful expedition of exploration that the British government had up to then sent into inner Africa.' By the end of the mission, even if the Niger problem was still not solved, central Sahara, Lake Chad and central Sudan had all been charted and revealed to the outside world.

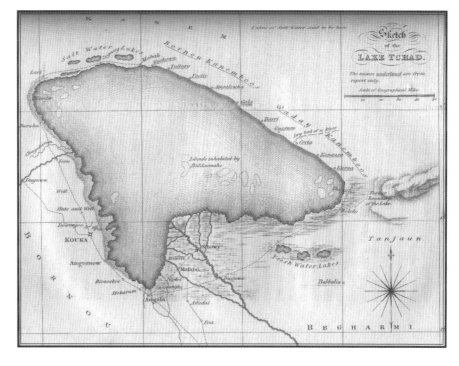

Figure 136. *Sketch of Lake Chad (RGS: Denham, D. 1828.* Narrative of travels and discoveries in northern and central Africa in the years 1822, 1823 and 1824. *3rd Edition. London: John Murray).*

BIBLIOGRAPHIC REFERENCES AND FURTHER READING

Bruce-Lockhart, J. and Wright, J. 2000. *Difficult and Dangerous Roads.* London: Sickle Moon Books.

Denham, D. 1828. *Narrative of Travels and Discoveries in Northern and Central Africa in the Years 1822, 1823 and 1824.* 3rd Edition. London: John Murray.

Gardner, B. 1968. *The Quest for Timbuctoo.* London: Cassell.

Hibbert, C. 1982. *Africa Explored. Europeans in the Dark Continent, 1769–1889.* London: Hamish Hamilton.

Sattin, A. 2003. *The Gates of Africa. Death, Discovery and the Search for Timbuktu.* London: HarperCollins.

ALEXANDER GORDON LAING

Figure 137. *Major Gordon Laing.*
Engraving by S. Freeman (RGS).

ALEXANDER GORDON LAING (Figure 137) was born into an educated and scholarly family in Scotland in 1794. He reached the fabled city of Timbuktu, but died at the hands of the Tuareg in 1826.

After studying at the University of Edinburgh and a short spell as a school teacher, Laing decided to make his life in the British army and served during the Napoleonic Wars in the West Indies and Honduras. In 1820 he was posted to Sierra Leone, and undertook explorations into the interior of Africa. He also spent a spell in the Gold Coast. However, with the support of the colonial secretary, Lord Bathurst, with whom he had ingratiated himself, Laing was sent to seek the Niger River. He was instructed to travel via Tripoli across the Sahara to Timbuktu and then on to the elusive river.

The idea prevalent in Europe at the time was of Timbuktu as a great desert metropolis and the heart of a vast trading empire. For European writers, it was an idealised, mythical site and a byword for unimaginable distance, isolation and remoteness. In 1788 the British set up 'The Association for Promoting the Discovery of the Interior Parts of Africa', which was generally known as the African Association. The association recruited a number of young British and European men – including Mungo Park, Johann Burckhardt and Friedrich Hornemann – to chart the great West African rivers and to establish the precise location of Timbuktu. The French were also active, and in December 1824 the Société de Géographie offered a prize of over 10,000 francs to the first person to provide a first-hand, verifiable and scientifically valid description of Timbuktu.

Laing decided to accept this French challenge. He arrived in Tripoli in May 1825 and fell in love with Emma, the daughter of the British consul general, Hanmer Warrington. Laing married her, and four days later, on 18 July, in the midst of the hot season, he set off southwards. With him were a guide named Sheikh Babani, two West African boat builders, a Jewish interpreter named Jacob Nahun and Laing's West African servant, Jack le Bore. Unfortunately, his companions were all to die before Laing reached Timbuktu. Laing's route was via Ghadames, now in north-western Libya, and In Salah in central Algeria. He missed his new wife and generally appears to have been depressed and neurotic. He was also worried that Clapperton, travelling from the west, might beat him to Timbuktu. He even worried about finance. In addition, Laing suffered from the usual privations of thirst and hunger.

In January 1826, beyond In Salah, the expedition was attacked by the Tuareg and Laing was fearfully wounded in 24 places. He described his injuries in his letters, though he may have exaggerated them to impress his father-in-law and his wife:

> To begin from the top, I have five saber cuts on the crown of the head & three on the left temple, all fractures from which much bone has come away, one on my left cheek which fractured the jaw bone & has divided the ear, forming a very unsightly wound, one over the right temple, and a dreadful gash on the back of the neck, which slightly scratched the windpipe; a musket ball in the hip, which made its way through my back … five saber cuts on my right arm & hand, three of the fingers broken, the hand cut three fourths across, and the wrist bones cut through; three cuts on the left arm, the bone of which as been broken, but is again uniting. One slight wound on the right leg, and … one dreadful gash on the left, to say nothing of a cut across the fingers of my left hand, now healed up.

'To begin from the top, I have five saber cuts on the crown of the head and three on the left temple...'

Laing also developed a fever and was robbed of virtually all his money. However, unlike most of his companions, he survived and on 13 August reached his destination. He had travelled some 3,600 km since leaving Tripoli. He stayed for some weeks researching old manuscripts, and then set off for the return trip home. However, just beyond Timbuktu, Laing was killed by another band of Tuareg, who it is thought either cut off his head or strangled him. His gruesome death was René Caillié's gain, for it was the latter who was awarded the Société de Géographie's prize. Unlike the Frenchman, Laing travelled as a European and a Christian, a fact that caused some British people to express their pride in Laing and their contempt for Caillié. Laing's memorial in Timbuktu describes him as the first European to reach the city, a claim that is in fact untrue, for French and Portuguese explorers had been there in previous centuries. Nonetheless, he deserved great credit for his bravery and for making one of the great journeys in the history of desert exploration.

BIBLIOGRAPHIC REFERENCES AND FURTHER READING

Fyfe, C. 2008, Laing, Alexander Gordon (1794–1826). *Oxford Dictionary of National Biography online.*
Gardner, B. 1968. *The Quest for Timbuctoo.* London; Cassell.
Hibbert, C. 1982. *Africa Explored. Europeans in the Dark Continent, 1769–1889.* London: Hamish Hamilton.
Kirk-Greene, A.H.M. 1989. *The Society and Alexander Laing, 1794–1826.* African Affairs, 88, 415–418.
Sattin, A. 2003. *The Gates of Africa. Death, Discovery and the Search for Timbuktu.* London: HarperCollins.
Wellard, J. 1964. *The Great Sahara.* London: Hutchinson.

RENÉ-AUGUSTE CAILLIÉ

RENÉ CAILLIÉ (Figure 138) was the first European to return alive from Timbuktu, a town on the south side of the Sahara in what is now Mali. Born in 1799, in France, his background was far from propitious, for his father was a drunkard and a convict. René himself was thin and frail looking. Both his parents died while he was still young and he received a limited education. However, reading of Daniel Defoe's *Robinson Crusoe* is said to have whetted his appetite for travel and in 1816, never having even been to Paris, he set out for Senegal as an officer's servant. The officer soon died but Caillié decided to remain, and made some gruelling preparatory journeys in the region. It was in 1824 that he decided to try to reach Timbuktu. He vowed to wear the clothes of a Moor and behave as a Moor, learn to speak a language the Moors would understand and how to be a good Mohammedan, and he would also travel light (Figure 139). To that end he spent eight months with the Brakna Moors, who lived north of the Senegal River. He told them he had been born in Egypt of Arab parents, but had been carried away by French soldiers who had invaded Egypt in his infancy, and that his master had bought him to Senegal. His ambition, he said, was to return to Egypt. In 1827 he set out with a Mandingo caravan across Sierra Leone and Guinea to the upper Niger at Kurussa, and on to Djenné in central Mali, whence he continued to Timbuktu by river.

Figure 138. *René Caillié (RGS: Caillié, R. 1830.* Travels through Central Africa to Timbuctoo, *volume 1, frontispiece).*

Figure 139. (above) *Caillié meditating on the Koran and taking notes (RGS: Caillié, R. 1830.* Travels through Central Africa to Timbuctoo, *volume 2, 73).*

Figure 140. (opposite) *Timbuktu as portrayed by Caillié (RGS: Caillié, R. 1830.* Travels through Central Africa to Timbuctoo, *volume 2, 75).*

Most of the route, however, he did on foot, suffering grievously from fever, an ulcerated foot and scurvy. He was forced to tarry in the village of Tiémé in north-west Ivory Coast for some time so that he could recover. He described his feelings when he realised that he had scurvy:

I soon experienced all the horrors of that dreadful disease. The roof of my mouth became quite bare, a part of the bones exfoliated and fell away, and my teeth seemed ready to drop out of their sockets. … To crown my misery, the sore in my foot broke out again and all hope of my departure vanished. … Alone in the interior of a wild country, stretched on the damp ground, with no pillow but the leather bag which contained my luggage, with no medicine. … I was soon reduced to a skeleton. … Suffering had deprived me of all energy. One thought alone absorbed my mind – that of Death. I wished for it, and prayed for it to God.

After recovering, aided by the attentions of an old negress who nursed him, he arrived in Timbuktu (Figure 140) in April 1828. Although Laing had reached Timbuktu before Caillié (in 1826), on leaving the city he had been murdered by the Tuaregs, so Caillié was the first European to travel to Timbuktu and survive. For this he received a prize of 10,000 francs from the Société de Géographie de Paris. In 1830 he published a two-volume account of his epic journey entitled *Travels through Central Africa to Timbuctoo.* To some it is a rambling and disappointing account, full of trivial detail, but it is also honest, not least about Timbuktu, and is generally informative about the people he encountered.

Timbuktu proved to be a great disappointment. It was smaller than he had expected, with, he estimated, only 10,000–12,000 inhabitants, its commerce appeared to be limited, it had poor water, was dreary, the market was inactive, and the area was terrorised by the Tuaregs.

On the other hand he liked the people, and especially the women (*Journal*, Volume 2, p. 61):

> The women of Timbuctoo are not veiled like those of Morocco: they are allowed to go out when they please, and are at liberty to see any one. The people are gentle and complaisant to strangers. In trade they are industrious and intelligent; and the traders are generally wealthy and have many slaves. The men are of the ordinary size, well made, upright, and walk with a firm step. Their colour is a fine deep black. Their noses are a little more aquiline than those of the Mandingoes, and like them they have thin lips and large eyes. I saw some women who might be considered pretty. They are all well fed: their meals, of which they take two a day, consist of rice, and couscous made of small millet, dressed with meat or dried fish. Those negroes who are in easy circumstances, like the Moors, breakfast on wheaten bread, tea, and butter made from cow's milk. Those of inferior condition use vegetable butter. … The inhabitants of Timbuctoo are exceedingly neat in their dress and in the interior of their dwellings. Their domestic articles consist of calabashes and wooden platters. They are unacquainted with the use of knives and forks, and they believe that, like them, all people in the world eat with their fingers.

Caillié noted that for the Tuaregs, the largest and fattest women were the most admired, especially those who were so obese that they were unable to walk without being supported by two assistants.

Caillié stayed in Timbuktu for two weeks and then joined a large caravan that was going north to Morocco. It took about three months to reach Fez in the north-east of the country and it was a very challenging experience, for he was subjected to periods of great thirst, to sandstorms and mirages, to insults concerning the colour of his skin, and to scorpions and snakes. He was also injured when he fell off a camel. In the south he was concerned about the Tuaregs (p.65):

'At Timbuctoo the slaves are never allowed to go out of the town after sun-set, lest they should be carried off by the Tooariks...'

These people visit Timbuctoo for the sole purpose of extorting from the inhabitants what they call presents, but what might be more properly called forced contributions. … When the chief of the Tooariks arrives with his suite at Timbuctoo, it is a general calamity, and yet every one overwhelms him with attention, and sends presents to him and his followers. He sometimes remains there two months, being maintained all that time at the expense of the inhabitants and the king, who sometimes give them really valuable presents, and they return home laden with millet, rice, honey, and preserved articles. … The Tooariks have terrified the negroes of their neighbourhood into subjection, and they inflict upon them the most cruel depredations and exactions. Like the Arabs, they have fine horses which facilitate their marauding expeditions. The people exposed to their attacks stand in such awe of them, that the appearance of three or four Tooariks is sufficient to strike terror into five or six villages. At Timbuctoo the slaves are never allowed to go out of the town after sun-set, lest they should be carried off by the Tooariks, who forcibly seize all who fall in their way. The condition of these unhappy beings is then more deplorable than ever. I saw some in the little canoes almost naked, and their masters were constantly threatening to beat them.

Caillié was graphic in his account of a sandstorm (p. 103):

On the 14th of May, a violent gale blew from the east, which unroofed several of the houses, and raised such a quantity of sand, that it was impossible to keep the doors open. The heat, though there was no sun, was stifling. The air was full of sand, which descended in the night. It would be impossible to express what I suffered during this storm. 1 was obliged to lie on the ground, with my head enveloped in a pagne, to protect myself from the burning sand, which entered through the chinks in the door. I experienced a continual thirst, and had nothing but warm and brackish water to quench it. This unwholesome drink caused a violent derangement of the stomach, and the heat, rising to a degree I had never before felt, produced a dreadful head-ache.

Mirages were also a frustration (p. 125):

In crossing the desert, I perceived, at a distance, immense tracts, which had the appearance of rivers or lakes, with islands of sand rising in the midst of them; they presented themselves to the eye, in the horizon of the desert, as places where one might quench one's thirst. This prospect broke for a time the uniformity of these vast deserts; on approaching, I was cruelly disappointed, for the water vanished, and I saw nothing but loose sand where I had hoped to quench my thirst. This illusion only rendered my situation more dreadful, when I was consumed with thirst, and saw the sea receding before me as by enchantment. It is impossible to form any correct idea of a *mirage* without having seen one.

Figure 141. (opposite) *An oasis in the far south of Morocco (author's image).*

It was a great relief to Caillié when they reached the oases of southern Morocco (Figure 141), where he made interesting observations on the Jewish people of Tafilet (p. 188):

> The Jews of Tafilet are excessively dirty, and always go barefoot, perhaps to avoid the inconvenience of frequently taking off their sandals, which they are compelled to do in passing before a mosque or the door of a sherif. … They shave their heads after the example of the Moors, but leave a tuft of hair which falls over the forehead. Some are pedlars, others artisans; they manufacture shoes and mats from palm leaves; some of them also are blacksmiths. They lend their money upon usury to the merchants trading in the Soudan, whither they never go themselves. … Money is always plentiful with the Jews: yet they affect the utmost poverty; because the Moors, who ascribe to them greater riches than they really possess, often persecute them for the purpose of extorting their gold. … The Jews live better than the Mahometans, couscous and gruel forming but a small portion of their food; their bread is of wheat, kneaded and baked by themselves and their principal beverage, beer of their own brewing, though in the season of the vintage they make a little wine. … The Jewesses whom I have seen in Tafilet are in general small, lively, and pretty: they have blue eyes, animated and expressive, aquiline nose, and a mouth of middling size ; they are inquisitive, and very fond of talking. Drawing water, washing linen, fetching wood for cooking, in short all the household labours, fall to their share.

Back in France, Caillié got married, took up farming and sired four children in quick succession. A man who exuded goodwill and stoicism, he died in the Charente-Maritime region of France in 1838, aged 38, from consumption and a recurrent fever caught in Africa. His account of Timbuktu encouraged later explorers, including Heinrich Barth.

BIBLIOGRAPHIC REFERENCES AND FURTHER READING

Caillié, R. 1830. *Travels through Central Africa to Timbuctoo; and across the Great Desert to Morocco; performed in the years 1824–1828.* 2 volumes. London: Colburn and Bentley.

Gardner, B. 1968. *The Quest for Timbuctoo.* London: Cassell.

Heffernan, M. 2001. "A dream as frail as those of ancient Time": the in-credible geographies of Timbuctoo. *Environment and Planning*, D, 19, 203–225.

Hibbert, C. 1982. *Africa Explored. Europeans in the Dark Continent, 1769–1889.* London: Hamish Hamilton.

HEINRICH BARTH

HEINRICH BARTH (Figure 142), born in Hamburg in 1821 and educated at the University of Berlin, was one of the most notable Saharan explorers. Unlike many of the great explorers he was essentially a scholar and linguist who had been stimulated by such great German geographers as Alexander von Humboldt and Karl Ritter. Moreover, he did not return from his travels with a slim journal merely cataloguing his route, events and a few meteorological statistics. He produced a large five-volume account, which though somewhat dull, is a masterpiece of geographical, historical, anthropological and philological research. He was also notable for his generally sympathetic attitude to the people through whose lands he travelled. He had great strength and physical stature, being well over six feet (1.8 m) tall. He was also stubborn, thorough, did not suffer fools gladly, and was humourless but mentally tough, which he needed to be, for his longest journey lasted five years and five months and involved a distance of 16,000–19,000 km.

After studying Arabic in London, Barth embarked on his first African journey in 1845, heading from Tangier to Egypt, up the Nile to Wadi Halfa, and then to Sinai, Syria, Turkey and Greece. In 1849 Barth joined the quaintly named Mixed Scientific and Commercial Expedition to Central Africa. At the request of British foreign secretary Lord Palmerston, the expedition was commanded by Captain James Richardson, a fervent anti-slavery campaigner who had already crossed the Sahara to Ghat, and also included a noted German geologist and astronomer, Adolf Overweg. The three men left Tripoli in the spring of 1850 and passing through Murzuk, reached the Tuareg town of Tin Tellust in the autumn. They passed through the Tassili n-Ajjer and Aïr mountains and made a detour to the decayed city of Agadez. In January 1851 they reached Damergou, which lies on the south side of the Sahara proper. At this point Barth and Overweg parted ways from Richardson (an unpredictable and autocratic leader), but planned to reunite with him on the shores of Lake Chad. In the event this was not possible, for Richardson was shortly to die from fever and exhaustion, in March 1851. Barth and Overweg also split up, with Barth heading off towards Kano, a city in what is now northern Nigeria. Overweg also died from malaria in September 1852 near Lake Chad. From Kano and Kukawa, Barth travelled to the Niger and reached Timbuktu in September 1853, having compared the people of Kano and Bornou (Borno) (*Travels*, 1890 edn., p. 385):

There is a great difference of character between these two towns. … The Bornu people are by temperament far more phlegmatic than those of Kano. The women in general are much more ugly, with square short figures, large heads, and broad noses, with immense nostrils, disfigured still more by the enormity of a red bead or coral worn in the nostril. Nevertheless they are certainly quite as coquettish, and, as far as I had occasion to observe, at least as wanton also, as the more cheerful and sprightly Hausa women.

'The women in general are much more ugly, with square short figures, large heads, and broad noses, with immense nostrils, disfigured still more by the enormity of a red bead or coral worn in the nostril.'

To reach Timbuktu (Figure 143), Barth assumed the guise of a travelling Muslim by the name of Abd el Kerim. He stayed there until March the following year, before returning to Kukawa. He then went back across the Sahara to Tripoli, travelling in the heat of summer, and reached the city in August 1855.

Barth was prone to self-congratulation, as is evident in the last paragraph of his *Travels* (1890 edn. p. 545):

I succeeded to my utmost expectation, and not only made known the whole of that vast region, which even to the Arab merchants in general had remained more unknown than any

Figure 142. (opposite) *Heinrich Barth (RGS).*

Figure 143. *Barth's caravan entering Timbuktoo. (Engraving by Eberhard Emminger (1808-85). From Denham, D. 1828. Narrative of Travels and Discoveries in Northern and Central Africa in the Years 1822, 1823 and 1824. 3rd Edition. London: John Murray.*

other part of Africa, but I succeeded also in establishing relations with all the most powerful chiefs. … I have the satisfaction to feel that I have opened to the view of the scientific public a most extensive tract of the secluded African world, and not only made it tolerably known, but rendered the opening of a regular intercourse between Europeans and those regions possible.

The Geographical Society awarded him its Patron's Medal in 1856, and Oxford gave him an honorary degree, but Barth died of a stomach disorder, probably a result of his great journey, in Berlin in 1865, aged just 44.

Prothero (1958) summarised Barth's significance thus:

He had been away for nearly five and a half years and during that time had travelled a total distance of over 10,000 miles. His single most important discovery was of the upper reaches of the River Benue; second to this were his journeys between Sokoto and Timbuktu. In the course of the latter he had spent a longer time in Timbuktu than René Caillié, the only European previously to visit the city and return alive. On his return journey from Timbuktu to Say along the Niger valley he was passing through country seen previously by Mungo Park, whose death further downstream had prevented any report of it from reaching the outside world. Between Kukawa and Sokoto the country had been traversed by Clapperton and in part by Richard Lander, but knowledge of it was advanced greatly by Barth's observations. Even though he made no startling original discoveries the range of his journeys was immense. What is most important is that he recorded in great detail all that he saw and heard. The immense industry displayed in his journals is amazing.

BIBLIOGRAPHIC REFERENCES AND FURTHER READING

Barth, H. 1890. *Travels* (p. 385). London: Ward Lock and Co.

Barth, H. 1890. *Travels* (p. 545). London: Ward Lock and Co.

Gardner, B. 1968. *The Quest for Timbuctoo.* London: Cassell.

Hibbert, C. 1982. *Africa Explored. Europeans in the Dark Continent, 1769–1889.* London: Hamish Hamilton.

Marozzi, J. 2010. Heinrich Barth. Crossing the Sahara (1821–1865). In R. Hanbury-Prothero, R.M. 1958. Heinrich Barth and the Western Sudan. *Geographical Journal*, 124, 326–337.

Tenison (ed) *The Great Explorers.* London: Thames and Hudson, 196–203.

Wellard, J. 1964. *The Great Sahara.* London: Hutchinson.

HENRI DUVEYRIER

Figure 144. *Henri Duveyrier (RGS: Duveyrier, H. 1864. Les Toureg du Nord, frontispiece).*

HENRI DUVEYRIER (Figure 144), born of mixed English and French parentage in Paris in 1840, had a very brief and very precocious career as a Saharan explorer, and is most notable for his respect for and ethnographic descriptions of the Tuareg. In 1857, after an education that took place in France, England, Italy, Switzerland and Germany, he travelled to Algeria, where he made a life-changing tour of Laghouat Province with Irishman Oscar MacCarthy. It was on this short tour that Duveyrier encountered the Tuareg, 'the people of the veil'.

On his return he visited Heinrich Barth in London to seek advice and information so that he could undertake a more ambitious and extensive journey. In 1859, aged only 19, Duveyrier once more set foot in Algeria and became the first European to visit the oasis of El Goléa. He also visited Ghadames, Gat and Murzuk in the deep south of Fezzan Province (in present-day Libya).

Duveyrier praised the virtues of the Tuareg. As Douglas Porch (*The Conquest of the Sahara*, 1985, p. 73) wrote:

Of all the European travellers, Henri Duveryier was the most impressed by the Tuareg. His description of the virtues of this noble race read like a cross between Sir Walter Scott and the Boy Scout Handbook: brave, hospitable, faithful, patient, tolerant of the defects of others, industrious, charitable, magnanimous, haters of oppression, and so on. The list is virtually inexhaustible. It was almost too good to be true. It *was* too good to be true.

Here are some quotes (translated) from his *Exploration du Sahara. Les Touareg du Nord* (p. 382 and 386):

> In general, the Tuareg are tall, some even seem real giants. All are lean, lean, sinewy, and their muscles seem steel springs. … The Caucasian type is that of their faces: face oval and elongated in some, in others round: wide forehead, dark eyes, small nose, high cheekbones, average mouth, thin lips, white teeth and beautiful, where such have not been decayed by the use of natron, and rare black beard, black hair and smooth. Some have blue eyes, but this nuance is found infrequently. Eyes, in all people who are over forty years, seem veiled and obscure. This effect is due to the intensity of the light and to the action of solar reverberation. Many are blind or become blind before old age. The trunk, both in men than in women, is largely developed. The upper and lower limbs, elongated, muscular, ending in small and shapely hands and feet. … Men are generally strong, robust, indefatigable, though their average power is much lower than the European. … Women, too are big, have an arrogant carriage and are usually beautiful. … Their appearance, however, is much closer to the European women than Arab women. A physical trait that a Touareg can recognize from a mile, is the attitude of his approach: serious, slow, jerky, striding, head erect, which attitude is reminiscent of the ostrich or camel walk, but that is mainly due to the habitual use of the spear. The bravery of the Touareg is proverbial. Whatever has been said, they do not poison their arrows or their spears; they disdain the use of firearms, which they call *weapons of treachery*, because a man hiding behind a bush can kill his opponent without running any risk. Defence of their hosts and their clients is still the supreme virtue of the Tuareg.

'The bravery of the Touareg is proverbial. Whatever has been said, they do not poison their arrows or their spears; they disdain the use of firearms, which they call *weapons of treachery...*'

However, the book is not only about the Tuareg. The first 245 pages give a comprehensive account of the physical geography of the area, its hydrography, geology, meteorology, astronomy, vegetation and wildlife (including lake crocodiles). The detail given and the observations made are spectacular in quantity, quality and breadth, which is remarkable for one so young. There are, for example, descriptions of the different types of dune, including linear seifs and star dunes, a discussion of the area they cover, and the direction of the winds that shape them. Duveyrier argued that the sand was the product of the intense disintegration of the desert surface brought about by temperature changes and other processes. He also appreciated the importance of the floods from the central Saharan mountains:

'The action of the water was enough to prompt a Nezla (tribe) full, camped at the mouth of two valleys, perished with all hands.'

We judge the action of the water by the following facts: In the spring of 1862, a rainstorm fell on the western slopes of the Ahaggar brought so much water in the valleys of Idjeloùdjàl and they led Tarhit part of the mountain. The action of the water was enough to prompt a Nezla (tribe) full, camped at the mouth of two valleys, perished with all hands. Thirty-four people and a large number of camels were drowned. A camel which was grazing quietly on the portion of the mountain washed away, was recovered unharmed, three days after the event, to a considerable distance, on the ground where she had been surprised and, after a long voyage, had come ashore on a bank of the wadi.

Duveyrier made two more journeys to North Africa in 1885 and 1886, but he shot himself in 1892 with his own revolver in the woods near his home in Sèvres, after suffering from depression that may have been linked with French colonial policy and aggressive European imperial expansion.

BIBLIOGRAPHIC REFERENCES AND FURTHER READING

Duveyrier, H. 1864. *Exploration du Sahara. Les Touareg du Nord.* Paris: Challamel aîné.
Heffernan, M. 1989. The limits of Utopia: Henri Duveyrier and the exploration of the Sahara in the nineteenth century. *Geographical Journal*, 155, 342–352.
Porch, D. 1985. *The Conquest of the Sahara.* London: Jonathan Cape.
Wellard, J. 1964. *The Great Sahara.* London: Hutchinson.

GEORGES-MARIE HAARDT
AND LOUIS AUDOUIN-DUBREUIL

GEORGES-MARIE HAARDT, though born in Naples in 1884, to Belgian parents, became a French citizen in 1914. Louis Audouin-Dubreuil was born in France in 1887. They joined forces to become two of the most important experimenters in the use of the motor car for desert exploration. Before their exploits, other Frenchmen had attempted forays into the Sahara by car, often with the encouragement of General François-Henry Laperrine, himself a pioneer motorist, but they had not been successful.

In 1922 André-Gustave Citroën, the innovative French carmaker, planned and organized what the French called a 'raid' across the Sahara, the object being to test his newly derived 'caterpillar' cars and to link the French Niger River and Mediterranean territories. The Citroën works produced a small fleet of 10-horsepower tractor cars (Figure 145), armed with aeroplane machine guns in case of attack from the untamed inhabitants of the desert. The expedition set off from the railhead at Touggourt (northern Algeria) on 17 December 1922 (Figure 146). They passed through In Salah and Tamanrasset in the Hoggar Mountains, before reaching the Niger at the town of Bourem. All five cars entered Timbuktu, their destination, on January 7 1923, just 20 days after setting out and having traversed around 3,500 km of immense terrain. With much Gallic pomp and ceremony, the first trans-Saharan mail delivered by car was handed over to Colonel Mangeot, the local regional commander. An immense crowd that had gathered under conditions of stifling heat greeted the occasion with thunderous applause. It was 'a motley crowd of all the races of the Soudan, from the veiled Tuareg, the Berabishes and the Moors with pointed profiles and long fuzzy hair to the negroes with enormous muscles, whose naked flesh

Figure 145. *The Citroens (RGS: Haardt and Audouin-Dubreuil. 1924.* Across the Sahara by Motor car: from Touggourt to Timbuctoo. *London: T. Fisher Unwin).*

exhaled the curious odour of stags.' (Haardt and Audouin-Dubreuil, *Across the Sahara by Motor car*, p. 129).

A fast camel caravan would have needed at least six months to accomplish the same crossing (Wellard, *The Great Sahara*, p. 308). The rubber caterpillar tracks were designed by Adolphe Kégresse and the team was led by Haardt, by then general manager of the Citroën factories. Audouin-Dubreuil, who had commanded a group of machine gun cars attached to the Saharian squadrons in southern Tunisia, was his deputy. Among those who also completed the crossing was the expedition mascot, Flossie, a Sealyham Terrier. Between 28 October 1924 and 26 June 1925, and encouraged by the success of this first 'raid', Citroëns accomplished a crossing of Africa from Algeria, all the way to the Cape of Good Hope. This was dubbed the Croisière Noire. Later they drove to China on what was called the Croisière Jaune.

The Citroëns and their rubber caterpillar tracks were not without their problems. As C.S Jarvis (Three Deserts, p. 106) remarked:

They were the last word in desert transport in those days, as they would climb any sand-dune and, despite the small size of their engines, could develop enough power to drag another car out of the sand. But they had two great disadvantages – they could never travel faster than fifteen miles an hour even in good going, and their cooling apparatus was not up to the heat developed by the engine, so that they consumed vast quantities of water.

In addition, the rubber tracks had a limited life, fuel consumption was high, and they had little advantage over hard surfaces. For the most part the British preferred Fords, and the Italians preferred Fiats. Curiously, the Germans never produced anything very good. As for the French, they soon abandoned the Citroen half-tracks and opted first for six-wheeler trucks and cars, and then for four wheelers with balloon tyres.

Haardt died in 1932, in Hong Kong of pneumonia contracted during the Croisière Jaune. Audouin-Dubreuil lived for many years in Zarzis, Tunisia, and died there in 1960.

BIBLIOGRAPHIC REFERENCES AND FURTHER READING

Haardt, G.M. and Audouin-Dubreuil, L. 1924. *Across the Sahara by Motor car: from Touggourt to Timbuctoo*. London: T. Fisher Unwin.

Jarvis, C.S. 1936. *Three Deserts*. London: John Murray.

Nöther, W. 2003. *Die Erschliessung der Sahara durch Motorfahrzeuge 1901–1936*. Munich: Belleville.

Thomas, B.E. 1952. Modern Trans-Saharan Routes. *Geographical Review*, 42, 267–282.

Wellard, J. 1964. *The Great Sahara*. London: Hutchinson.

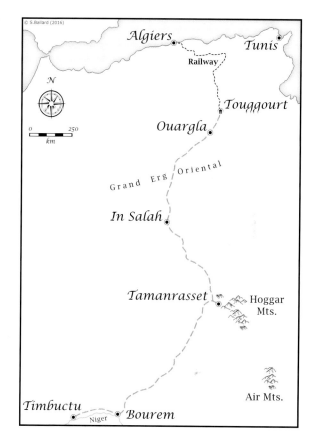

Figure 146. *The route of the first crossing of the Sahara by motor car. (Map drawn by Sebastian Ballard).*

THÉODORE ANDRÉ MONOD

THÉODORE MONOD was undoubtedly the greatest French desert naturalist of the twentieth century. Born in Rouen in April 1902, the son of Wilfred Monod, he attended the city's Lycée Pierre Corneille. His father was a pastor of the Temple Protestant de l'Oratoire du Louvre which Theodore also attended. He remained a devout Christian throughout his life.

Théodore went to the Ecole Alsacienne, a Protestant foundation, and at the age of 15, started a school newspaper with some friends. This touched on many topics, and included articles about caterpillars and kingfishers. He went on to take a degree in Natural Science at Paris University and, almost immediately afterwards, was appointed to a post at the Muséum National d'Histoire Naturelle in the capital. His travels (Figure 147) began in 1922, when, aged 20, he was sent by the museum on a research expedition to Mauritania. His brief was to study the fish in the region of the port of Nouadhibou. He found himself, as he put it, between two oceans – the water where he searched and the sands and the rocks of the desert which he contemplated. After a year, instead of returning to France, he extended his trip and headed south by camel to Nouakchott, on the Atlantic coast. Made by mehari camel, the journeys were termed *meharées*.

In 1927 Monod was chosen to take part in a scientific expedition across the Sahara, from Algiers to Dakar via Timbuktu. One of his best-known discoveries in what is now northern Mali's Kidal region was the skeleton of Asselar Man, dating back to the Neolithic. When on military service in a mobile camel corps at Hoggar, Algeria, in 1928–29, Monod wrote a book on the archaeology of Ahnet, where he had discovered rock drawings and pottery. Between March 1934 and June 1935, he carried out a large-scale expedition across the western Sahara during which he visited for the first time the circular feature Guelb er Richat, also known as the Eye of the Sahara, in the Adrar massif of Mauritania.

In 1938 Monod moved to Dakar as director of the newly created Institut Français d'Afrique Noire. Two years later, after the outbreak of the Second World War, in spite of his pacifism, he was ordered to spy on Italian military installations. His mission led to an expedition into the Libyan Desert, where he found more satisfaction in exploring than in observing the movements of Italian army trucks. Nevertheless, his account of the geography of northern Tibesti proved of value to the Long Range Desert Group.

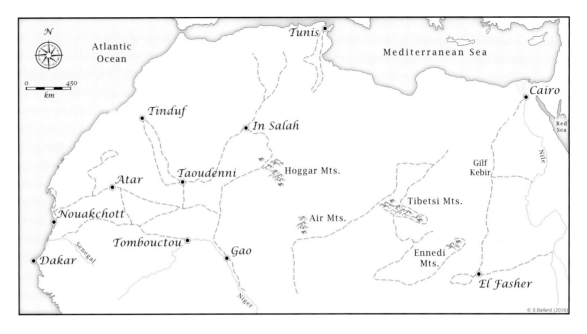

Figure 147. *The routes of Monod in the Sahara (Map drawn by Sebastian Ballard).*

Between 1953 and 1964, he organized six expeditions to Majabat al-Kubra, a huge sand-covered area, half the size of France, lying between Mauritania and Mali.

Truly a polymath, on his many journeys, he studied a vast range of topics, including meteorite craters, dunes, stratigraphy, the travels of Alexander Gordon Laing, prehistory, rock art, pastoralism, zoology and botany, Libyan Desert Glass and the lost oasis of Zerzura. He wrote detailed studies of parts of the Sahara, including a monograph on the Majabat al-Koubra, an enormous work full of information on all aspects of the region, including its dunes. Remarkably, between 1916 (he he started writing while at school) and 2000, he published 1881 volumes, summaries, articles and memoirs, including nearly 700 dedicated to the natural sciences. He accumulated over 20,000 samples during his travels. Two genera and 35 plant species, and eight genera and 130 animal species are named after him. Popular accounts of his travels are presented in *Méharées – Explorations au vrai Sahara* (1937) and *L'Emeraude des Garamantes. Souvenirs d'un Saharien* (1984).

Monod spoke out regularly against pollution, and took stands on many subjects besides. He was fiercely outspoken on animal rights and on the question of hunting. A strict vegetarian, he once trekked 1,000 km in the Sahara without visiting a single water hole to prove that he had sufficient stamina to do so without eating meat. He styled himself a humanist and a pacifist, declaring that he was 'violently non-violent'. Other protests he was involved in ranged from attacks on the drink and tobacco industries, bullfighting, nuclear power, child slavery, world hunger, environmental damage and poverty, fascism and French policy in Algeria. Some of his mature musings on such matters are discussed in *Terre et Ciel* (1997).

Monod loathed the petrol engine and as a consequence was particularly unhappy about the annual Paris–Dakar motor rally in which dozens of rugged vehicles roared through the Sahara, churning up the sands. He believed that the only transport compatible with desert life was the camel, travelling at three miles an hour.

For his explorations and scientific work he was awarded a gold medal by the Royal Geographical Society in 1960, and was also recognized by the American and French geographical societies. He dismounted a camel for the last time on 9 January 1994. He was then 91. He died at Versailles, near Paris, in November 2000, aged 98.

BIBLIOGRAPHIC REFERENCES AND FURTHER READING

Hall, D.N. 2001. Théodore Monod, 1902–2000. *Geographical Journal*, 167, 191–192.

Hureau, J. C. (2001). Un exceptionnel naturaliste éclectique. *Autres Temps. Cahiers d'éthique sociale et politique*, 70(1), 25–38.

Jarry, I. 2001. *Théodore Monod*. Paris: Payot.

Monod, T. 1928. Une traversée de la Mauritanie occidentale. *Revue de Géographie Physique et de Géologie Dynamique* 1, 3–25, 88–106.

Monod, T. 1932. L'*Adrar Ahnet – Contribution à l'étude archéologique d'un District Saharien*, Paris: Institut d'Ethnologie.

Monod, T. 1937. *Méharées – Explorations au vrai Sahara*. Paris.

Monod, T. 1958. Majâbat Al-Koubrâ. *Memoirs de L'Institut Français D'Afrique Noire*, 52, 406 pp.

Monod, T. 1984. *L'Emeraude des Garamantes. Souvenirs d'un Saharien*. Paris: Harmattan.

Monod, T. 1997. *Terre et Ciel*. Arles: Actes Sud.

Monod, T. and Diemer, E. 2000. *Zerzura: L'Oasis Légendaire du Désert Libyque*. Paris: Editions Vent de Sable.

BIBLIOGRAPHY

GENERAL READING ON DESERTS

Giles, E. 1889. *Australia Twice Traversed; The Romance of Exploration, Being a Narrative Compiled from the Journals of Five Exploring Expeditions into and Through Central South Australia and Western Australia, from 1872 to 1876.* London: Sampson Low, Marston, Searle and Rivington.

Goudie, A.S. 2002. *Great Warm Deserts of the World.* Oxford: Oxford University Press.

Goudie, A.S. 2013. *Arid and Semi-arid Geomorphology.* New York: Cambridge University Press.

Hassanein, Ahmed. 1925. *The Lost Oases.*

Ives, J.C. 1861. *Report upon the Colorado river of the west.* Washiongton, D.C., Government Printing Office.

Laity, J. 2008. *Deserts and Desert Environments.* Chicheser; Wiley-Blackwell.

Manley, D. 1991. *The Nile. A Traveller's Anthology.* London: Cassell.

Mason, Michael. 1936. *The Paradise of Fools: Being an Account, by a Member of the Party, of the Expedition which Covered 6,300 Miles of the Libyan Desert by Motor-car in 1935.* London: Hodder and Stoughton.

Moorehead, Alan. 1963. *Cooper's Creek.* London: Harper & Row.

Nicholson, S. 2011. *Dryland Climatology.* Cambridge: Cambridge University Press.

Parsons, A.J. and Abrahams, A.D. (eds) 2009. *Geomorphology of Desert Environments* (2nd edition). Springer.

Porch, D. 1984. *The Conquest of the Sahara.* London: Jonathan Cape.

Reclus, É. 1871. *The Earth: A descriptive history of the phenomena of the life of the globe.* London: Chapman & Hall.

Somerville, M. 1858. *Physical Geography.* London: John Murray.

Thomas, D.S.G. (ed.) 2011. *Arid Zone Geomorphology.* Chichester: Wiley Blackwell.

Welland, M. 2015. *The Desert. Lands of Lost Borders.* London: Reaktion Books.

FULL BIBLIOGRAPHY

Al-Hajri, H.S. 2003. *Oman through British Eyes: British Travel Writing on Oman from 1800 to 1970* (Doctoral dissertation, University of Warwick).

Al Yahya, E. 2006. *Travellers in Arabia. British Explorers in Saudi Arabia.* London: Stacey International.

Almásy L. 1934. *The Unknown Sahara* (p. 6–7). Budapest: Franklin Tarsulat.

Almásy, L. 1939. *Unbekannte Sahara.* Leipzig: Brockhaus.

Almásy, L. 2001. *With Rommel's Army in Libya* (p. xii). Bloomington, Indiana: 1st Books Library.

Andrews, R.C. 1927. Explorations in Mongolia: a review of the Central Asiatic Expeditions of the American Museum of Natural History. *Geographical Journal*, 69, 1–19.

Anon. 1885. Dr Gustav Nachtigal. *Proceedings of the Royal Geographical Society of London and Monthly Record of Geography*, 7, 466.

Anon. 1902. Obituary: Edward John Eyre. *Geographical Journal*, 19, 99–100.

Anon, 1941. Obituary: Dr John Ball. *Geographical Journal*, 98, 301–303.

Bagnold, R.A. (1933). A Further Journey Through the Libyan Desert. *The Geographical Journal*, 82(2), 103–126.

Bagnold, R.A. 1935. *Libyan Sands* (p. 95). London: Hodder and Stoughton.

Bagnold, R.A. 1941. *Physics of Blown Sand and Desert Dunes*. London: Methuen.

Bagnold, R.A. 1990. *Sand, Wind and War. Memoirs of a Desert Explorer*. Tucson: University of Arizona Press.

Baigent, E. 2004. Bankes, William John (1786–1855). *Oxford Dictionary of National Biography online*.

Bald, M. 2010. *From the Sahara to Samarkand. Selected Travel Writings of Rosita Forbes, 1919–1937*. Mount Jackson, VA: Axios Press.

Ball, J. 1917. *Desert reconnaissance by motorcar. Primarily a handbook for patrol-officers in Western Egypt*. Western Frontier Force. 49 pp. MS in Royal Geographical Society.

Ball, J. 1924. Note on the cartographical results of Hassanein Bey's journey. *Geographical Journal*, 64, 367–386.

Ball, J. 1927. Problems of the Libyan Desert. *Geographical Journal*, 70, 21–38, 105–118, 209–224.

Ballard, J.S. 2000. Andrews, Roy Chapman. *American National Biography online*.

Barth, H. 1890. *Travels* (p. 385). London: Ward Lock and Co.

Barth, H. 1890. *Travels* (p. 545). London: Ward Lock and Co.

Beale, E. 1979. *Chipped Idol. A Study of Charles Sturt the Explorer*. Sydney: Sydney University Press.

Bell, G. 1907. *The Desert and the Sown*. New York: E.P. Dutton.

Bell, G. 1911. *Amurath to Amurath*. London: William Heinemann.

Benson, L.K. 2008. *Across China's Gobi*. Norwalk, CT: EastBridge.

Bermudez, O. 1975. Esbozo biografico de William Bollaert. *Norte Grande*, 1, 313–318.

Beuk, G. 2012. Arthur Weigall: a man out of time. *Egyptological* (http://www.egyptological.com/2012/02/arthur-weigall-a-man-out-of-time-part1-7525) and (http://www.egyptological.com/2012/02/arthur-weigall-a-man-out-of-time-part2-8394).

Bevis, R. 1972. Spiritual Geology: C.M. Doughty and the Land of the Arabs. *Victorian Studies*, 163–181.

Bey, H. 1925. *The Lost Oases*. London: Thomas Butterworth.

Bierman, J. 2004. *The Secret Life of Laszlo Almasy*. London: Viking.

Blanch, L. 1954. *The Wilder Shores of Love*. New York: Carroll and Graf.

Blunt, A. 1879. *Bedouin Tribes of the Euphrates*. London: John Murray.

Blunt, A. 1881. A Pilgrimage to Nejd, the Cradle of the Arab Race. London: John Murray.

Blunt, W.S. 1880. A visit to Jebel Shammar (Nejd). New routes through Northern and Central Arabia. *Proceedings of the Royal Geographical Society and Monthly Record of Geography*, 2, 81–102.

Bollaert, W. 1851. Observations on the Geography of Southern Peru, including survey of the Province of Tarapaca, and route to Chile by the coast of the Desert of Atacama. *Journal of the Royal Geographical Society*, 21, 99–130.

Bollaert, W. 1854. Observations on the history of the Incas of Peru, on the Indians of South Peru, and on some Indian remains in the Province of Tarapaca. *Journal of the Ethnological Society of London*, 3, 132–164.

Bollaert, W. 1867/8, Additional notes on the Geography of southern Peru. *Proceedings of the Royal Geographical Society of London*, 12, 126–134.

Brent, P. 1978. *Far Arabia. Explorers of the Myth*. Newton Abbot: Readers Union.

Brinton, J. 1969. *Wreck on the Tigris*. Saudi Aramco World, 20, 24–29.

Brodie, F.M. 1967. *The Devil Drives*. London: Eyre & Spottiswoode.

Brower, D. 1994. Imperial Russia and its

orient: the renown of Nikolai Przhevalsky. *Russian Review*, 53, 367–381.

Browne, W.G. 1799. *Travels in Africa, Egypt and Syria, from the Years 1792 to 1798*. London: Adell and Davies.

Bruce-Lockhart, I. and Wright, J. 2000 *Difficult and Dangerous Roads*. London: Sickle Moon Books.

Burckhardt, J.L. 1819. *Travels in Nubia*. London: John Murray.

Burckhardt, J.L. 1822. *Travels in Syria and the Holy Land*. London: John Murray.

Burckhardt, J.L.1829. *Travels in Arabia*. London: John Murray.

Burnes, A. 1833. Substance of a geographical memoir on the Indus. *Journal of the Royal Geographical Society*, 3, 113–156.

Burnes, A. 1834. Papers descriptive of the countries on the North-West Frontier of India: The Thurr, or Desert: Joodpoor and Jaysulmeer. *Journal of the Royal Geographical Society*, 4, 88–129.

Burnes, A. 1834. *Travels into Bokhara 1831–33*. London: John Murray.

Burnes, A. 1834. Memoir on the Eastern Branch of the River Indus, giving an account of the alterations produced on it by an earthquake, also a theory of the formation of the Runn, and some conjectures on the route of Alexander the Great; drawn up in the years 1827–1828. *Transactions of the Royal Asiatic Society of Great Britain and Ireland*, 3, 550–588.

Burnes, A. 1837. On Sind. *Journal of the Royal Geographical Society*, 7, 11–20.

Burton, R.F. 1854. Journey to Medina, with route from Yambu. *Journal of the Royal Geographical Society of London*, 24, 208–225.

Burton, R.F. 1874. *Personal Narrative of a Pilgrimage to Mecca and Medina*. B. Tauchnitz.

Bustard, L. 1990. The ugliest plant in the world. The story of *Welwitschia mirabilis*. *Curtis's Botanical Magazine*, 7, 85–90.

Cable, M. and French, E. 1942. *The Gobi Desert*. London: Hodder and Stoughton.

Cable, M. 1942. A new era in the Gobi. *Geographical Journal*, 100, 193–205.

Caillié, R. 1830. *Travels through Central Africa to Timbuctoo; and across the Great Desert to Morocco; performed in the years 1824–1828*. 2 volumes. London: Colburn and Bentley.

Canton, J. 2011. *From Cairo to Baghdad. British Travellers in Arabia*. London: I.B. Tauris.

Cardona, M.K. (2012). Alexine Tinné: Nineteenth-Century Explorer of Africa. *Terrae Incognitae*, 44(2), 124–138.

Chaffin, T. 2002. *Pathfinder. John Charles Frémont and the Course of American Empire*. Norman: University of Oklahoma Press.

Chappell, J.E. 1970. Climate change reconsidered: another look at "The Pulse of Asia". *Geographical Review*, 60, 347–373.

Chesney, F.R. 1868. *Narrative of the Euphrates Expedition*. London: Longmans Green.

Christie, T.L. 1967. Shaikh Burckhardt: explorer. *Saudi Aramco World*, 18 (5), 15–17.

Clifford, B.E.H. 1929. A journey by motor lorry from Mahalapye through the Kalahari Desert. *Geographical Journal*, 73, 342–358.

Clifford, B.E.H. 1930. A reconnaissance of the Great Makarikari Lake. *Geographical Journal*, 75, 16–26.

Clifford, B.E.H. 1938. Across the Great Makarikari Salt Lake. *Geographical Journal*, 91, 233–241.

Cotton, H.E.A. (1921). Tod's Rajasthan Annals and Antiquities of Rajasthan, or the Central and Western Rajput States of India. By Lieut.-Col. James Tod, late Political Agent to the Western Rajput States. Edited, with an introduction and notes, by William Crooke. *Bulletin of the School of Oriental and African Studies*, 2, 139–145.

Cowan, R.S. 2005. Galton, Sir Francis (1822–1911). *Oxford Dictionary of National Biography online*.

Cox, F.J. 1952. Munzinger's observations on the Sudan, 1871. *Sudan Notes and Records*, 33, 189–201.

Craig, J. 2008. Philby, Harry St John Bridger (1885–1960). *Oxford Dictionary of National Biography online*.

Crowley, F.K. 'Forrest, Sir John (1847–1918)', Australian Dictionary of Biography, National Centre of Biography, Australian National University, http://adb.anu.edu.au/biography/forrest-sir-john-6211/text10677, published in hardcopy 1981, accessed online 22 April 2014.

Cumpston, J.H.L. 1951. *Charles Sturt. His Life and Journeys of Exploration*. Melbourne: Georgian House.

Curzon, G.N. 1889. *Russia in Central Asia in 1889 and the Anglo-Russian Question*. London: Longmans, Green and Co.

Curzon, G.N. 1892. *Persia and the Persian Question*. 2 vols. London: Longmans, Green and Co.

Curzon, G.N. 1896a. The Pamirs and the source of the Oxus. *Geographical Journal*, 8, 1: 15–54; 2: 97–119; 3: 239–64.

Curzon, G.N. 1896b. Makran. *Geographical Journal*, 7, 5: 557.

Darlow, M. and Bray, B. 2010. *Ibn Saud. The Desert Warrior and his Legacy*. London: Quartet Books.

Davidson, K. 2000. Huntington, Ellsworth. *American National Biography online*.

De Cosson, A. 1935. *Mareotis*. London: Country Life.

De Villers, M. and Hirtle, S. 2003. *Sahara. The Life of the Great Desert*. London: HarperCollins.

Deasey, D. Warburton, Peter Egerton (1813–1889), *Australian Dictionary of Biography*, National Centre of Biography, Australian National University, http://adb.anu.edu.au/biography/warburton-peter-egerton-4798/text7993, published in hardcopy 1976, accessed online 22 April 2014.

Denham, D. 1828. *Narrative of Travels and Discoveries in Northern and Central Africa in the Years 1822, 1823 and 1824*. 3rd edition. London: John Murray.

Doughty, C.M. 1888. *Arabia Deserta*. Cambridge: Cambridge University Press.

Dutton G. 'Eyre, Edward John (1815–1901)', *Australian Dictionary of Biography*, National Centre of Biography, Australian National University, http://adb.anu.edu.au/biography/eyre-edward-john-2032/text2507, published in hardcopy 1966, accessed online 22 April 2014.

Duveyrier, H. 1864. *Exploration du Sahara. Les Touareg du Nord*. Paris: Challamel aîné.

Edwards, F.M. 1957. George Forster Sadleir. *Journal of the Royal Central Asian Society*, 44, 38–49.

Egan, F. 1977. *Fremont, Explorer for a Restless Nation*. Reno: University of Nevada Press.

Esch, H. von der 1944. *Weenak – die Karavane ruft*. Leipzig: Brockhaus.

Eyre, E.J. 1845. *Journals of Expeditions of Discovery into Central Australia and Overland from Adelaide to King George's Sound in the year 1840–1*. London: T. and W. Boone.

Eyre, E.J. 1846. Considerations against the supposed existence of a Great Sea in the interior of Australia. *Journal of the Royal Geographical Society of London*, 16, 200–211.

Fancher, R.E. 1982. Galton in Africa. *American Psychologist*, 37, 713–714.

Farini, G.A. 1886. A recent journey in the Kalahari. *Proceedings of the Royal Geographical Society*, 8, 437–453.

Farini, G.A. 1886. *Through the Kalahari Desert. A Narrative of a Journey with Gun, Camera and Notebook to Lake N'Gami and back (1886)*. New York: Scribner and Welford.

Fitzpatrick, K. 1969. Burke, Robert O'Hara (1821–1861). *Australian Dictionary of Biography*, Volume 3, Melbourne University Press, pp. 301–303.

Flannery, T. (1998). *The Explorers. Stories of Discovery and Adventure from the Australian Frontier*. New York: Grove Press.

Forbes, R. 1921. *The Secret of the Sahara: Kufara*. London: Cassell.

Forrest, J. 1871. Journal of an expedition to explore the country from West Australia to Port Eucla, and thence to Adelaide, South Australia. *Journal of the Royal Geographical Society of London*, 41, 361–372.

Forrest, J. 1875. *Explorations in Australia.* 3 volumes. London: Sampson Low.

Forrest, J., Weld, F.A. and Fraser, M. 1875. Journal of the Western Australian Exploring Expedition through the centre of Australia from Champion Bay to the Overland Telegraph Line between Adelaide and Port Darwin. *Journal of the Royal Geographical Society of London*, 45, 249–299.

Fowler, D.D. 2000. Powell, John Wesley. *American National Biography online.*

Freeman, L.R. 1923. *The Colorado River, Yesterday, To-day and To-morrow.* London: William Heinemann.

Freeth, Z. and Winstone, V. 1978. *Explorers of Arabia.* London: Allen and Unwin.

Freitag, J. 2009. *Serving Empire, Serving Nation: James Tod and the Rajputs of Rajasthan.* Leiden and Boston: Brill.

Frémont, J.C. 1845. *Report of the Exploring Expedition to the Rocky Mountains in the Year 1842, and to California in the year 1843–'44.* Washington, D.C.: Senate of the United States.

French, P. 1994. *Younghusband. The Last Great Imperial Adventurer.* London: Harper Collins.

Freshfield, D.W. 1911. Obituary: Sir Francis Galton, F.R.S. etc. *Geographical Journal*, 37, 323–325.

Fyfe, C. 2008, Laing, Alexander Gordon (1794–1826). *Oxford Dictionary of National Biography online.*

Galton, F. 1852. Recent expedition to the interior of South-Western Africa. *Journal of the Royal Geographical Society*, 22, 140–163.

Galton, F. 1853. *Narrative of an Explorer in Tropical South Africa being an Account of a Visit to Damaraland in 1851.* London: John Murray.

Galton, F. 1872. *The Art of Travel, or, Shifts and Contrivances Available in Wild Countries.* London: John Murray.

Gammage, B. 2004. Sturt, Charles (1795–1869). *Oxford Dictionary of National Biography online.*

Gardner, B. 1968. *The Quest for Timbuctoo.* London: Cassell.

Garnett, R. 2004. Browne, William George (1768–1813). *Oxford Dictionary of National Biography online.*

Geikie, James. 1874. *The Great Ice Age and its relations to the Antiquity of Man.* London, W. Ibister & Co.

Gibbney, H.J. 'Sturt, Charles (1795–1869)', *Australian Dictionary of Biography*, National Centre of Biography, Australian National University, http://adb.anu. edu.au/biography/sturt-charles-2712/text3811, published in hardcopy 1967, accessed online 22 April 2014.

Ghose, I. 2006. Imperial Player: Richard Burton in Sindh. In T.Youngs (ed) *Travel Writing In the Nineteenth Century: Filling the Blank Spaces*, Chapter 5. London: Anthem.

Gilbert, E.W. 1933. *The Exploration of Western America.* Cambridge: Cambridge University Press.

Giles, E. 1889. *Australia Twice Traversed; The Romance of Exploration, Being a Narrative Compiled from the Journals of Five Exploring Expeditions into and Through Central South Australia and Western Australia, from 1872 to 1876.* London: Sampson Low, Marston, Searle and Rivington.

Gillham, N.W. 2001. *A Life of Sir Francis Galton.* Oxford: Oxford University Press.

Gilmour, D. 1994. *Curzon.* London: John Murray.

Gladstone, P. 1970. *Travels of Alexine. Alexine Tinne, 1835–1869.* London: John Murray.

Godsall, J.R. 1993. Fact and fiction in Richard Burton's *Personal Narrative of a Pilgrimage to El-Medinah and Meccah* (1855–6). *Journal of the Royal Asiatic Society* (Third Series), 3, 331–351.

Goldberg, J. 1986. Captain Shakespear and Ibn Saud: a balanced reappraisal. *Middle Eastern Studies*, 22(1), 74–88.

Gordon, J.W. 1987. *The Other Desert War. British Special Forces in North Africa, 1940–1943*, New York: Greenwood Press.

Goudie, A.S. 2002. *Great Warm Deserts of the World*. Oxford: Oxford University Press.

Goudie, A.S. 2008. *Wheels Across the Desert. Exploration of the Libyan Desert by Motor-car 1916–1942*. London: Silphium Press.

Goudie, A.S. 2013. *Arid and Semi-arid Geomorphology*. New York: Cambridge University Press.

Grayson, D.K. 1993. *The Desert's Past. A Natural History of the Great Basin*. Washington: Smithsonian Institution Press.

Gregory, H.E. 1945. Scientific explorations in southern Utah. *American Journal of Science*, 243(10), 527–549.

Gross, K., Rolke, M. and Zboray, A. 2013. *Operation Salam*. Munich: Belleville Verlag.

Guest, J.S. 1992. *The Euphrates Expedition*. London: Kegan Paul.

Guinn, J.M. 1896. Captain Jedediah S. Smith: the pathfinder of the Sierras. *Annual Publication of the Historical Society of Southern California*, Los Angeles, 3, 45–63.

Haardt, G.M. and Audouin-Dubreuil, L. 1924. *Across the Sahara by Motor car: from Touggourt to Timbuctoo*. London: T. Fisher Unwin.

Hall, D.N. 2001. Théodore Monod, 1902–2000. *Geographical Journal*, 167, 191–192.

Halle, C. 1913. *To Menelek in a Motor-Car*. London: Hurst and Blackett.

Hamilton, A. 2010. *An Arabian Utopia: the Western Discovery of Oman*. Oxford: Oxford University Press and Arcadian Library.

Hankey, J. 2001. *A Passion for Egypt*. London: I.B. Tauris.

Harding, J. 1877. The Desert of Atacama (Bolivia). *Journal of the Royal Geographical Society*, 47.

Harold, J. 2003. Deserts, cars, maps and names. Encountering traces of Claud H. Williams M.C., author of the one hundred and seventy-one page secret *Report on the Military Geography of the North-Western Desert of Egypt*. Paper presented at the ASTENE Conference, Worcester College, Oxford, July 2003.

Harris, C.A. 2004. Warburton, Peter Egerton (1813–1889). *Oxford Dictionary of National Biography online*.

Hassanein, Ahmed. 1925. *The Lost Oases*.

Hassanein Bey, A.M. 1924. Crossing the untraversed Libyan Desert. *National Geographic Magazine*, 46(3), 49pp.

Hedin, S. 1903. *Central Asia and Tibet*. London: Hurst and Blackett.

Hedin, S. 1926. *My Life as an Explorer*. London: Cassell and Company.

Hedin, S., 1914. *From Pole to Pole*. London: Macmillan.

Hedin, S., 1940. *The Wandering Lake*. London: George Routledge and Sons.

Heffernan, M. 1989. The limits of Utopia: Henri Duveyrier and the exploration of the Sahara in the nineteenth century. *Geographical Journal*, 155, 342–352.

Heffernan, M. 2001. "A dream as frail as those of ancient Time": the incredible geographies of Timbuctoo. *Environment and Planning*, D, 19, 203–225.

Herr, P. 2000. Frémont, John Charles. *American National Biography online*.

Hibbert, C. 1982. *Africa Explored. Europeans in the Dark Continent, 1769–1889*. London: Hamish Hamilton.

Hogarth, D.G. 1905. *The Penetration of Arabia. A Record of the Development of Western Knowledge Concerning the Arabian peninsula*. London: Alston Books.

Hogarth, D.G. 1926. Obituary. Gertrude Lowthian Bell. *Geographical Journal*, 68, 363–368.

Hogarth, D.G. 1927. Gertrude Bell's Journey to Hayil. *Geographical Journal*, 70.

Hopkirk, P. 1980. *Foreign Devils on the Silk Road*. Oxford: Oxford University Press.

Hopkirk, P. 1990. *The Great Game*. Oxford: Oxford University Press.

Hornemann, F. 1802. *Travels from Cairo to Mourzouk*. London: African Association.

Howell, G. 2006. *Daughter of the Desert.* London: Macmillan.

Huntington, E. 1905. The depression of Sistan in eastern Persia. *Scottish Geographical Magazine*, 21, 379–385.

Huntington, E. 1907. *The Pulse of Asia.* Boston and New York: Houghton, Mifflin and Company.

Huntington, E. 1910. Problems in exploration: Central Asia. *Geographical Journal*, 35, 395–419.

Huntington, E. 1945. *Mainsprings of Civilization.* New York: Wiley.

Hureau, J.C. (2001). Un exceptionnel naturaliste éclectique. *Autres Temps. Cahiers d'éthique sociale et politique*, 70(1), 25–38.

Ikle, F.W. 1968. Sir Aurel Stein. A Victorian Geographer in the tracks of Alexander. *Isis*, 59, 144–155.

Ives, J.C. 1861. *Report upon the Colorado river of the west.* Washington, D.C., Government Printing Office.

Jarry, I. 2001. *Théodore Monod.* Paris: Payot.

Jarvis, C.S. 1936. *Three Deserts.* London: John Murray.

Jarvis, C.S. 1938. *Desert and Delta* (p. 86). London: John Murray.

Jones, D.D. and Grissom, J.W. 1949. Francis Rawdon Chesney: a reappraisal of his work on the Euphrates route. *Historian*, 11, 185–203.

Joyce, E.B. and McCann, D.A. 2011. *Burke and Wills: the Scientific Legacy of the Victorian Exploring Expedition.* Collingwood, Victoria: CSIRO.

Keay, J. 1982. *Eccentric Travellers.* London: John Murray.

Kelly, J.B. 1977. Review of Philby of Araba by Elizabeth Monroe. *Middle Eastern Studies*, 13, 144–146.

Kelly, S. 2002. *The Hunt for Zerzura. The Lost Oasis and the Desert War.* London: John Murray.

Kennedy, Dane. 2013. *The Last Blank Spaces. Exploring Africa and Australia.* Cambridge, Massachusetts: Harvard University Press.

Kiernan, R.H. 1937. *The Unveiling of Arabia.* London: Harrap.

King, P. (ed.). 1986. *Curzon's Persia.* London: Sidgwick and Jackson.

Kirk-Greene, A.H.M. 1989. The Society and Alexander Laing, 1794–1826. *African Affairs*, 88, 415–418.

Kowalewski, M. 2000. Manly, William Lewis. *American National Biography online.*

Kroll, G. 2000. Roy Chapman Andrews and the business of exploring: cetology and conservation in progressive America. *Endeavour*, 24, 79–84.

Kirchner, J.W. 2013. The physics and chemistry of Earth's dynamic surface (Ralph Alger Bagnold Medal Lecture). In *EGU General Assembly Conference Abstracts* (Vol. 15, p. 14258).

Kreutzmann, H., 2004, Ellsworth Huntington and his perspective on Central Asia. Great Game experiences and their influence on development thought. *GeoJournal*, 59, 27–31.

Laity J., 2008. *Deserts and Desert Environments.* Chicheser; Wiley-Blackwell.

Lane-Poole, S. 2004. Chesney, Francis Rawdon (1789–1872). *Oxford Dictionary of National Biography online.*

Laughton, J.K. 2004. Wellsted, James Raymond (1805–1842). *Oxford Dictionary of National Biography online.*

Limerick, P.N. 1985. *Desert Passages. Encounters with the American Deserts.* Albuquerque: University of New Mexico Press.

Longford, E. 2007. *A Pilgrimage of Passion: the Life of Wilfrid Scawen Blunt.* London: I.B. Tauris.

Lukitz, L., Bell, Gertrude Margaret Lowthian (1868–1926). *Oxford Dictionary of National Biography*, Oxford University Press, 2004, article 30686.

Main, M. 1987. *Kalahari. Life's Variety in Dune and Delta.* Johannesburg: Southern Book Publishers.

Maitland, A. 2006. *Wilfred Thesiger. The Life of the Great Explorer.* London: Harper Press.

Makin, W.J. 1929. *Across the Kalahari Desert*. London: Arrowsmith.

Manley, D. 1991. *The Nile. A Traveller's Anthology*. London: Cassell.

Manly, W.L. 1894. *Death Valley in '49*. San Jose, CA: Pacific Tree and Vine Company.

Marozzi, J. 2010. Heinrich Barth. Crossing the Sahara (1821–1865). In R. Hanbury-Prothero, R.M. 1958. Heinrich Barth and the Western Sudan. *Geographical Journal*, 124, 326–337.

Marshall-Cornwall, J. 1965. Three soldier-geographers. *Geographical Journal*, 131, 357–365.

Martin, G.J. 1973. *Ellsworth Huntington: His Life and Thought*. Hamden, CT: Archon Books.

Massey, W.T. 1918. *The Desert Campaigns*. London: Constable.

Matless, D. 2004. Younghusband, Sir Francis Edward (1863–1942). *Oxford Dictionary of National Biography*.

Mason, Michael. 1936. *The Paradise of Fools: Being an Account, by a Member of the Party, of the Expedition which Covered 6,300 Miles of the Libyan Desert by Motor-car in 1935*. London: Hodder and Stoughton.

McGuirk, R. 2013. *Light Car Patrols, 1916–1919*. London: Silphium Press and Royal Geographical Society.

McLaren, I.F. 1976. Wills, William John (1834–1861). *Australian Dictionary of Biography*, Volume 6, Melbourne University Press, 410–411.

McLynn, F. 1990. *Burton: Snow upon the Desert*. London: John Murray.

Meyer, K.E. and Brysac, S.B. 1999. *Tournament of Shadows*. Washington, D.C.: Counterpoint.

Mitchell, A. 2000. 'Amid th'encircling gloom': the moral geography of Charles Sturt's narratives. *Journal of Australian Studies*, 24, 85–94.

Monod T. 1928. Une traversée de la Mauritanie occidentale. *Revue de Géographie Physique et de Géologie Dynamique* 1, 3–25, 88–106.

Monod, T. 1932. *L'Adrar Ahnet – Contribution à l'étude archéologique d'un District Saharien*. Paris : Institut d'Ethnologie.

Monod, T. 1937. *Méharées – Explorations au vrai Sahara*. Paris.

Monod, T. 1958. Majâbat Al-Koubrâ. *Memoirs de L'Institut Français D'Afrique Noire*, 52, 406 pp.

Monod, T. 1984. *L'Emeraude des Garamantes. Souvenirs d'un Saharien*. Paris: Harmattan.

Monod, T. 1997. *Terre et Ciel*. Arles: Actes Sud.

Monod, T. and Diemer, E. 2000. *Zerzura: L'Oasis Légendaire du Désert Libyque*. Paris: Editions Vent de Sable.

Monroe, E. 1973a. Across the Rub 'Al Khali. *Saudi Aramco World*, 24, 6–13.

Monroe, E. 1973b. *Philby of Arabia*. London: Faber and Faber.

Montell, G. 1954. Sven Hedin the explorer. *Geografiska Annaler*, 36, 1–8.

Moorehead, A. 1963. *Cooper's Creek*. London: Hamish Hamilton.

Morgan, D.L. 1953. *Jedediah Smith and the Opening of the West*. Lincoln: University of Nebraska Press.

Morris, D. 'Stuart, John McDouall (1815–1866)', *Australian Dictionary of Biography*, National Centre of Biography, Australian National University, http://adb.anu.edu.au/biography/stuart-john-mcdouall-4662/text7707, published in hardcopy 1976, accessed online 22 April 2014.

Munzinger, W. 1859. *Über die Sitten und das Recht der Bogos (The Laws and Customs of the People of Bogos)*. J. Wurster: Winterthur.

Munzinger, W. 1868–1869. Journey across the Great Salt Desert from Hanfila to the foot of the Abyssinian Alps. *Proceedings of the Royal Geographical Society*, 13, 219–224.

Munzinger, W. 1869. Narrative of a journey through the Afar Country. *Journal of the Royal Geographical Society*, 39, 188–232.

Munzinger, W. and Miles, S.B. 1871. Account of an excursion into the interior of southern Arabia. *Journal of the Royal Geographical Society of London*, 41, 210–245.

Murray, G.W. (1951). Obituary: Ladislas Almásy. *Geographical Journal*, 117(2), 253–254.

Nachtigal, G. 1876. Journey to Lake Chad and neighbouring regions. *Journal of the Royal Geographical Society of London*, 46, 396–411.

Nachtigal, G. 1879–1881. *Sahara and Sudan*. 3 volumes. Berlin and Leipzig: F.A. Brockhaus.

Nesbitt, L.M. 1934. *Hell-hole of Creation. The Exploration of Abyssinian Danakil*. New York: Knopf.

Nicholson, T.R. (1965). *A Toy for the Lion*. London: W. Kimber.

Nicholson, S. 2011. *Dryland Climatology*. Cambridge: Cambridge University Press.

Nicolson, H. 1928. *Curzon*. Foreign Affairs, 7: 221–33.

Nicolson, H. 1934. *Curzon: the Last Phase 1919–1925*. London: Constable.

Nöther, W. 2003. *Die Erschliessung der Sahara durch Motorfahrzeuge 1901–1936*. Munich: Belleville.

Oldham, C.E.A.W. 1943. Sir Aurel Stein – obituary. *Proceedings of the British Academy*, 29, 453–465.

Omrani, B., 2006, "Will we make it to Jalalabad?" 19th century travels in Afghanistan. *Asian Affairs*, 37, 161–174.

Ondaatje, C. 1996. *Sindh Revisited*.

A Journey in the Footsteps of Captain Sir Richard Francis Burton. London: Harper Collins.

Palgrave, W.G. 1864. Observations made in Central, Eastern, and Southern Arabia during a journey through that country in 1862 and 1863. *Journal of the Royal Geographical Society*, 34, 111–154.

Palgrave, W.G. 1865. *Personal Narrative of a Year's Journey through Central and Eastern Arabia (1862–63)*. 2 volumes. London: Macmillan.

Parker, J. 2004. *Desert Rats*. London: Headline.

Parsons, A.J. and Abrahams, A.D. (eds.) 2009. *Geomorphology of Desert Environments* (2nd edition). Springer.

Peacock, S. 1995. *The Great Farini. The High-wire Life of William Hunt*. Harmondsworth: Penguin Books.

Philby, H. St. J.B. 1933. *The Empty Quarter*. London: Constable.

Philby, H. St. J.B. 1946. *A Pilgrim in Arabia*. London: Robert Hale.

Philby, H. St. J.B. 1920. Southern Najd. *Geographical Journal*, 55, 161–185.

Philby, H. St .J.B. 1923. Jauf and the North Arabian Desert. *Geographical Journal*, 62, 241–249.

Pittaway, J. 2008. *Long Range Desert Group, Rhodesia. The Men Speak*. Avondale, South Africa: Dandy Agencies.

Porch, D. 1985. *The Conquest of the Sahara*. London: Jonathan Cape.

Powell, J.W. 1878. *The Lands of the Arid Region of the United States*. Washington, D.C.: Government Printing Office.

Powell, J.W. 1961. *The Exploration of the Colorado River and its Canyons*. New York, NY: Dover Publications.

Prior, K. 2004. Burnes, Sir Alexander (1805–1841). *Oxford Dictionary of National Biography*.

Przhevalsky, N. 1879. *From Kulja, Across the Tian Shan to Lob-Nor*. London: Sampson Low.

Pyne, S.J. 1998. *How the Canyon Became Grand*. Harmondsworth: Penguin Books.

Ravenstein, E.G. 1896. Gerhard Rohlfs. *Geographical Journal*, 8, 184–185.

Rawlinson, H.C. 1871/2. Address to the Royal Geographical Society. *Proceedings of the Royal Geographical Society of London*, 16, 291–377.

Rawlinson, H.C. 1875–1876. Address to the Royal Geographical Society. *Proceedings of the Royal Geographical Society of London*, 20, 377–448.

Rayfield, D. 1976. *The Dream of Lhasa. The Life of Nikolay Przhevalsky (1839–1888) Explorer of Central Asia*. London: Paul Elek.

Reclus, É. 1871. *The Earth: A descriptive history of the phenomena of the life of the globe*. London: Chapman & Hall.

Roberts, D. (2002). *A Newer World: Kit Carson, John C. Frémont and the Claiming of the American West.* New York: Simon and Schuster.

Roeckell, L.M. 2010. Bollaert, William (1807–1876). *Oxford Dictionary of National Biography online.*

Rohlfs, G. 1864–1865. Account of a journey across the Atlas Mountains and through the Oases Tuat and Tidikelt to Tripoli, by way of Ghadames, in the year 1864. *Proceedings of the Royal Geographical Society of London*, 9, 312–314.

Rohlfs, F.G. 1874. *Adventures in Morocco and Journey along the Oases of Draa and Tafilet.* London: Sampson Low.

Rohlfs, F.G. 1875. *Drei Monate in der Libyschen Wüste.* Cassel: Theodor Fischer.

Rolle, A. 1982, Exploring an explorer: psychohistory and John Charles Frémont. *Pacific Historical Review*, 51, 135–163.

Rose, K. 1969. *Superior Person, A Portrait of Curzon and His Circle in Late Victorian England.* London: Weidenfeld and Nicolson.

Ross, J. 2010. Charles Sturt. In R. Hanbury-Tenison (ed). *The Great Explorers.* London: Thames and Hudson. pp. 204–208.

Sabini, J. 1981. *Armies in the Sand. The Struggle for Mecca and Medina.* London: Thames and Hudson.

Sadlier, G.F. 1866. *Diary of a Journey Across Arabia from El Khatif in the Persian Gulf to Yambo in the Red Sea, during the Year 1819.* Bombay: Education Society Press.

Sattin, A. 2003. *The Gates of Africa. Death, Discovery and the Search for Timbuktu.* London: HarperCollins.

Seaver, G. 1952. *Francis Younghusband, Explorer and Mystic.* London: John Murray.

Sebba, A. 2004. *The Exiled Collector.* London: John Murray.

Sim, K. 1981. *Jean Louis Burckhardt. A Biography.* London: Quartet Books.

Sinclair, A. T. 1908. Tattooing—Oriental and Gypsy. *American Anthropologist*, 10(3), 361–386.

Skrine, C. 1953. Obituary: Sven Hedin. *Geographical Journal*, 119, 252–253.

Sluglett, P. 2004. Leachman, Gerard Evelyn (1880–1920). *Oxford Dictionary of National Biography online.*

Sluglett, P. 2004. Shakespear, William Henry Irvine (1878–1915). *Oxford Dictionary of National Biography online.*

Smith H.A. 2004. Clifford, Sir Bede Edmund Hugh (1890–1969). *Oxford Dictionary of National Biography online.*

Smith, J. Diary, http://mtmen.org/mtman/html/jsmith/jedexped1.html, accessed online 15 November 2015.

Somerville, M. 1858. *Physical Geography.* London: John Murray.

Stein, M.A. 1909. Explorations in Central Asia, 1906–8. *Geographical Journal*, 34, 5–36, 241–264.

Stein, M.A. 1916. A third journey of exploration in Central Asia. *Geographical Journal*, 48, 97–130.

Stein, M.A. 1920. Explorations in the Lop Desert. *Geographical Review*, 9, 1–34.

Stein, M.A. 1925. Innermost Asia: its geography as a factor in history. *Geographical Journal*, 65, 377–403.

Stenger, W. 1954. *Beyond the Hundredth Meridian.* New York: Houghton Mifflin Company.

Stuart, J.M. 1863. Explorations from Adelaide across the continent of Australia, 1861–2. *Journal of the Royal Geographical Society of London*, 33, 276–321.

Sturt, C. 1847. A condensed account of an exploration in the interior of Australia. *Journal of the Royal Geographical Society of London*, 17, 85–129.

Sturt, C. 1848–49. *Narrative of an expedition into central Australia, performed under the authority of Her Majesty's Government, during the years 1844, 5, and 6: together with a notice of the province of South Australia, in 1847.* London: T. and W. Boone, 2 vols.

Swinscow, T.D.V. 1972. Friedrich Welwitsch, 1806–72. A centennial memoir. *Biological Journal of the Linnean Society*, 4, 269–289.

Sykes, E.C. 1898. *Through Persia on a Side-Saddle*. London: A.D. Innes & Co.

Sykes, P.M. 1902. *Ten Thousand Miles in Persia; or Eight Years in Iran*. London: John Murray.

Sykes, E.C. and Sykes, P.M. 1920. *Through Deserts and Oases of Central Asia*. London: Macmillan.

Tabachnick, S.E. 2004. Doughty, Charles Montagu (1843–1926). *Oxford Dictionary of National Biography online*.

Tate, M.L. 2011. Bollaert, William. *Handbook of Texas online*.

Tenison (ed). *The Great Explorers*. London: Thames and Hudson, 196–203.

Thesiger, W. 1934. Review. *Geographical Journal*, 84, 527–528.

Thesiger, W. 1935. The Awash River and the Aussa Sultanate. *Geographical Journal*, 85, 1–19.

Thesiger, W. 1948. Across the Empty Quarter. *Geographical Journal*, 111, 1–19.

Thesiger, W. 1949. A further journey across the Empty Quarter. *Geographical Journal*, 113, 21–44.

Thesiger, W. 1950. Desert borderlands of Oman. *Geographical Journal*, 116, 137–168.

Thesiger, W. 1959. *Arabian Sands*. London: Longmans.

Thesiger, W. 1987. *The Life of my Choice*. London: Collins.

Thesiger, W., 1960. Obituary. *Geographical Journal*, 126, 563–566.

Thomas, B. 1932. *Arabia Felix: Across the Empty Quarter of Arabia*. London: Jonathan Cape.

Thomas, B.E. 1952. Modern Trans-Saharan Routes. *Geographical Review*, 42, 267–282.

Thomas, D.S.G. (ed.) 2011. *Arid Zone Geomorphology*. Chichester: Wiley Blackwell.

Thompson, J. 2004. Palgrave, William Gifford (1826–1888). *Oxford Dictionary of National Biography online*.

Tidrick, K. 1990. *Heart Beguiling Araby. The English Romance with Arabia*. London: I.B. Tauris.

Tillotson, G. (ed.). 2007. *James Tod's Rajasthan. The Historian and His Collections*. Mumbai: Marg Publications.

Tod, J. 1829–1832. *Annals and Antiquities of Rajasthan*. London: Smith Elder.

Tod, J. 1839. *Travels in Western India, Embracing a Visit to the Sacred Mounts of the Jains, and the Most Celebrated Shrines of Hindu Faith Between Rajpootana and the Indus: With an Account of the Ancient City of Nehrwalla*. London: W.H. Allen and Company.

Tuson, P. 2014. *Western Women Travelling East 1716–1916*. Oxford: The Arcadian Library in association with the Oxford University Press.

Ure, J. 2010. Nikolai Przhevalsky. In R. Hanbury-Tenison (ed.) *The Great Explorers*. London: Thames and Hudson. pp. 93–97.

Ure, J. 2010. Harry St John Philby. In R. Hanbury-Tenison (ed.) *The Great Explorers*. London: Thames and Hudson. pp. 215–219.

Usick, P. 2002. *Adventures in Egypt and Nubia. The Travels of William John Bankes (1786–1855)*. London: The British Museum Press.

Verrier, A., 1991. *Francis Younghusband and the Great Game*. London: Jonathan Cape.

Vicente, F. L. 2003. Travelling objects: The story of two natural history collections in the Nineteenth Century. *Portuguese Studies*, 19, 19–37.

Visher, S.S. 1948. Memoir to Ellsworth Huntington, 1876–1947. *Annals of the Association of American Geographers*, 38, 38–50.

Walker, A. 1995. *Aurel Stein. Pioneer of the Silk Road*. London: John Murray.

Wallach, J. 1996. *Desert Queen*. London: Weidenfeld and Nicholson.

Walpole, R. 1820. *Travels in Various Countries of the East; being a Continuation of Memoirs relating to European and Asiatic Turkey, &c*. London: Longman, Hurst, Rees, Orme, and Brown.

Warburton, P.E. 1874–5. Journey across the Western Interior of Australia. *Proceedings of the Royal Geographical Society*, 19, 41–51.

Warburton, P.E. 1875. *Journey Across the Western Interior of Australia.* London: Sampson Low.

Ward, P. 1987. *Travels in Oman.* Cambridge: Oleander Press.

Weigall, A., 1909. *Travels in the Upper Egyptian Deserts.* Edinburgh and London: William Blackwood and Sons.

Weiss, S.C. 1999. John C. Frémont 1842, 1843–'44 Report and Map. *Journal of Government Information*, 26, 297–313.

Welland, M. 2015. *The Desert. Lands of Lost Borders.* London: Reaktion Books.

Wellard, J. 1964. *The Great Sahara.* London: Hutchinson.

Wellsted, R. 1836. Observations on the coast of Arabia between Ras Mohammed and Jiddah. *Journal of the Royal Geographical Society*, 6, 51–96.

Wellsted, J.R. 1838. *Travels in Arabia.* 2 volumes. London: John Murray.

Whitfield, S. 2010. Marc Aurel Stein. In R. Hanbury-Tenison (ed). *The Great Explorers.* London: Thames and Hudson. pp. 106–111.

Wheeler, S. 2004. Tod, James (1782–1835). *Oxford Dictionary of National Biography online.*

Williams, C.H. 1919. *Report on the Military Geography of the North-Western Desert of Egypt.* War Office Handbook.

Williams, C.H. undated. *Light Car Patrols in the Libyan Desert.* 85 pp. manuscript in the Royal Geographical Society.

Winstone, H.V.F. 1976. *Captain Shakespear.* London: Jonathan Cape.

Winstone, H.V.F. 1982. *Leachman. O.C. Desert.* London: Quartet Books.

Winstone, H.V. F. 2003. *Lady Anne Blunt: A Biography.* Manchester: Barzan Publishing.

Worster, D. 2001. *A River Running West. The Life of John Wesley Powell.* New York: Oxford University Press.

Wright, D. 1987. Curzon and Persia. *Geographical Journal*, 153, 343–350.

Wynn, A. 2003. *Persia in the Great Game.* London: John Murray.

Younghusband, F. 1928. in *Geographical Journal*, 71, 5: 4.

Younghusband, F., 1937. *The Heart of a Continent.* London: John Murray.

INDEX